Ultimate Festival & Travel Guide: Venice & the Veneto

Unforgettable Experiences, Unmissable Events, Unique
Itineraries & Best Times to Travel to Venice, Verona, Padua,
and the Veneto Region

Katerina Ferrara

IMMERSION TRAVEL PUBLISHING

ISBN (Paperback): 978-1-966874-08-9

ISBN (Hard Cover): 978-1-966874-09-6

ISBN (eBook): 978-1-966874-07-2

Audible (AudioBoook)

Library of Congress Control Number: 2025914205

DISCLAIMER

DISCLAIMER

The author is not a travel agent. All opinions, experiences, and views expressed in this book are based on personal travel experiences.

Festival and event dates are set by local comuni and may change with little or no notice due to weather, logistics, or local decisions. Some festivals follow variable calendars tied to religious feasts or seasonal events. For this reason, it is strongly advised to confirm dates directly with official sources before booking travel.

Businesses and websites recommended in this book may also change, change ownership, rebrand, or close. The author has received no compensation or sponsorship for any recommended businesses.

Contents

Explore More and Stay Connected

Thanks for exploring Italy with me

Unlock the Secrets of Italy with Insider Expertise!

Allow me to be your personal guide, sharing insider tips, unique experiences, and essential information to uncover the treasures of Italy like never before.

Sign up for my free newsletter today and receive your **FREE downloadable guides** filled with curated itineraries, expert advice, and practical tips to make your adventures across Italy unforgettable and stress-free! https://katerinaferrara.com/

KaterinaFerrrara
.com

With your complimentary subscription, you'll enjoy:

- Monthly updates with insider secrets for Italy, top experiences, hidden spots, and seasonal highlights

- Italy and Vatican News you can use

Don't miss out on exclusive insights and bonus content to enhance your Italian journey! **Sign up today and let's start exploring!**

Travel Italy Book Series

Available now:

Book 1: *Ultimate Festival and Travel Guide Sicily (Available in English, Italian, & Dual-Language)*

Book 2: *Rome 2025 Jubilee Year Travel Guide*

Book 3: *Ultimate Festival and Travel Guide Rome and Beyond*

Book 4: *Ultimate Festival and Travel Guide Puglia*

Book 5: *Ultimate Festival and Travel Guide Venice and the Veneto*

Book 6: *Ultimate Festival and Travel Guide Miland and Lombardy*

Book 7: *Ultimate Festival and Travel Guide Umbria*

Arriving in 2026:

Book 8: *Ultimate Festival and Travel Guide Florence and Tuscany*

Arriving in 2027:

Book 8: *Ultimate Festival and Travel Guide Bologna & Emilia-Romagna*

Arriving in 2028:

Book 9: *Ultimate Festival and Travel Guide Naples, Amalfi and Beyond*

CHAPTER ONE

The Joy of Festival Travel

Experience Italy in Celebration

P icture yourself gliding along silent canals at dusk, the golden light of sunset reflecting off Byzantine facades as gondolas drift by. The distant sound of music grows closer, and suddenly you're swept into a procession that has wound through these same narrow calli for centuries. The air is rich with the aroma of feast-day delicacies: frutti di mare, risotto al nero di seppia, sweet frittelle. Around you, locals share prosecco and laughter, welcoming you not as a tourist but as part of their living tradition. As evening falls, the lagoon itself becomes a stage for illuminated boats and floating pageants that have celebrated Venetian identity since the days of the Doges. This is Festival Travel, where you don't just visit a destination; you become part of its story.

Welcome to a side of Venice and the Veneto that many travelers overlook: one of ancient traditions and an unforgettable cultural heritage. As someone who has traveled to Italy for over 25 years and immersed myself in its vibrant culture, I've discovered that Venice's heart beats the strongest during its festivals.

This kind of travel allows you to become a part of a story that began millennia ago and continues to unfold with each festival, each feast, each celebration. These magical moments define festival travel in the Veneto: experiences that pierce the veil between past and present, between visitor and local, between watching and belonging. Here, in the festivals and sagre of Venice and its enchanting region, every celebration is a gateway to understanding the soul of a place through its most joyous expressions.

Your Key to Venice and the Veneto

This book springs from my experience at these extraordinary events. It's more than a travel guide; it's your gateway to discovering the living spirit of Italy. While it includes all the essential travel information you need (top sights, walking tours, restaurant and hotel recommendations), it offers something unique that you won't find elsewhere: an invitation to become part of Venice's living history.

Venice's rich tapestry of culture, woven over millennia, reveals itself in every corner of the Veneto. The magnificent Basilica di San Marco stands as an eternal symbol of the Republic's former glory, while the Roman arena in Verona whispers tales of ancient spectacles. In Padua, Giotto's revolutionary frescoes illuminate centuries of artistic innovation, and in Treviso, medieval arcades frame scenes of daily life unchanged for generations. Throughout the region, Byzantine mosaics, Renaissance villas, and Gothic palaces remind us that Venice once ruled a maritime empire.

But Venice is far more than its monuments: it's a living testament to an unbroken cultural heritage where past and present dance together. The region's vibrant traditions and festivals infuse every campo and piazza with infectious energy, transforming ancient stones into stages for modern celebration. Here, history isn't confined to museums: it lives in the festivals that fill the calendar, in recipes passed down through generations, and in the daily rhythms of life that echo through time.

What This Guide Offers:

- **City Highlights:** Discover what makes each place unique, from Venice's floating majesty to Vicenza's architectural elegance. Each city profile reveals the character that only locals usually know.

- **Living History:** Uncover how Roman, Byzantine, and Renaissance influences weave through daily life here.

- **Natural Wonders:** Journey from the misty lagoons of Venice to the vineyard-covered hills of Valpolicella to the dramatic peaks of the Dolomites. I'll show you where to find the postcard views.

- **Local Life:** Find those authentic moments that make travel meaningful: from morning markets where locals shop for dinner to quiet campi, where time seems to stand still.

- **Food Finds**: Through countless meals and recommendations from our Venetian friends, we've curated a list of restaurants that serve authentic regional specialties at honest prices.

- **Festival Focus:** While this guide covers all aspects of the Veneto, I've highlighted the celebrations that transform ordinary places into extraordinary experiences, helping you time your visit for maximum magic.

Finding Festival Culture

I didn't always know about this incredible world of Italian festivals. My husband and I started our international travels on our honeymoon in 1997, and we have made it a priority to return to Italy each year. Our journey began like that of many travelers, exploring Italy's famous landmarks and savoring its cuisine. But it was during a visit to a small town in Sicily that everything changed.

Surrounded by the festival's sights, sounds, and smells in the town square, I felt a change, something delightful. The locals welcomed me with such warmth and pride in their traditions that I couldn't help but be drawn in. That moment sparked my love for Festival Travel: a way of engaging with Italy that goes beyond sightseeing to truly becoming part of its living traditions.

Each festival since has only deepened this connection. I'll never forget following the scent of roasting chestnuts to a tiny village square on a crisp fall day, or watching in awe as a solemn religious procession illuminated a medieval street. These experiences are windows into the heart and soul of Venice and the Veneto, revealing the genuine spirit of its people. They've inspired me to create the **Travel**

Italy Book Series, which will eventually grow to include 22 Festival and Travel Guides covering all of Italy's diverse regions.

Understanding Feste and Sagre

What Sets a Festa Apart from a Sagra?

As you explore this guide, you'll naturally pick up some Italian along the way, starting with two essential festival terms: 'festa' and 'sagra.'

A **festa** (plural: feste) often grows from Roman Catholic traditions, like Venice's Festa del Redentore or Marostica's Partita a Scacchi. Yet not all feste are religious, as they encompass everything from Venice Film Festival to Verona's historic Vinitaly wine fair, and Conegliano's Prosecco celebrations. Among the most spectacular are Chioggia's Palio della Marciliana, where streets transform into medieval marketplaces, and Verona's Carnival, a vibrant tradition dating back centuries.

While Catholic traditions shape many Italian festivals, these celebrations welcome everyone, regardless of faith. They're joyful expressions of history, tradition, and community spirit where all can create lasting memories.

A **sagra** (plural: sagre), by contrast, springs from ancient harvest celebrations. The word itself derives from "sacro," meaning "sacred" in Latin. Originally held in temple yards to thank the Roman gods for bountiful harvests, these festivals live on in small towns and villages as community fundraisers for schools and local projects, powered entirely by volunteers.

While feste celebrate various aspects of culture, sagre focus specifically on local cuisine. From Bassano del Grappa's Sagra degli Asparagi Bianchi, which showcases the region's prized white asparagus, to festivals honoring radicchio, mushrooms, risotto, baccalà, chestnuts, and wines, there's a celebration for every palate.

Here's my essential sagra tip: arrive hungry. Purchase your meal ticket at the event booth: for 12 to 15 euros, you'll enjoy an exceptional zero kilometro meal with local wine. ("Zero kilometro" refers to food produced within roughly 150 kilometers, ensuring peak freshness and supporting local farmers.)

For feste, I recommend staying two to three nights minimum, as celebrations often continue into the late evening. Sagre, however, work perfectly as day trips, since they often occur in tiny villages that may not even have hotels. Many visitors base themselves in larger nearby towns and venture out to experience these local food festivals.

Whether you're traveling solo, with family, or planning a multi-generational trip, these festivals offer rich experiences for everyone. Photographers, influencers, and creatives discover endless possibilities, from vibrant processions to intimate cultural moments. Music festivals showcase Italy's performing arts, while markets built around the festivals highlight local artisans creating unique treasures. Many festivals offer hands-on experiences with traditional crafts or cooking techniques.

Families particularly appreciate the child-friendly atmosphere, complete with puppet shows, parades, and special treats. Importantly, these events support sustainable tourism and directly benefit local communities, helping to preserve these cherished traditions for future generations. Consider this guide not only a travel guide but also your personal festival planner for creating authentic experiences beyond the typical tourist path.

Why Festival Travel?

- Experience cities at their most alive and authentic, when streets pulse with music, color, and celebration.

- Join in centuries-old traditions that most tourists never witness, from solemn processions to joyous feasts.

- Savor once-a-year delicacies and festival-specific dishes that rarely appear on restaurant menus.

- Discover the fascinating stories and cultural significance behind each celebration, passed down through generations.

- Connect meaningfully with local communities as they welcome visitors into their cherished traditions.

- Capture extraordinary moments, from elaborate costumes to breathtaking ceremonial displays.

- Share in activities that delight all ages, making these festivals perfect for family memories.

- Support and help preserve local traditions while contributing directly to community economies.

- Travel sustainably by supporting community-run events that preserve cultural heritage and benefit local economies rather than mass tourism.

An Insider's Perspective

Because of my love for Italy and our goal to move there one day, I started studying Italian in 2020 when our son Augustus left for university. I don't do anything halfway, so when I decided to learn Italian, I really committed myself to it and became fluent quickly (somewhat thanks to lockdowns). What began as a personal challenge soon opened up a whole extra dimension of Italian culture to me.

Every morning, I tune into Di Buon Mattino on TV2000. What started as a simple language immersion exercise blossomed into a genuine passion. The show, broadcasting from Rome, goes beyond typical news coverage; it journeys across Italy, discovering festivals, traditions, and local specialties. Between watching Italian TV series, chatting with Italian friends, reading Italian newspapers, and my daily dose of Di Buon Mattino, I kept discovering one fascinating festival after another. Even now, each day the show transports me to a new celebration somewhere in Italy, revealing another region's unique culture. It's a daily way to learn about new cities, regions, saints, or celebrated foods.

As I explored deeper, I realized these festivals truly embody Italian culture; they're living celebrations of community, history, folklore, and tradition. This sparked an idea: why not experience these festivals firsthand? When I began planning our travels around them several years ago, I was thrilled that my husband, son, cousins, and friends were just as excited to join the adventure.

While there are cultural festivals in the U.S., they're different. Italian festivals are lifelong commitments, drawing people back year after year, even from far away. These aren't just celebrations; they are cherished reunions with family and friends.

A huge part of what makes these festivals special is the food, dishes and desserts you can only find during these celebrations, flavors that stay hidden from restaurant menus the rest of the year. As I researched these festivals for our trips, the cuisine emerged as a crucial part of the story, deeply woven into local traditions and memorable experiences.

I'll never forget hunting down the Testa del Turco at the Festa della Madonna delle Milizie in Scicli. Following the enticing aromas through the centro storico, my anticipation grew with each step. That first bite, the delicate, crisp pastry with its rich, creamy filling, was unlike anything I had tasted before. It was not just delicious; it was a gateway into the festival's spirit, a flavor that captured the essence of celebration and tradition. Don't worry, I have included all these special festival foods in the chapters.

My friend Annalisa's story perfectly captures this festival spirit. Like many Italians, she moved to Rome for work but returns to her hometown every year for her patron saint's festival. When I asked to join her one year, she laughed and said, "Katerina, you wouldn't be able to keep up! I run all over town just to see the procession of Sant'Ambogio at every important viewpoint!" Her enthusiasm showed me how deeply these festivals are woven into Italian life.

What to Expect in This Book

Now that you understand the magic and significance of festival travel, let me show you how this guide will help you experience it firsthand. In the chapters that follow, we'll delve deep into Venice and the Veneto's most captivating festivals, exploring their origins, significance, and the best ways to experience them. Whether you're planning a trip or simply armchair traveling, this book will be your guide to the heart of Venetian culture through its vibrant celebrations.

Whether you're timing your visit to join in centuries-old celebrations or creating your own path through this enchanting region, you'll find the insights here to make every moment count.

Festival Travel transforms ordinary tourism into extraordinary experiences. Instead of viewing Venice through the lens of a typical tourist, you'll experience it through the joy of its celebrations, the warmth of its communities, and the depth of its traditions.

San Marco and the Basin

The Magic of the Veneto's Festivals

Venice may be the jewel in the Veneto's crown, but the region's soul truly awakens in its festival-filled towns and villages. Picture yourself here: following torch-lit processions through the medieval streets of Bassano as ancient traditions come alive, swaying to music under a star-filled sky at a summer festival in the Prosecco hills, or raising a glass of just-pressed wine at a centuries-old sagra in the Verona. These are the moments most travelers never experience. The pulse of Italian life reaches its peak during its celebrations.

This guide opens doors most visitors never know exist. Beyond just telling you when and where festivals happen, I'll share the secrets that transform you from observer to participant: the hidden campos where locals gather for the best views of processions, the family-run bacari where festival specialties have been perfected over generations, and the timeless traditions that welcome visitors into their ancient rhythms.

Let me invite you to venture beyond the guidebook landmarks and into living history. Here, every festival writes a new chapter in stories centuries old, every feast celebrates the flavors of heritage, and every celebration offers the chance to become part of something extraordinary. From Venice's grand spectacles echoing the days of the Doges to intimate village festivals where everyone feels like family, these experiences will transform your Italian journey into a treasured memory.

Join me in discovering the real Italy: one festival at a time. Let's embark on this journey together, where every canal echoes with history, every local dish tells a story, and every celebration invites you to become part of Europe's living heritage.

Welcome to Festival Travel, where your most extraordinary Italian adventures are about to begin!

CHAPTER TWO

How to Use This Unique Guide

Organize, Explore, Enjoy

W hile festivals are a unique and vibrant thread throughout this guide, its purpose is far broader. It is meant to help you explore Venice and the Veneto with depth, curiosity, and ease. Whether you are planning your first visit or returning for a richer experience, this book serves as a **complete travel companion,** offering insight into the region's culture, history, and hidden corners. The festivals make this guide special, but its true strength lies in the immersive city descriptions, the living traditions, and the practical suggestions that make your travels rewarding with or without a festival.

Each chapter offers an immersive look at the towns and cities of the region, complete with historical background, must-see landmarks, restaurant recommendations, transportation tips, and authentic cultural insights. Even if you are not planning your trip around a specific festival, you can use this book to discover hidden gems, enjoy local food traditions, and experience Venice and its surrounding areas like a well-prepared traveler rather than a tourist.

If you are interested in festivals, you'll find a curated calendar that outlines events by month and location, helping you align your travel dates with local celebrations. Festival chapters include detailed descriptions of what to expect, from parades and processions to music, markets, and traditional food. But whether you attend a festival or not, the surrounding city guides are filled with rich cultural content, day trip ideas, and personal travel insights to help you make the most of your time.

Use the book in whatever way best suits your travel style, whether you're designing a full itinerary, planning one unforgettable day, or simply flipping through for inspiration over a cappuccino.

Quick Start Guide

Want to include a Festival? Follow these steps:

1. **Check the Festival Calendar Chapter** to see what's happening during your visit.

2. **Read Chapter 1** to understand the magic of festival travel and the difference between feste and sagre.

3. **Use the Maps (Chapters 3-4)** to visualize festival locations and plan your route.

4. **Pick 1-2 festivals.** One or two festivals are all you need to capture the spirit; you can always come back for more.

5. **Book accommodation early** for major festivals like Carnevale or Regata Storica.

6. **Arrive the evening before** any festival for the best experience.

Already Chosen the Cities You Plan to Visit? Use the Alphabetical Index of Locations Chapter to find festivals in towns you're already visiting.

Planning a Festival-Focused Trip? Start with the Calendar of Events chapter and build your itinerary around multiple celebrations using FestaFusion techniques.

Chapter Organization

Chapters are organized to get you everything you need to attend the festival as well as enjoy the town:

1. Town and Main Festival Information

2. Must-See Sights in Walking Tour order

3. Logistics, how to arrive and get around

4. Restaurant Recommendations

5. Accommodation Recommendations

6. Day Trips, Nearby Sights to See

7. Events in Town throughout the Year

Maximize Your Festival Experience with #FestaFusion

Why see just one festival when you can experience several during your visit? I've coined the term FestaFusion to help you discover the magic of timing your visit to catch multiple celebrations. With so many festivals throughout Italy, experiencing several during one trip is not only possible but enriching. For example:

- Join FestaFusion Venezia during the Festa della Sensa and the Vogalonga.

- Experience FestaFusion Verona, combining the Opera Festival with the Sagra dei Gnocchi.

- During the carnival season, savor multiple celebrations throughout the region.

- Mix and match festivals across chapters using the Calendar of Events - they're all within easy reach.

These festival combinations aren't just convenient; they're transformative. Each celebration adds new layers to your understanding of Italian culture, revealing hidden connections in traditions, foods, and customs. With some planning, this guide makes it easy to experience several events in one trip: exactly what my husband and I plan to do in our retirement: una festa ogni settimana, a festival every week!

Immersion Experiences: Beyond the Festivals

While festivals are at the heart of this book, I've discovered that Italy's magic extends far beyond its celebrations. That's why I've included special Immersion Experience chapters. Think of these as your guide to authentic adventures near each festival location: experiences that let you dive deeper into local life, whether you're between festivals or creating your own unique journey.

These year-round experiences invite you to:

- **Get Your Hands Dirty:** Learn to make risotto alongside local nonnas (grandmothers) or watch master glassblowers at work in their centuries-old crafts.

- **Embrace Nature's Drama**: Boat through the marshes of the lagoon, explore hidden islands, or hike the rolling Prosecco hills.

- **Live the History:** Watch opera in Verona's ancient arena, make a mosaic with a master craftsman, or discover secret historical sites tourists rarely see.

- **Go Behind the Scenes:** Visit family vineyards in Valpolicella, learn the secrets of radicchio farming, or try your hand at traditional mask making.

- **Be a Local:** Stay in an agriturismo in the Euganean Hills, walk ancient paths on a cammino, or join seasonal grape harvest celebrations.

Each Immersion Experience chapter is your insider guide, packed with:

- The Full Story: What makes this experience special and what to expect.

- Making It Happen: Booking tips, websites, packing essentials, perfect timing, and how to get there.

- Insider Secrets: Little-known tips to make your experience even better.

Planning Your Festival Travel

Want to make the most of your festival experience? Arrive the evening before. This golden rule has served me well: it gives you time to discover the town's rhythm, wander its streets without rushing, and scout the perfect spots for tomorrow's celebrations. My first stop is always finding the main piazza and central church (whether it's called a cattedrale, duomo, or chiesa madre). These are the heart of most festivals, and knowing their location helps you navigate the festivities like a local.

How Long to Stay

For major festivals, I recommend two to three nights. Don't let accommodation costs worry you: outside major cities, Italian hotels are surprisingly affordable. (One of my favorite stays was right in Piazza Duomo in Ragusa for just $100 a night!) Longer stays let you fully immerse yourself in evening events, especially during those magical summer festivals, without worrying about late-night drives. Plus, festival schedules can be delightfully unpredictable: having extra time lets you go with the flow.

For food festivals (sagre), you can often make it a day trip. These typically happen in smaller towns that might not have many accommodation options.

Early Bird Benefits

Arrived with time to spare? Perfect! Use these precious hours to:

- Follow my walking tour to uncover the town's hidden gems.

- Sample regional specialties at local restaurants.

- Stop by cafes to chat with locals. They often share insider festival tips and stories that you won't find in any guide.

Consider a Local Guide: While I've crafted over 30 self-guided walking adventures for you, there's something special about exploring with a local guide. If your budget allows and you have extra time, I recommend booking through Tours By Locals or With Locals, especially in smaller towns where local knowledge is invaluable. Locals can offer in-depth festival background and history, share their own families' experiences, show you where events occur, and ensure you see the festival information flyers that are posted around town. Their stories and insights can transform a simple walk into an unforgettable journey.

As the festival draws near, keep an eye out for event programs yourself as well. In my experience, they're usually posted on cathedral doors and other prominent spots around town. Check if there are any traditional dress codes or color schemes. Taking part in these customs not only shows respect but makes you feel part of the celebration.

Feel the Rhythm of the Festival

Once the festival begins, let yourself be swept up in the experience. Join in the activities, savor those once-a-year festival treats, and connect with the community. While capturing memories is important, remember that some of the most magical moments happen when you put the camera down and simply participate.

Festival Categories and Planning

Embrace the spontaneity of Italian travel, particularly during festive seasons. While this guide offers well-researched information, the dynamic nature of festivals means schedules can evolve. To enhance your experience, I've included a variety of options and activities for each destination. This way, you're guaranteed an enriching adventure, with plenty of room for delightful surprises along the way.

Italian festivals fall into two categories: fixed-date celebrations that occur annually on specific dates, and moveable feasts that align with weekends, harvests, or religious calendars. Each festival listing includes timing details to help you plan effectively.

My website offers sample itineraries that show how to combine festival experiences with broader regional exploration, making it easier to create your perfect Italian journey: https://katerinaferrara.com/

While other travel guides simply list attractions and leave you to puzzle out the logistics, I've designed this book differently. Each town features carefully crafted walking tours that present sites in a logical, walkable sequence, complete with practical details to help you plan efficiently.

Though festivals are our focus, this guide serves equally well as a companion for general travel. You'll find detailed city guides, walking tours, cultural context, and practical advice valuable for any visit to the region.

A Note on Organization

For festivals outside Venice, each chapter is a complete guide with everything you need: walking routes, local stories, practical details, places to stay, and where to find the best meals.

But Venice, with its wealth of festivals, needed a different approach. To avoid telling you where to stay and eat in Venice twenty different times, I've created special chapters:

- Regional Dishes and Venetian Specialities

- Best Dining, Gelato & Drinks in Venice

- Best Coffee and Pastries in Venice

- Itineraries for Venice and Must-See Sights

- Accommodation Detail Venice

- Transportation Detail Venice

This lets each Venetian festival chapter focus on what makes that celebration unique while keeping all the city information easily accessible.

Consider this guide your key to unlocking Italy's vibrant spirit. Whether you're here for the festivals or seeking to explore the region's rich tapestry of experiences, you'll discover everything needed to create a memorable adventure.

CHAPTER THREE

Discover Venice and the Veneto

Tradition & Timeless Beauty

V enice: The Enchanting Heart of the Lagoon

There is nowhere in the world quite like Venice. Built on more than 100 small islands and laced with over 150 canals, this floating city seduces visitors with its dreamlike beauty and haunting elegance. Life here unfolds not along boulevards but along narrow calli and gliding gondolas, where echoes of Vivaldi drift through the mist and every stone seems to whisper a story. It is a city where art, faith, and ingenuity coalesce, a marvel of human ambition rising improbably from the sea.

Over centuries, Venice was built slowly and ingeniously atop wooden pilings driven deep into the mud of the lagoon. These submerged foundations, hardened over time by the lack of oxygen, still support many of the city's most iconic buildings, a testament to both engineering brilliance and resilience.

Each of Venice's six sestieri San Marco, Dorsoduro, Cannaregio, Castello, San Polo, and Santa Croce, offers its own flavor of Venetian life. In San Marco, you'll find the heart of the former Republic, where the domes of Saint Mark's Basilica glitter beside the Gothic arches of the Doge's Palace.

Dorsoduro balances quiet charm with artistic grandeur, home to the Gallerie dell'Accademia and Peggy Guggenheim Collection. Cannaregio, where the Jewish Ghetto was established in 1516, is vibrant and less trodden, a place to experience daily life unfolding along quiet canals.

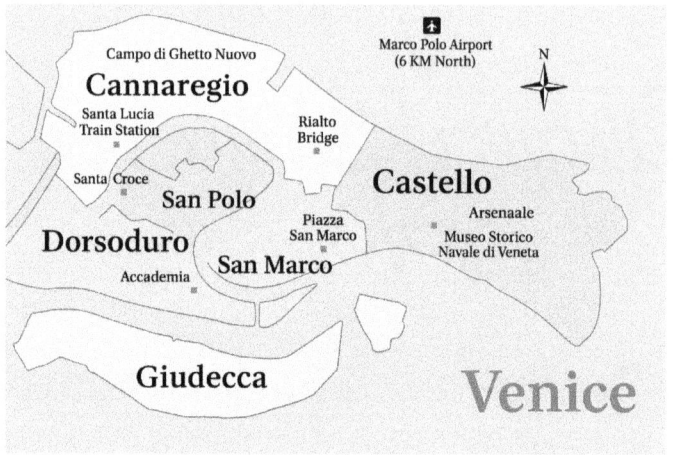

Six Sestieri (Neighborhoods) of Venice

Castello stretches toward the eastern edge of the city, blending monumental churches with local gardens and hosting the Biennale's artistic energy. San Polo, the smallest sestiere, pulses with life around the bustling Rialto Market and bridge, Venice's oldest crossing. Santa Croce, often overlooked, offers a more laid-back feel, with quiet squares, artisan workshops, and easy access to the city's arrival points.

But Venice is more than its sites; it's a feeling. It's the thrill of getting lost in the labyrinth of alleys, only to stumble into a luminous campo where locals sip spritz and children kick soccer balls under the watchful gaze of Baroque façades.

It's the stillness of dawn on the Grand Canal, the hush before the city awakens. And it's the pageantry of festivals that echo centuries of civic pride, spiritual devotion, and creative flair. The Carnival of Venice, the Festa della Sensa, the Redentore, these are not performances but living traditions.

And yet, to truly appreciate Venice, one must understand that its story doesn't end at the edge of the lagoon. It's merely the beginning.

Grand Canal Venice

Exploring Venice and Beyond: Hidden Treasures of the Veneto

Venice may feel like a world unto itself, suspended between sea and sky, but one of the greatest surprises of traveling through the Veneto is just how easy it is to step off the beaten path and into something magical.

I remember one quiet afternoon when my husband and I took a spontaneous day trip from Venice. We hopped on a local train, no reservations needed, and in just thirty scenic minutes we arrived in Treviso, a town that felt like a secret we'd stumbled upon. The canals were quieter, the streets less hurried. We strolled under vine-covered arcades and across cobbled piazzas, admired pastel frescoes on medieval facades, and stopped at a cozy café for cappuccinos and warm sfogliatine pastries, made of delicate flaky layers filled with fruit or cream and dusted with powdered sugar.

Afterwards, we wandered beyond the town center and discovered the beautiful ancient water mill of Treviso, its weathered stones and moss-covered wheel turning gently beside a tranquil stream, a tangible link to the town's medieval past.

There was an ease to the day, a joy in discovering somewhere so close to Venice, yet filled with its own distinct character; we wandered the Pescheria (fish market) island, watched bikes roll by flower-lined bridges, and later met friends for an aperitivo at a bar on the water's edge, sampling classic cicchetti (small bites) such as baccalà mantecato, sarde in saor, crostini con fegatini and schie fritte alongside chilled Prosecco before buying a small bottle to take back with us on the return train. It was the kind of moment that stays with you, not because of grand monuments, but because it felt real, local, and beautifully unexpected.

Treviso was just the beginning. That short ride opened our eyes to the rich variety that the Veneto offers beyond its most famous city, and it left us wondering, what else lies just beyond the next bend in the tracks?

Why Venture Beyond Venice?

Venice may be the glittering jewel of the Veneto, but it is far from the whole treasure. Just beyond the lagoon lies a mosaic of cities, towns, and landscapes that have shaped, and been shaped by, centuries of culture, commerce, and creativity. From the Renaissance elegance of Vicenza to the vineyard-laced hills of Soave, the Roman splendor of Verona to the scholarly spirit of Padua, each subregion of the Veneto tells its own interesting story.

Venturing beyond Venice reveals a more intimate, authentic side of northern Italy. Here, you can sip world-renowned wines in the shadow of Palladian villas, soak in ancient thermal springs once favored by emperors, or hike through the Dolomites where age-old mountain traditions endure. You'll encounter artisans preserving centuries-old crafts, festivals rooted in mountain lore or rural devotion, and piazzas where locals still gather to share stories over espresso. Whether you're drawn by art, food, history, or nature, the wider Veneto offers something richer: a deeper connection to Italy's enduring soul.

Concise History of the Veneto

Venice, the shimmering city rising from the Adriatic Sea, is more than its canals, gondolas, and opulent architecture. It is a living museum of history, a cultural beacon that has shaped and been shaped by centuries of commerce, politics, religion, and art. To understand the festivals of Venice and the greater Veneto region, one must first journey through their shared past, rich with triumph, tragedy, innovation, and tradition.

Origins and Roman Roots

The origins of Venice trace back to the early Middle Ages, around the 5th and 6th centuries AD, when inhabitants of the mainland fled barbarian invasions, notably by the Huns and Lombards. Seeking refuge in the marshy lagoons of the Adriatic, these displaced people laid the foundations of a new society atop wooden pilings sunk into the mud. Though difficult to settle, the lagoons offered protection and access to maritime trade routes.

The Veneto region, however, has deeper roots. Before Venice rose, Veneto was part of the Roman Empire, with cities like Verona, Padua (Padova), Vicenza, and Treviso thriving as Roman municipia. These cities were connected by Roman roads and served as vital military and trade hubs. Their legacy is still visible in ancient arenas, forums, and aqueducts that dot the region.

Venice canal at dusk

The Rise of the Venetian Republic

Venice grew from a collection of fishermen's huts perched on stilts to a formidable maritime power. In 697 AD, the first Doge (chief magistrate), Paolo Lucio Anafesto, was elected, an event traditionally considered the beginning of the Venetian Republic. Over time, the city evolved into a self-governing and independent entity, distinct from both the Eastern and Western Roman Empires. Its independence and geographic isolation within the lagoon provided a unique political and cultural trajectory.

The city's ancient architecture reflected its ingenuity in adapting to the aquatic environment. Buildings were constructed atop thousands of wooden piles driven deep into the lagoon bed, a foundation system that has lasted centuries. The layout of the city emerged in concentric rings around the Grand Canal, with neighborhoods (sestieri) connected by bridges and narrow pedestrian paths. Venice became a masterpiece of urban planning on water.

By the 11th century, Venice had become a dominant maritime republic. Its navy and merchant fleet controlled key trade routes across the Mediterranean, the Adriatic, and even into the Black Sea and the Levant. It was not just military might that propelled Venice to prominence; it was its keen commercial instincts and skillful diplomacy.

The Venetians brokered trade deals with the Byzantine Empire, Islamic caliphates, and Christian kingdoms alike. This international commerce brought immense wealth, fostering an elite class of merchant-aristocrats who reinvested their fortunes into the city's infrastructure, palaces, churches, and civic institutions.

Venetian architecture in this period flourished in a distinct style known as Venetian Gothic, which fused Byzantine, Islamic, and Gothic elements. The Doge's Palace (Palazzo Ducale), completed in its current form in the 14th century, is the pinnacle of this architectural style. Its delicate tracery, pointed arches, and ornamental stonework speak to Venice's role as a crossroads of East and West. Similarly, the development of the Rialto district as a commercial and financial center further illustrated the city's burgeoning importance.

Venetian Tracery Windows, Gothic Architecture

Venice's governing institutions also became more refined. The Republic developed a complex system of administration, with power concentrated in the hands of the Doge, the elected leader of Venice, and the Great Council, composed of aristocratic families. This oligarchic structure allowed the city to maintain stability, avoid dynastic struggles, and pursue its wide-reaching maritime ambitions.

As Venice grew richer, it also expanded its territories, establishing colonies and trading posts throughout the Adriatic, the Aegean, and the Middle East. These outposts supported the Republic's economy and acted as defensive strongholds, protecting its merchant ships and asserting dominance over rival maritime powers such as Genoa and Pisa. Venice became known as "La Serenissima," the Most Serene Republic, for its longevity, wealth, and political equilibrium.

Doge's Palace

The Crusades and Expansion

Venice's pivotal role in the Crusades, especially the Fourth Crusade (1202–1204), drastically increased its wealth and influence. The diversion of the Crusade to Constantinople led to the sacking of the Byzantine capital, from which Venice looted immense treasures. Many of these, including the famous bronze horses atop St. Mark's Basilica, remain in Venice today.

As Venice expanded, it acquired territories on the mainland and across the seas, including parts of modern-day Greece, Cyprus, and Crete. The mainland expansion into the Veneto, known as the Terraferma, included cities such as Verona, Padua, and Vicenza. These cities added agricultural resources, strategic advantages, and further cultural richness to the Republic.

Culture, Art, and the Renaissance

Venice was not merely a trading empire; it was a cultural superpower. During the Renaissance, the city became a haven for artists, musicians, architects, and scholars. Figures like Titian, Tintoretto, Veronese, and Bellini transformed the visual arts, while Andrea Palladio, based in Vicenza, revolutionized architecture with his harmonious classical style.

Printing also flourished in Venice. Aldus Manutius, a pioneer of publishing, introduced the portable octavo book and italic type. Venetian presses became the most prolific in Europe, spreading knowledge far and wide.

Festivals during this period reflected both religious devotion and civic pride. Elaborate processions, regattas, masked balls, and holy day observances highlighted Venice's wealth and artistic brilliance.

One lesser-known but extraordinary Venetian art is the work of the battiloro, the goldbeaters. These artisans specialized in transforming gold into impossibly thin leaf used for everything from painted wooden panels to the glowing tesserae (small glass tiles) in Byzantine mosaics. The tradition of the battiloro spanned centuries in Venice, and until recently, it continued in one final workshop housed in a building once lived in by Titian himself.

In 2024, I had the rare opportunity to visit this remarkable place before it closed its doors. Watching the process unfold was unforgettable; the mother carefully prepared the parchment packets, the father beat the gold with rhythmic precision, and their daughter oversaw both the artistry and the business. The family was selling the workshop and preparing for retirement in the cool air of the mountains. It was a poignant reminder that Venice's legacy of craftsmanship is not only preserved in its museums but also in the fading echoes of living traditions, carried for generations and now lovingly passed into memory.

Decline and Fall

Despite its grandeur, the Venetian Republic faced increasing challenges from the 16th century onward. The rise of the Ottoman Empire, competition from

Portuguese and Spanish explorers who opened new trade routes, and shifting political alliances all weakened Venice's grip on global commerce.

The Republic held out longer than many other city-states, maintaining its independence until 1797. That year, Napoleon Bonaparte arrived in Venice and ended over a millennium of republican government. The Treaty of Campo Formio ceded the city to Austria, beginning a period of foreign domination.

Venice and Veneto in Modern Times

In the 19th century, the Veneto region became a center of resistance during the Risorgimento, the movement for Italian unification. After various struggles and revolts, the region, including Venice, officially joined the Kingdom of Italy in 1866.

Since then, both Venice and the Veneto have continued to strengthen. Venice transformed into one of the world's most iconic tourist destinations, while the Veneto developed into one of Italy's most economically productive regions. Cities like Verona, Vicenza, and Padua remain vibrant centers of culture, education, and industry.

Festivals: Echoes of the Past

The festivals celebrated today across Venice and the Veneto are steeped in the region's long and diverse history. Some commemorate saints or miraculous events. Others recall victories, civic rituals, or seasonal traditions. Events like the Festa della Sensa (celebrating Venice's marriage to the sea), the Redentore Festival (marking deliverance from the plague), and the famed Carnival of Venice (with its roots in the 12th century) all draw on centuries of shared identity.

In the Veneto, cities like Verona, Bassano del Grappa, and Treviso host festivals tied to agricultural cycles, medieval fairs, or historical reenactments. From wine and cherry festivals to grand processions and operatic tributes, each event reveals another layer of regional pride and historical continuity.

As we move into the specific festivals of May and beyond, understanding the layered history of Venice and the Veneto allows us to better appreciate the meaning behind the masks, parades, fireworks, and sacred rituals that continue to breathe life into this timeless corner of Italy.

Key Subregions of the Veneto

Venezia: The Floating Center of the Maritime Empire

Where land meets water in a breathtaking embrace, Metropolitan Venice captures the soul of the Venetian Republic.

This subregion encompasses the world-famous city of Venice with its shimmering canals, the artisan islands of Murano, Burano, and Torcello, the bustling mainland hub of Mestre, and the fishing town of Chioggia. Once the seat of a powerful maritime empire, Venice rose from the marshes as a haven of trade, art, and religious devotion. Today, it continues to enchant with its floating palaces, mosaic-studded basilicas, and vibrant lagoon culture.

Veneto
Provinces of the Veneto

Verona: A Stage of Romance and Roman Glory

Romance, ruins, and rolling vineyards define the Veronese, a land where Roman amphitheaters stand beside Renaissance palazzi. Verona, the jewel of the region and a UNESCO World Heritage Site, offers Shakespearean charm, but the magic continues outward, through the vine-covered hills of Valpolicella, the tranquil shores of eastern Lake Garda, and into the Lessini Mountains. The Veronese has long been a cultural and economic crossroads, with a legacy steeped in viticulture, opera, and noble traditions.

Treviso: Where Prosecco Bubbles and Canals Whisper

Gentle rivers, winding canals, and sparkling wine define the Trevigiano, a landscape of quiet beauty and festive tradition. Treviso, often called "Little Venice," offers charming waterways and frescoed facades, while the nearby hills of Conegliano and Valdobbiadene produce the world's finest Prosecco. Once the proud Marca Trevigiana under Venetian rule, the region retains a noble air, where old-world elegance meets the joyful rhythm of local markets, vineyards, and seasonal festivals.

Canal Views Treviso

Vicenza: Land of Villas, Visionaries, and Mountain Valor

Elegant and industrious, the Vicentino blends the grandeur of Palladio's villas with the spirit of artisanal innovation. Vicenza itself, a World Heritage Site, is a showcase of 16th-century harmony and classical ideals. Beyond the city, the Berici Hills and Monte Grappa frame a land of historic battles, mountain treks, and rustic flavors. This subregion thrives on a legacy of architecture, craftsmanship, and resilience, from silk-making to goldsmithing and alpine defense.

Belluno: Peak of Tradition and Soul of the Dolomites

A dramatic realm of peaks and pine forests, the Bellunese rises into the eastern Dolomites, where nature and tradition reign supreme. Belluno, the gateway to this alpine world, leads to remote valleys shaped by Ladin and Tyrolean heritage. In winter, ski legends are born in Cortina d'Ampezzo; in summer, hikers follow centuries-old paths. Belluno is celebrated for its woodcarving, mountain dairies, and sacred festivals that blend Catholic faith with ancient alpine rites.

Padua: Where Faith, Frescoes, and Thermal Waters Flow

12th century Baptistry, Padua

The heart of learning and spirituality, the Padovano is anchored by Padua (Padova in Italian), one of Europe's oldest university cities. Its cobbled streets echo with medieval scholarship and the genius of Giotto, whose frescoes shaped Renaissance art.

Surrounding the city are vast agricultural plains and the volcanic Euganean Hills, a patchwork of vineyards, olive groves, and thermal springs that have drawn visitors since Roman times. This is a land of reflection and renewal, where faith, science, and natural beauty converge.

Rovigo: Italy's Quiet Delta of Rebirth and Reflection

Tucked between the Po and Adige Rivers, the Polesine is a land of waterways, reclaimed fields, and enduring rural life. Once marshland prone to floods, this fertile plain was transformed through centuries of land reclamation and irrigation. Rovigo, the regional capital, reflects both agricultural roots and baroque elegance. Off the beaten path, the Po Delta beckons with serene wetlands, bird sanctuaries, and timeless fishing villages. The Polesine moves at the pace of its rivers, quiet, generous, and full of hidden treasures.

The Magic Beyond the Lagoon

There's a phrase Italians use that beautifully captures the charm of the Veneto: "Il bello della provincia", the beauty of the provinces. While Venice may be the crown jewel, beyond its shimmering canals lies an Italy that is just as captivating, yet far less discovered.

Why Journey Beyond?

In the towns and countryside beyond Venice, you'll find treasures that no gondola ride or palace tour can quite match. This is where the heartbeat of the Veneto truly lives.

Here, history isn't confined to museums; it flows through everyday life. Entering the gate to the castle and town of Sirmione, we stepped into a world where ancient stone meets the shimmering lake. The medieval walls gave way to cobbled lanes lined with gelaterias and flower-filled balconies, while the thermal springs reminded us that this town has drawn visitors since Roman times. We wandered past Roman ruins at the Grotte di Catullo and sat by the water's edge, watching swans drift across the turquoise lake as the sun set.

In the hills of Valdobbiadene, we found ourselves invited into a vineyard during the Prosecco harvest, sipping wine and sharing laughter with locals whose passion for the land runs as deep as their roots. In Bassano del Grappa, we crossed the wooden Ponte degli Alpini as the Brenta River shimmered below, then lingered in artisan workshops where hands still shape clay and glass into timeless beauty.

Castello Scaliger, Sirmione

Life moves to a gentler rhythm. Picture yourself joining an evening passeggiata in Vicenza, where Palladian architecture glows golden in the fading light. Or taking a cable car in Malcesine for views over Lake Garda that stretch from ancient Roman ruins to alpine peaks. And then there's the joy of stumbling upon a small-town festival in a mountain village, where the music of tamburi echoes through narrow streets and the scent of roasted chestnuts or fresh polenta fills the air.

Here, festivals aren't staged for tourists; they are heartfelt celebrations, passed down through generations, where you're welcomed not as a guest, but as part of the family.

Your Journey Begins

After years of exploring the Veneto, I've learned that its true magic lies in these unexpected encounters, in quiet moments shared with strangers, in age-old traditions celebrated under open skies, and in the deep sense of place that exists beyond the lagoon.

That's what this book offers, not just a guide to Venice's marvels, but an invitation to explore the region that surrounds it, places like Arquà Petrarca, where the poet Petrarch's hillside home still gazes over olive groves and medieval lanes, Marostica, where human chess games unfold in the town square, and Burano, where lace making traditions live on and canals reflect houses painted in joyful, sun washed hues.

Whether you're drawn to:

- The echo of opera in Verona's ancient arena.

- A crisp glass of Prosecco in the hills of Conegliano.

- The stillness of a sunrise in Chioggia's fishing harbor.

- The spectacle of mountain festivals in Cortina d'Ampezzo.

- Bike rides around Lake Garda.

- Or my personal favorite: the surprise of finding beauty in the every day, a quick train ride out of the more touristed Venice, where the magic of the Veneto quietly reveals itself.

This journey beyond the Grand Canal offers something precious: the chance to experience Italy not just as a postcard, but as a living story you get to step into.

Let this book be your guide, your key, and your companion as you uncover the hidden wonders of Venice and the Veneto. Adventure is calling, and it's just a train ride away.

Note on Historical Terms / Glossary:
Because I want to keep the history sections concise and get you to the festivals and travel information as quickly as possible, I have included many historical terms in the **Glossary of Key Terms** section. If you come across a ruling family, architectural style, or historical reference that is not fully covered in the history section, please refer to the glossary for additional details.

CHAPTER FOUR

Venice and Veneto Maps

Lakes, Mountains, Cities and Sea

Navigating Venice: A Guide to the Six Sestieri

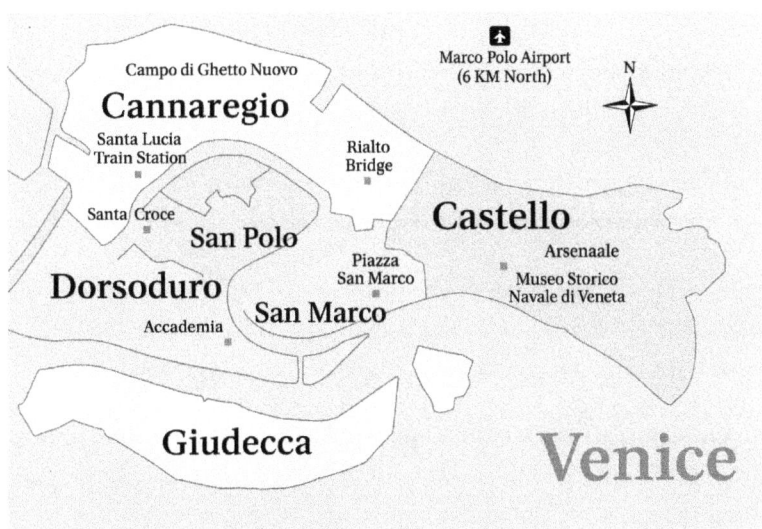

The Neighborhoods, Sestieri of Venice

Venice may be a city without cars, but it's a place best explored on foot, or by boat. The city is divided into six historic districts, known as *sestieri*, each with its own distinct character, rhythm, and charm. Understanding the layout of the *sestieri* will help you make sense of Venice's winding alleys, hidden courtyards, and countless bridges.

At the heart of the city lies the Grand Canal, curving like a backward S through the city and separating Venice into two sides. Crossing the Grand Canal are only a few bridges, Rialto, Accademia, and Scalzi, so knowing where you are within the *sestieri* can help you plan your route and avoid backtracking.

Each sestiere offers something unique:

1. **San Marco** is the ceremonial heart of Venice, home to St. Mark's Basilica, the Doge's Palace, and elegant cafés like Caffè Florian.

2. **Cannaregio** is a vibrant, residential neighborhood filled with local eateries, the Jewish Ghetto, and a laid-back charm.

3. **Dorsoduro** blends culture and beauty, with the Peggy Guggenheim Collection, sunny Zattere promenade, and sweeping canal views.

4. **San Polo** is one of the oldest districts and home to the lively Rialto Market and some of the best *bacari*.

5. **Santa Croce** is the city's main transport hub, with easy access to Piazzale Roma and the train station, plus quiet streets and hidden gems.

6. **Castello**, the largest *sestiere*, stretches from busy Riva degli Schiavoni to quiet local corners near the Biennale Gardens.

Venice is compact but layered, with every turn offering something new to discover. Use the following map and neighborhood guide to find your bearings, plan your walks, and uncover the true magic of the floating city.

See the **Transportation Detail Chapter (Chapter 38)** for helpful information on how to get around Venice using *vaporetti* (water buses), water taxis, gondolas, and private boats.

A Landscape of Lakes, Mountains, Cities, and Sea

To truly appreciate the Veneto, one must start with its geography. This northern Italian region stretches from the shimmering Adriatic Sea in the east to the soaring Dolomites in the north, and from the shores of Lake Garda in the west to the fertile plains that edge the River Po. The variety of landscapes is extraordinary, and so is the way each subregion shapes its culture, cuisine, architecture, and traditions.

The Veneto is more than Venice. While the floating city captures the imagination, the region is also home to elegant cities like Verona, Padua, and Vicenza, each a jewel with its own character and history. Hill towns like Asolo and Marostica crown the landscape with medieval charm, while coastal gems like Chioggia carry on the seafaring traditions of the Republic.

Map of the Subregions of the Veneto

Veneto

Subregions of the Region of the Veneto

The Islands of the Venice Lagoon

Venice, the airport, and the Islands of the Lagoon

Scattered across the serene waters of the Venetian Lagoon are dozens of islands, each with its own story, rhythm, and charm. Murano is world-renowned for its glassmaking traditions, while Burano dazzles with colorful houses and delicate lacework. Torcello, once more powerful than Venice itself, offers a peaceful retreat filled with ancient ruins and mosaics. San Michele is the quiet island cemetery of Venice, and San Giorgio Maggiore, with its iconic church and panoramic views, stands just across the water from St. Mark's.

These islands are easily reached by vaporetto and make unforgettable day trips or peaceful escapes from the bustling center of Venice. Together, they reveal the rich layers of culture, craftsmanship, and history that have shaped life in the lagoon for over a thousand years.

CHAPTER FIVE

Map of Must See Celebrations

Explore the Festivals of the Veneto on our Interactive Map

Festival & Sagra Map: Your Essential Guide

Immerse yourself in the Veneto's most cherished traditions. Our detailed festival map pinpoints every vibrant celebration across the region, from ancient religious processions to mouthwatering food sagre. Each marker reveals event dates and locations, making it easy to weave these authentic Italian experiences into your journey. Find the map here:

https://katerinaferrara.com

Interactive Google Map: Plan Your Adventure

Take your exploration further with our comprehensive Google Map. This dynamic tool brings the festival cities to life, helping you visualize your route, estimate travel times, and preview each destination through local photos. From North to South, plan your journey here:

https://maps.app.goo.gl/iNQ1u2Dp8YwNyQzP8

Venice & the Veneto Festival Map. The Festival Map is also available in color on the book's page. https://katerinaferrara.com/

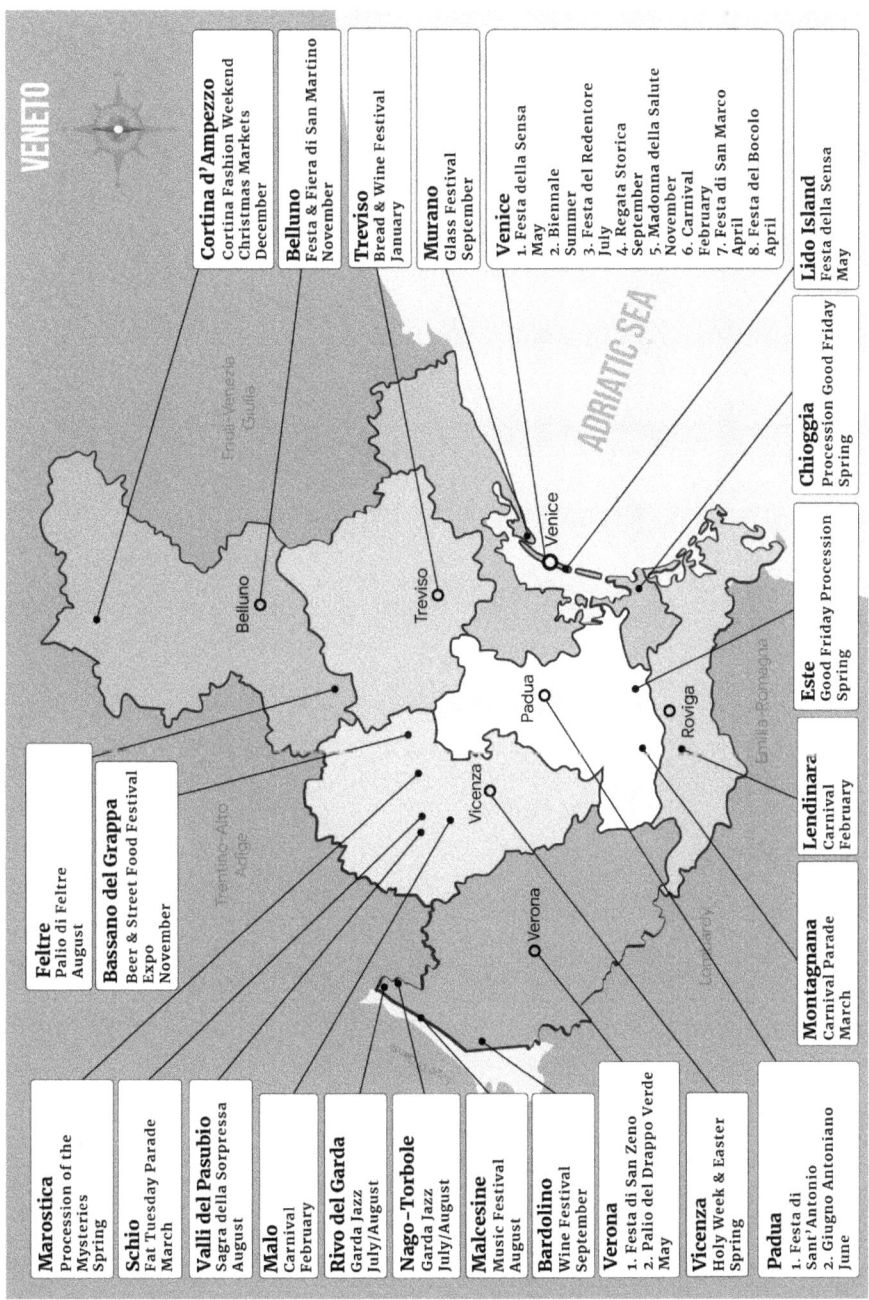

CHAPTER SIX

Arrive and Explore

A Visitors Guide to the City & the Veneto

V enice is unlike any other city in the world, a maze of canals, bridges, and centuries-old architecture rising from the sea. But the magic of the Veneto doesn't end at the edge of the lagoon. Whether you're flying in from abroad or arriving by train from elsewhere in Italy, this guide will help you settle in and prepare for unforgettable excursions beyond the Grand Canal.

Getting to Venice

Venice welcomes travelers primarily through Marco Polo Airport (VCE), about 13 kilometers (8 miles) north of the city center. Treviso Airport (TSF), a smaller airport about 25 miles away, has budget airlines.

From Marco Polo Airport, you have several scenic and convenient options to reach Venice's historic center:

Alilaguna water buses provide a picturesque ride across the lagoon, stopping at key points like San Marco, Rialto, and Fondamenta Nove (tickets start around €8–€15).

ATVO and ACTV buses run frequently to Piazzale Roma, Venice's land-accessible entry point, in 20–30 minutes for €10 or less.

Water taxis offer direct service to your hotel or nearby canal, costly (around €100–€130), but ideal for a romantic or effortless arrival.

From Treviso Airport, shuttle buses connect directly to Venice's Piazzale Roma in about 70 minutes, with tickets priced around €12.

If arriving by train, Venezia Santa Lucia Station brings you right to the Grand Canal. From there, you can explore on foot or via vaporetto (public water bus). Trains from major cities like Milan, Florence, and Verona are frequent, efficient, and scenic.

For complete travel logistics, see Transportation Detail (Chapter 39).
This chapter includes everything you need to know about arriving in and navigating Venice and the Veneto. It covers Vaporetti (water buses), water taxis, getting to Venice from the airport, car rentals, regional bus lines, ferry routes, and which cities offer convenient train service. Whether you're planning a smooth arrival or looking to explore the region with ease, Chapter 33 is your go-to resource for transportation tips and insider advice.

Choosing Your Base in Venice

Staying in the heart of Venice allows you to experience the city before and after the day trippers leave. Neighborhoods like San Marco, Dorsoduro, Cannaregio, and Castello each offer a unique vibe, whether it's the glamor of Piazza San Marco, the artsy calm of Dorsoduro, or the authentic charm of Cannaregio's canal-side trattorias.

Cannaregio is our favorite neighborhood to stay in Venice. We have stayed in the past in the Rialto area and in San Marco, but we truly love the authentic neighborhood feel of Cannaregio. It stretches from one end of the Grand Canal to the quiet edges where local life unfolds. In the mornings, when I would go for an early walk, I'd see grandparents delivering kids on scooters to school and neighbors handing off their recyclables directly to the boats as they moved along the smaller canals. There is something grounding and beautiful in witnessing the rhythm of daily life continuing in such a historic place.

On our most recent visit, we stayed near Campo Santa Maria Formosa, a quiet yet central square just minutes from both San Marco and Rialto. The early mornings were serene, with the sound of church bells echoing over the rooftops. In the evening, we'd return to a cozy inn tucked into an alleyway just beyond the crowds, grateful for the convenience of being close to everything, but far enough to rest.

For those planning to explore the Veneto region with day trips to Padua, Verona, Treviso, Vicenza, or the Dolomites, consider splitting your stay between Venice and a second location on the mainland such as Padua Lake Garda, or Verona, which offer easy train access and a more local feel.

See the **Accommodation Detail (Chapter 38)** for more guidance and neighborhood-specific hotel recommendations.

Getting Around Venice and Beyond

Venice is best discovered on foot or by boat. Once you've settled in, wandering through its alleyways, crossing arched bridges, and following the sound of church bells becomes part of the adventure. The vaporetto system makes getting around the city's islands simple, while gondola ferries let you cross the Grand Canal at various points for just a couple of euros.

For broader Veneto exploration, Venice serves as a perfect base. Trenitalia and Italo trains connect the lagoon city to Padua (30 min), Treviso (30 minutes), Verona (1 hour), Vicenza (45 minutes), and even Cortina d'Ampezzo via bus and rail connections. Each of these towns offers unique charm, from frescoed chapels and Palladian villas to lakeside castles and alpine festivals.

Regional buses and ferries provide additional transport for reaching smaller towns, the Po Delta, or lakefront villages along Lake Garda. Renting a car is ideal if you want to explore the Prosecco Hills or Dolomite trails, but parking must be done outside Venice (typically in Mestre or Tronchetto). For local taxis, ride apps like FreeNow are helpful, especially when traveling from airports or mainland hotels. The Transportation Detail chapter has everything you need to get around Venice and the Veneto.

Summer Celebrations

May Through August

CHAPTER SEVEN

FestaFusion Verona

A Saint's Feast and a City's Run Through History

F estaFusion Verona

#1. Festa di San Zeno. Verona's heartfelt celebration of its patron saint, blending solemn mass, medieval parades, and lively street festivities in the historic San Zeno district.

#2. Palio del Drappo Verde. An ancient footrace through Verona's medieval streets, where athletes and locals compete for honor, tradition, and the coveted green banner.

#FestaFusion: When two festivals converge in the same town around the same time, your journey becomes twice as magical.

Where: Verona

When: May 21 (Festa di San Zeno). Palio del Drappo Verde is held on the weekend closest to May 21.

Average Temperatures: High 27°C (81°F). Low 13°C (55°F).

Verona: A Symphony of Time

Verona's story spans more than 2,000 years, unfolding along the banks of the Adige River in northern Italy. First settled in the 2nd century BC, the city rose to prominence under the Roman Empire, which laid out its enduring street grid and transformed Verona into a major urban center. Roman citizenship was granted to its inhabitants in the 1st century AD, and the city's prosperity and influence grew.

After the empire's decline, Verona became a strategic frontier, fortified against invasions and ruled successively by Ostrogoths, Lombards, and eventually Charlemagne. In the medieval era, it emerged as a powerful, free municipality.

Verona's golden age came in the 13th and 14th centuries under the rule of the Scaliger (Della Scala) family, especially Cangrande I, who brought political stability, economic strength, and a flourishing of the arts. During this time, Verona became home to exiled poet Dante Alighieri and the legendary setting for the tragic romance of Romeo and Juliet.

In 1405, Verona joined the Republic of Venice, entering a new chapter of artistic and architectural refinement. The city remained under Venetian rule until 1797, when it was ceded to Austria, and eventually became part of unified Italy in 1866.

Verona endured hardship during World War II, including Nazi occupation and the execution of Mussolini's son-in-law, Galeazzo Ciano, on the riverbank. Yet the city emerged with its heritage intact, honored today as a UNESCO World Heritage Site for its exceptional preservation of Roman, medieval, and Renaissance architecture.

Today, Verona is a thriving city of around 260,000 residents. Its strategic location near Lake Garda, Valpolicella wine country, and the Venetian Prealps, along with frequent rail and air connections, make it both historically rich and effortlessly accessible.

A Personal Love Affair with Verona

One summer morning, my husband, son, and I arrived by car from Sirmione and spent the day wandering through the city's walkable center. Verona revealed itself slowly, with Roman ruins beside medieval churches, Renaissance palaces glowing in the sun, and piazzas alive with the laughter of locals. The soft pink of its buildings shimmered in the warmth, giving the city a dreamy, romantic air.

That evening, we dined near the Arena, watching the elegant Veronese arrive for the opera in tailored suits and high heels, graceful even on the cobblestones. It felt like a scene from another era, with golden light stretching across the piazza and the ancient stones echoing centuries of gatherings.

The performance was magnificent, but what moved me most was how the locals embraced it as a living tradition. This was not just a spectacle for tourists, it was a heartfelt celebration of their culture and history.

Verona remains one of my favorite cities because it blends the past and present so seamlessly. Every stone seems to hold a story, and every piazza pulses with both memory and life.

#1. Festa di San Zeno

The Festa di San Zeno is one of Verona's oldest and most cherished traditions, with roots reaching back to the early medieval era. Celebrated annually in honor of the city's patron saint, it blends solemn religious rites with joyful civic festivities that have strengthened over sixteen centuries.

Originally centered on San Zeno's tomb after his canonization in the late 4th century, the celebration began as a pilgrimage and a day of special Masses and processions. As Verona grew in prominence during the Middle Ages, the festival expanded in scale and meaning.

Under the patronage of the powerful della Scala family in the 13th and 14th centuries, the day transformed into a major civic event. Grand processions carried the saint's relics through the streets, accompanied by guilds and confraternities in elaborate displays. Public feasts, open-air markets, tournaments, and pageantry attracted visitors and merchants from across northern Italy.

Today, Veronese families continue to gather near the Basilica of San Zeno, sharing traditional meals and attending the blessing ceremony. For many, the festival remains a living expression of faith, community, and cultural pride, an unbroken link to the city's enduring past.

Who is San Zeno?

San Zeno, Verona's beloved patron saint, was born around AD 300 in Mauritania (North Africa) and became Verona's eighth bishop in the 4th century. Known for his humility, wisdom, and sense of humor, he ministered to the common people, preaching along the Adige River and encouraging baptisms in its waters. During his time as bishop, he defended Christian orthodoxy against Arianism and helped strengthen the Church during a pivotal moment in history.

He died around AD 371 and was soon venerated as a saint. Often depicted with a fishing rod or a fish, Zeno is remembered both for his pastoral care and as a "fisher of men." His legacy lives on in the Basilica di San Zeno Maggiore, one of Italy's finest Romanesque churches. Built over his tomb, the basilica features bronze doors with biblical scenes, a rose window known as the "Wheel of Fortune," and richly frescoed interiors that continue to inspire visitors and pilgrims alike.

Rose Window, Basilica di San Zeno

Timeline of Events for the St. Zeno Festival

10:30 a.m.

Solemn Mass at the Basilica di San Zeno

This central religious observance, presided over by Verona's bishop, starts the day. The basilica, one of Italy's finest Romanesque churches, fills with devoted Veronese and visitors alike. This feast day features the saint's relics, usually housed within the crypt, now displayed for veneration in a chapel. Church bells ring throughout the morning, announcing the celebration to the entire city.

12:00 p.m. to 7:00 p.m.

San Zeno Fair and Food Stalls

Following Mass, the piazza outside the basilica transforms into a vibrant marketplace reminiscent of medieval festival traditions. Local artisans display crafts that often incorporate imagery of San Zeno or the basilica.

Wine stands offer tastings of local varietals, primarily Valpolicella and Soave. Musicians perform traditional folk songs, and children's activities include games that have been played during the festival for centuries.

3:00 p.m.

Historical Parade in the Borgo di San Zeno

This parade recreates medieval celebrations from the time San Zeno was first honored as Verona's patron saint. Participants wear meticulously researched period costumes reflecting different eras of Veronese history. Local parishes, cultural associations, and civic groups join in, with floats portraying scenes from San Zeno's life or moments when his intercession was believed to have protected the city.

A distinctive tradition is the distribution of white lilies, symbols of the saint's purity, and sweet pastries shaped like smiling faces, a nod to San Zeno's nickname, il santo che ride ("the smiling saint"). The route winds through the oldest parts of the San Zeno quarter, where the bishop himself once walked in the 4th century.

9:30 p.m.

Fireworks along the Adige River

The day culminates with this spectacular display, visible from several vantage points, including the Ponte Scaligero and Castelvecchio bridge.

Special Festival Foods

Gnocchi di San Zeno: The signature potato dumplings, served with various sauces, with many families following recipes passed down through generations

Bollito con pearà: The peppery bread sauce (pearà comes from the Italian word for pepper) is simmered for hours before being served with tender boiled meats

Risotto all'Amarone: A luxurious risotto cooked with the region's famous Amarone wine

Pastissada de caval: A heritage dish of horse meat stew, still prepared for special occasions by traditional families

---

#2. The Palio del Drappo Verde: Racing Through Eight Centuries

First held in 1208, the Palio del Drappo Verde is one of Europe's oldest footraces, created to celebrate Verona's victory over feudal rivals. The race, whose name means "Race for the Green Banner," became a cherished civic tradition and was held every year for nearly six centuries until political upheaval ended it in 1797.

In 2008, the Palio was revived, once again bringing runners through the streets of Verona during springtime celebrations. Originally mandated in Verona's statutes of 1271 and confirmed by Cangrande I della Scala, the Palio awarded a green cloth to the winner and, amusingly, a live rooster to the last-place runner. By 1393, a women's race was added, with the green banner awarded to the female victor.

Even Dante referenced the Palio in his Divine Comedy, highlighting its fame across medieval Italy. The course historically ran 7 to 10 kilometers along the city walls and through key gates and streets, finishing at Piazza Sant'Anastasia. More than a race, the Palio remains a living connection to Verona's medieval pride, endurance, and identity.

4:00 p.m.

Opening Ceremony and Flag-Throwers

The festivities begin in Verona's elegant Piazza dei Signori, where trumpets sound and the city's famed sbandieratori (flag-throwers) dazzle the crowd with spinning, soaring flags. The green banner is proudly presented as costumed officials and representatives from Verona's districts parade through the square. A herald reads the ancient race rules in both Italian and the Veronese dialect, while musicians and performers bring history to life with medieval melodies and theatrical reenactments, including the legendary 1208 victory that inspired the race.

5:00 p.m.

Children's and Amateur Races Begin

The competitive aspect begins with the youngest participants, ensuring the tradition passes to new generations. Children from Verona's schools, many wearing Renaissance-inspired tunics in their neighborhood colors, take to a shortened version of the route with unbridled enthusiasm. Parents and grandparents line the course, many sharing stories of their own participation in previous years, creating a living chain of memory.

Amateur adult runners follow, many choosing to wear historically inspired attire or representing their workplaces or social clubs. This inclusive race welcomes participants of all abilities, embodying the communal spirit that has always been central to the Palio's identity.

6:00 p.m.

Palio del Drappo Verde, the Main Race

The elite competition begins with a ceremonial cannon shot that reverberates off the ancient stone buildings. Top runners from across Italy and beyond surge forward along a course that links Verona's most significant landmarks. Streets cleared for this official heat fill with spectators waving banners and cheering their favorites.

True to historical tradition, the first man and woman to cross the finish line receive the coveted green flag, a length of fine green cloth symbolizing victory and prosperity. In a touching nod to ancient custom, the last male finisher still receives a rooster, a humorous but honored consolation prize that connects directly to medieval practice.

7:00 p.m. to 9:00 p.m.

Public Feast and Awards Ceremony

As twilight settles over Verona, the city comes together for a festive communal meal, echoing medieval traditions. Long tables fill the piazza, where locals and visitors share Veronese specialties like risotto all'Amarone, grilled sausages with polenta, and traditional pastries. Pop-up stalls offer local crafts and food, creating a lively market atmosphere.

The awards ceremony adds theatrical flair, with winners draped in green banners and honored with medals and wine. As music and dancing fill the evening air, Verona's ancient stones seem to glow with joy, linking past and present in a celebration of community.

Walking Tour of Verona

#1. Piazza Bra and the Verona Arena

Begin your walk in Piazza Bra, Verona's grand entrance plaza, filled with cafés, gardens, and elegant palaces. The crown jewel here is the Arena di Verona, a remarkably well-preserved Roman amphitheater built in the 1st century AD during the reign of Emperor Augustus. It originally held over 30,000 spectators who came to watch gladiator games, public celebrations, and tournaments.

The Arena was constructed with pink and white limestone from Valpolicella and once had a complete outer ring, much of which was lost in a major earthquake in AD 1117. Despite the damage, it has remained in use for nearly 2,000 years. Today, it seats around 15,000 people and is internationally renowned for the Verona Opera Festival, held each summer. The acoustics are superb, and watching an opera under the stars in this ancient structure is one of the city's most unforgettable experiences.

On our visit, we enjoyed dinner at Ristorante Vittorio Emanuele in Piazza Bra, savoring the view and atmosphere as beautifully dressed Italians arrived for the evening performance at the Arena. It was a perfect mix of history, elegance, and summer romance.

Arena of Verona

Verona has a live webcam facing the Arena. If you are interested in seeing how busy it is here is the link;

https://www.skylinewebcams.com/en/webcam/italia/veneto/verona/arena-di-verona.html

#2. Via Mazzini

From Piazza Bra, walk northeast along Via Mazzini, Verona's stylish pedestrian corridor. Though filled with high-end shops, the street follows the path of a Roman road and leads directly to the oldest heart of Verona. Under the modern pavements lie fragments of the Roman city plan, visible in glass-covered excavations along the way.

#3. Piazza delle Erbe

Piazza delle Erbe was once the Roman forum, now a vibrant and colorful square surrounded by palaces, towers, and lively market stalls. At the center is the Madonna Verona Fountain, created in AD 1368, which uses a Roman-era statue as its base. The Torre dei Lamberti, rising over 80 meters (275 feet), offers panoramic views of the city if you climb to the top. The square's frescoed buildings include Casa Mazzanti, decorated with mythological scenes from the Renaissance.

#4. Piazza dei Signori and Loggia del Consiglio

Just behind Piazza delle Erbe lies Piazza dei Signori, once the seat of government during the rule of the Scaligeri. It is flanked by elegant civic buildings, including the Palazzo della Ragione, Palazzo del Capitano, and the Loggia del Consiglio, built in the 15th century as Verona's first Renaissance structure.

During the Palio del Drappo Verde, this square becomes a ceremonial center, hosting the opening speeches, flag-throwing displays, and the awards ceremony. The statue of Dante Alighieri, who lived in Verona during his exile, watches over the square in thoughtful silence.

Piazza dei Signori

#5. Arche Scaligere and the Chiesa di Santa Maria Antica

Steps away are the Arche Scaligere, a group of elaborate Gothic tombs built for the Scaligeri lords who ruled Verona in the 13th and 14th centuries. Raised on ironwork platforms, the canopied tombs are dramatic and unique. Adjacent is Santa Maria Antica, the private church of the Scaliger family. Dating from the 8th century, it was rebuilt in the Romanesque style and remains a quiet, powerful space.

#6. Juliet's House (Casa di Giulietta)

On Via Cappello is the Casa di Giulietta, the house traditionally linked to Juliet Capulet of Shakespearean fame. The 14th-century building features a small inner courtyard, the iconic balcony (added in the 20th century), and a bronze statue of Juliet. Visitors leave love notes on the walls and touch Juliet's statue for luck in love. While the story is fictional, the site draws thousands of admirers each year.

#7. Ponte Pietra and the Roman Theatre

Continue north along the river to reach Ponte Pietra, the oldest bridge in Verona, originally built in 100 BC. It was partially destroyed during World War II and later reconstructed using original materials.

Crossing the bridge brings is the Roman Theatre and Archaeological Museum, built into the hillside in the 1st century BC. The theater could seat up to 3,000 spectators and is still used today for performances during the summer. The adjoining Archaeological Museum includes mosaics, statues, inscriptions, and ancient tools, and its terraces offer stunning views across the rooftops of Verona.

#8. Castelvecchio and Ponte Scaligero

Make your way back across the Adige River to Castelvecchio, a red-brick fortress built in the 14th century by Cangrande II della Scala. Designed both as a defensive military structure and a residence, it includes a deep moat, tall towers, and a fortified bridge for escape in times of siege.

The Ponte Scaligero, with its massive merlons, which are the upright stone blocks that crown the top of the bridge's battlements, and its fortified towers, was also constructed by the Scaligeri in the 1350s and became a model for military bridges throughout the Veneto. It was destroyed in 1945 and faithfully rebuilt after World War II.

Today, the castle houses the Civico Museo d'Arte, with a collection that includes works by Pisanello, Bellini, and Tintoretto, along with weapons, medieval sculpture, and fine decorative arts. The walkway atop the walls provides some of the best photo opportunities in Verona, with views of the bridge, river, and city skyline.

#9. Basilica di San Zeno Maggiore

End the walking tour at the magnificent Basilica di San Zeno Maggiore. This church is a masterpiece of Romanesque architecture, built between the 10th and 12th centuries, on the site where San Zeno was buried in AD 371.

The façade features a grand rose window called the Wheel of Fortune, and the famous bronze doors, created in the 11th and 12th centuries, depict scenes from the Bible and the life of San Zeno. Inside, the church is filled with

13th-century frescoes, a splendid 14th-century wooden ceiling, and beautiful symmetry throughout the nave and apse.

The crypt holds the relics of San Zeno, still venerated today. Behind the altar, you'll find the crowning jewel: the San Zeno Altarpiece, painted by Andrea Mantegna around AD 1457–1460, a luminous Renaissance triptych that remains one of Verona's greatest artistic treasures.

Logistics

Train: Verona's primary station, Verona Porta Nuova, is a major rail hub served by high-speed, regional, and international trains. It offers direct connections to Venice (1 hour 10 minutes), Milan (1 hour 15 minutes), Bologna (50 minutes), Florence (1 hour 30 minutes), and Rome (3 hours). From the station, it's a 15–20-minute walk or a short taxi/bus ride into the historic center and principal attractions like Piazza Bra and the Arena.

Bus: Bus services are offered in Verona by ATV (Azienda Trasporti Verona), the main local transit provider. ATV operates frequent buses throughout the city and surrounding towns, including routes to San Zeno, the train station, and the outskirts of Verona. Buses run from early morning until late evening, and tickets can be purchased at tabacchi shops, newsstands, or directly via the ATV mobile app.

For regional travel, FlixBus and Itabus provide low-cost connections between Verona and cities across Italy, including Milan, Venice, Florence, and Rome. These buses typically depart from Verona Porta Nuova Station and are a great option for travelers looking for flexible, affordable transportation between major destinations.

Car: Verona is easily accessible by car from the A4 (Milan-Venice) and A22 (Brenner-Modena) motorways. However, the centro storico is largely a ZTL (limited traffic zone). Visitors arriving by car are encouraged to park in one of the city's designated garages outside the ZTL and explore the city on foot. We rented a car at the Verona main station.

Parking: Paid public parking is available at: Parcheggio Cittadella (Via Città di Nimes, 14), just a short walk from Piazza Bra. Parcheggio Arena (Via Bentegodi,

8), also near the Arena and historic district. Or Parcheggio Centro (Piazza Renato Simoni), within walking distance from both the train station and the center.

Restaurant Recommendations

Ristorante Vittorio Emanuele. Address: Piazza Bra, 16

Set right on Piazza Bra, with the Arena di Verona as its stunning backdrop, Ristorante Vittorio Emanuele offers the perfect combination of scenic dining and classic Italian cuisine. We sat outside here one evening and watched the beautiful people arrive for the opera, dressed in evening gowns and tuxedos, as the sun set over the square. It was one of those magical Verona moments we will never forget.

The atmosphere is elegant but relaxed, with tables spilling out onto the piazza just steps from the Arena's ancient arches. The pasta is fresh, the steak tender and flavorful, and the wine list well-curated. Whether you're looking for a romantic dinner before a show or a leisurely lunch in the heart of the city, this is a place to savor the view, the food, and the unforgettable energy of Verona.

Antica Bottega del Vino. Address: Via Scudo di Francia, 3

One of Verona's oldest wine taverns, this atmospheric restaurant, dates back to the 16th century and is beloved for its walls lined with vintage bottles and its deep wine list. Try the Amarone-braised beef, risottos, or pasta with duck ragù while soaking in the candlelit charm. A must for wine lovers.

Osteria Le Vecete. Address: Via Pellicciai, 32

A small and traditional spot near Piazza delle Erbe, Le Vecete serves hearty Veronese fare such as pastissada de caval (slow-cooked horse stew), bigoli with duck sauce, and seasonal risottos. It's ideally located in the city center for an authentic local culinary experience.

Ristorante Il Desco. Address: Via Dietro San Sebastiano, 5/7

For a more upscale and refined evening, Il Desco offers a Michelin-starred menu in an elegant setting. Modern interpretations of classic Veneto cuisine are paired with curated wines. Ideal for festival evenings, romantic Verona in Love dinners, or post-opera relaxation.

Accommodations

Normally for a festival, I recommend a minimum of two nights in town. Verona has a wide range of options, sites nearby to visit, so I am going to recommend three or four nights.

Hotel Accademia. Address: Via Scala, 12

A 4-star hotel in a renovated 18th-century palace, located just steps from Juliet's House and Piazza delle Erbe. Elegant interiors, excellent service, and one of the best locations in the city.

Relais Balcone di Giulietta. Address: Via Cappello, 23

A romantic boutique hotel with rooms that overlook Juliet's courtyard and balcony. Perfect for couples in Verona for Verona in Love or anyone seeking a stay with a literary feel.

Hotel Indigo Verona–Grand Hotel Des Arts. Address: Corso Porta Nuova, 105

Stylish, art déco inspired hotel near the Arena and train station, with modern rooms, a charming internal garden, and luxury touches. A solid base for festival-goers who want beauty and comfort within easy walking distance.

Day Trip Options: Nearby Sites, Cities, and Towns

Valpolicella. 15 kilometers (9 miles) from Verona. Just north of Verona, Valpolicella is a historic wine region whose name means "valley of many wine cellars." With roots in Roman viticulture, the area is known for its scenic hills, vineyards, olive groves, and Romanesque churches. Highlights include the elegant Villa della Torre, a Renaissance villa turned winery and cultural site, and the 8th-century Pieve di San Giorgio, offering sweeping views over Lake Garda and remnants of a pagan altar.

Valpolicella is famed for Amarone, a bold wine made from partially dried corvina, rondinella, and molinara grapes. Visitors can enjoy tastings at centuries-old estates and explore quiet roads by car or bike. It's an ideal day trip for those who enjoy a relaxed pace, beautiful landscapes, and a deep connection to the region's winemaking and artistic heritage.

Soave. 25 kilometers (15 miles) from Verona. East of Verona, the walled town of Soave blends medieval architecture with world-class wine. Its star attraction is the hilltop Castello Scaligero, a 10th-century fortress expanded in the 14th century, complete with towers, ramparts, and sweeping vineyard views. The surrounding city walls, dotted with 24 towers, embrace a charming historic center of narrow streets and Romanesque churches.

Soave is also a wine lover's haven, famous for its crisp white wines made from the Garganega grape. Visitors can stroll along Via Roma, visit artisan shops, and tour local wine cellars for tastings. Soave offers a perfect pairing of history and hospitality, ideal for those who want to experience a fortified town with deep winemaking roots.

Lazise. 23 kilometers (14 miles) from Verona. On the southeastern shore of Lake Garda, Lazise is a romantic lakeside town with deep historical roots. Once a Roman port, it became one of Italy's first free communes under Otto I in the 10th century. The Scaliger Castle, with its five towers and crenellated walls, still stands over the harbor, and the preserved medieval walls wrap around the cobbled streets and colorful waterfront.

Today, Lazise is a perfect blend of past and present. Visitors can explore the historic Church of San Nicolò, stroll the lakefront promenade, or unwind at the Thermal Park Villa dei Cedri, a serene estate with hot spring-fed pools. With gelato in hand and boats bobbing in the harbor, Lazise is an ideal escape for those seeking lakeside charm, relaxation, and just a touch of grandeur.

Verona Festivals and Sagre Throughout the Year

VeroVerona in Love

Around February 14 (Valentine's Day)

This romantic festival celebrates Verona's connection to Shakespeare's Romeo and Juliet. The historic center is decorated with heart-shaped lanterns and red lighting, and special events include concerts, love-themed walking tours, artisan markets, and the reading of letters to Juliet.

Vinitaly (Wine Event)

April (usually mid-month)

Held at VeronaFiere, this is one of the world's largest wine exhibitions. Vinitaly brings together winemakers, sommeliers, importers, and enthusiasts from across the globe. Visitors can attend tastings, masterclasses, and exhibitions that highlight Italian and international wines. Though industry-focused, several public events such as Vinitaly in the City bring wine-themed festivities into Verona's piazzas.

Verona Opera Festival

June to September

Held in the Arena di Verona, this internationally acclaimed summer festival transforms the ancient Roman amphitheater into one of the world's most spectacular open-air opera venues. Featuring grand productions of Verdi, Puccini, and Bizet, with full-scale sets, orchestras, and candlelit audience participation, the festival attracts opera lovers from around the world.

Website for tickets: https://www.arena.it/en/

Tocatì–International Festival of Street Games

September (usually mid-month)

Tocatì, meaning "It's your turn" in Veronese dialect, is a celebration of traditional street games and sports from different cultures. The historic center becomes a massive play area where visitors of all ages can try games like skittles, tug-of-war, stilts, and ancient board games. The festival promotes cultural exchange, physical play, and historical traditions from around the world.

Verona Jazz Festival

October

This long-running music festival features Italian and international jazz musicians performing in theaters and open-air venues across Verona. From avant-garde jazz to swing and Latin fusion, the festival attracts a diverse audience. Concerts are often held in prestigious venues, such as Teatro Ristori and Teatro Filarmonico.

Fiera di Santa Lucia

December 13

This traditional winter fair honors Saint Lucy, the protector of eyesight and bringer of gifts for children. Stalls are set up in Piazza Bra, selling toys, sweets, books, roasted chestnuts, and handcrafted goods. According to the Veronese tradition, children receive gifts from Santa Lucia rather than from Santa Claus. The fair creates a festive, family-friendly atmosphere leading up to Christmas.

Natale a Verona (Christmas in Verona)

December through January 6

Verona's historic center glows with lights, Christmas markets, and Nativity scenes. The Arena hosts a Stella Cometa (Star of Bethlehem) art installation, and nearby, visitors can explore the International Exhibition of Nativity Scenes. The streets are filled with carolers, roasted chestnuts, mulled wine, and festive displays.na Festivals and Sagre Throughout the Year.

CHAPTER EIGHT

Venice's Marriage to the Sea

Feast of the Ascension

Festa della Sensa

Where: Venice and Lido Island

When: Sunday closest to the Feast of the Ascension (typically late May).

Average Festival Temperatures: High 26°C (79°F). Low 15°C (59°F).

Venice's Marriage to the Sea

Venice in May feels sacred and theatrical. The lagoon shimmers under bright sunlight, and a gentle wind rolls in from the Adriatic. Boats of all shapes gather in the water for one of Venice's most ancient rituals. In 2024, my husband and I had the chance to attend the Festa della Sensa. It was one of the most moving and meaningful celebrations we've ever experienced.

That morning, we took a vaporetto toward the Lido, the heart of the festival. We recommend arriving early and watching from the Lido side, especially near the

Church of San Nicolò, where the commemorative mass and ceremonial events unfold. The mood was reverent but joyful. Rowers in traditional costumes glided through the water. The mayor stood aboard the ceremonial boat, and a timeless energy filled the air.

When the gold ring was cast into the sea, renewing Venice's eternal bond with the waters, we stood in silence, deeply touched by the city's maritime identity. Venice, in that moment, felt less like a city and more like a living republic in conversation with the sea.

Venetian Boats on Parade

A Ritual Born from History

The Festa della Sensa, or Ascension Festival, began in the 9th century, forged from gratitude and ambition. In the year 1000, Venice dispatched a fleet to aid the Byzantine Empire, asserting itself as a maritime power. When the ships returned victorious, the people gave thanks and marked the occasion with a ceremony.

By 1177, the festival had grown in political importance. That year, Venice hosted Pope Alexander III and Emperor Frederick Barbarossa, historic rivals who signed the Treaty of Venice during the festival. This landmark moment turned the local sea ritual into a global diplomatic spectacle.

Feast of the Ascension 1740 by Canaletto

The Ceremony: Poetry in Motion

Imagine the Bucintoro, a gilded floating palace, gliding toward the open sea. Aboard stood the Doge, Venice's elected leader, draped in robes of crimson and gold. As the ship reached the lagoon beyond the Lido, silence would fall. The Doge would rise, hold a golden ring, and declare:

> "Desponsamus te, mare. In signum veri perpetuique domini."

> "We wed thee, sea, as a sign of true and everlasting dominion."

Venice did not conquer the sea, it married it. This sacred contract affirmed a relationship of mutual respect. The sea gave protection, trade routes, and abundance. Venice answered with innovation, naval strength, and enduring tradition.

Revolution and Revival

When Napoleon dissolved the Venetian Republic in 1797, many feared the ceremony was lost. The Bucintoro was burned, and its gold stripped. But the spirit remained. Venetians preserved the tradition quietly, and in time, revived it publicly.

Today, the Mayor of Venice carries on the Doge's role aboard the ceremonial boat Serenissima. The ritual has become more inclusive, with thousands of rowers and spectators from around the world joining in a grand, living celebration.

The vows are still spoken. The ring still flies. Venice still honors the sea.

View of St. Marks Basin from the Torre dell'Orologio

Festival Events

The Procession and Sea Marriage Ritual

Sunday morning, on Ascension Sunday in May (late May to early June)

9:00 a.m.

Ceremonial Boat Departs

The highlight of the festival begins precisely at 9:00 a.m. when the ceremonial boat departs from San Marco Basin, with the Mayor and city dignitaries aboard. As we waited along the waterfront, we first heard the deep, steady beats of the drums echoing across the water, long before the boats came into view.

For a moment, it felt like we had stepped back to 1750, hearing the ancient rhythms carrying over the lagoon just as they must have for centuries. Soon, we spotted many teams of young participants, including teenagers dressed in costume, proudly rowing in their boats and adding a youthful energy to this timeless tradition.

10:30 p.m.

Procession reaches San Nicolo

The procession reaches the waters off San Nicolò on the Lido, where the historic ring-casting ceremony takes place amid the pealing of church bells.

11:15 a.m.

Mass

12:30 p.m. - 3:00 p.m.

Boat Parade

Throughout the late morning and early afternoon, hundreds of decorated boats, from traditional Venetian rowing vessels to private crafts, form a spectacular floating parade that can be viewed from prime locations along Riva degli Schiavoni, Giardini, and the Lido shoreline. As the vibrant parade unfolded, we were struck not only by the colorful spectacle but also by how few of the surrounding tourists seemed to grasp the deeper meaning of the event.

Festival Boats in Procession, Grand Canal

While many stumbled upon it by chance, we had journeyed specifically to Venice to witness and be part of this historic celebration. The experience deepened our appreciation for the rich traditions that continue to shape the soul of the city, making us feel connected not just to Venice, but to generations who had shared in the same ritual over centuries.

Related Events

Vogalonga

Sunday Morning, 8:30 a.m.

While not part of the Festa della Sensa, this 30-kilometer non-competitive rowing event is held on the same weekend. Created in 1974 as an environmental protest, Vogalonga begins with a cannon blast and brings thousands of rowers through Murano, Burano, and the Grand Canal. It ends with celebrations citywide.

Adriatic Twinning Ceremonies

Saturday Afternoon, 3:00 – 6:00 p.m.

In the Doge's Palace, Venetian leaders welcome representatives from other Adriatic cities to renew cultural and diplomatic bonds through a twinning ceremony. This symbolic event celebrates partnerships between cities, often called sister cities, that share historical, cultural, or regional ties. The ceremony includes official speeches, the exchange of gifts, and traditional folk performances that highlight the shared heritage of the Adriatic region.

Sensa Market at the Arsenale

Saturday and Sunday, 10:00 a.m. – 8:00 p.m.

The historic shipyards transform into a lively market with 80+ artisan booths, Venetian cicchetti (appetizers), wine tastings, and live music at noon, 3:00, and 6:00 p.m.

Visitor Tips

Arrive early for the best views. The Church of San Nicolò on the Lido is the most meaningful vantage point, but you can also watch the boat's departure from Riva degli Schiavoni. Both spots fill quickly, so arrive 30 to 45 minutes early.

Lido Island Walking Tour

#1. Santa Maria Elisabetta Vaporetto Stop

Disembark from the vaporetto here, the island's major transport hub. You'll immediately find yourself on Gran Viale Santa Maria Elisabetta, the lively main boulevard lined with shops, cafes, and gelaterias. This is the perfect place to grab a coffee and orient yourself.

#2. Palazzo del Cinema

Home of the Venice International Film Festival, held every year in late August and early September. Walk 15 minutes down Gran Viale and turn toward Lungomare Guglielmo Marconi. The Palazzo has hosted global stars since the 1930s. If you're visiting outside festival season, you can still stroll past the red carpet space and see movie posters commemorating past festivals.

#3. Blue Moon Beach

Continue past the Palazzo toward the Adriatic Sea. Here, you'll find Lido's most famous beach. The wide sandy stretch is equipped with sunbeds and umbrellas, and there's a modern boardwalk with bars and casual eateries. Dip your toes in the sea or rent a cabana for a true beach day.

#4. Murazzi Sea Wall

Walk or rent a bike south along the waterfront to reach the Murazzi, a long stretch of stone embankments built in the 1700s to protect the lagoon. It's quiet, windswept, and ideal for a scenic seaside stroll or photos at sunset.

#5. San Nicolò al Lido Church and Monastery

A short walk north from the vaporetto stop brings you to the Church and Monastery of San Nicolò al Lido, one of the most historically significant sites on the island. The church, with its serene Romanesque façade, has long been a place of spiritual importance.

According to tradition, it once safeguarded the relics of Saint Nicholas, the beloved patron saint of sailors and children, before they were taken to Bari by sailors from the southern region of Apulia in 1087. This legend reinforces

Venice's strong maritime devotion to Saint Nicholas, and his image remains deeply embedded in the city's culture, especially during festivals like the Feast of the Sensa, which includes a Mass here.

#6. Parco delle Rimembranze (Park of Remembrance)

End your walk with a pause in this leafy park at the north tip of the island. It's a quiet memorial site to WWI soldiers, ideal for relaxing under the trees before heading back to Venice proper.

Restaurants on the Lido Island

Trattoria Andri. Address: Via Lepanto, 21
A charming, family-run trattoria with retro furnishings and home-cooked Venetian classics. Known for risotto, gnocchi, and a cozy atmosphere.

Ristorante La Tavernetta. Address: Via Sandro Gallo, 136/B
Elegant and romantic, this spot near the Palazzo del Cinema offers refined seafood and local specialties. Ideal for dinner after a beach stroll or festival screening.

Al Canton del Gallo. Address: Gran Viale Santa Maria Elisabetta, 33/a
Centrally located, casual, and great for a pizza or pasta stop. Friendly staff and outdoor seating on the primary avenue make it a reliable choice after sightseeing.

Accommodation on the Lido Island

Hotel Excelsior Venice Lido Resort. Address: Lungomare Guglielmo Marconi, 41
Legendary 5-star hotel with Moorish architecture and private beach access. Hosts many stars during the Film Festival and offers opulent rooms and lagoon views.

Hotel Villa Pannonia. Address: Via Doge Domenico Michiel, 48
A boutique 4-star hotel with a modern art vibe and tranquil garden. Just a short walk from the vaporetto stop and beach, ideal for couples or solo travelers.

Ausonia Hungaria Wellness & Lifestyle. Address: Gran Viale Santa Maria Elisabetta, 28

Housed in an art nouveau building with colorful tile work, this stylish hotel blends luxury with Lido charm. Features a rooftop spa and vibrant design.

A Note on Venetian Festival Chapters

Unlike chapters covering festivals outside Venice, this and other Venetian festival chapters focus solely on the celebrations, their history, events, and their cultural significance.

But Venice, with its wealth of festivals, needed a different approach. To avoid telling you where to stay and eat in Venice twenty different times, I've created special chapters under the **Navigating Venice** section toward the back of the book. They include:

- Regional Dishes and Venetian Specialties

- Best Dining, Gelato, and Drinks in Venice

- Best Coffee and Pastries in Venice

- Itineraries for Venice and Must-See Sights

- Accommodation Detail Venice

- Transportation Detail Venice

This organization allows you to plan your Venetian holiday holistically, while exploring each festival's unique character. This also avoids repeating essential elements throughout Venice's festival chapters.

CHAPTER NINE

Immersion Experience: Brenta Canal

The Canal's Villa Lined Shores

The Ancient Path of the Venetian Nobility

Imagine traveling as Venetian aristocrats once did, gliding along calm waters past magnificent villas that served as summer retreats and lavish party venues during the height of the Venetian Republic. The Brenta Canal, connecting Venice to Padua, offers precisely this experience: a journey through centuries of history, architectural splendor, and the refined lifestyle of La Serenissima's elite.

The burchiello experience is named after the elegant flat-bottomed boats that noble Venetian families used during the 17th and 18th centuries to travel between their city palaces and countryside villas. Today's modern vessels may have exchanged oars and horse-drawn propulsion for motors, but they follow the same historic waterway, stopping at the same architectural treasures that have graced these shores for centuries.

A Day of Floating Through History

This full-day immersion transports you from the watery streets of Venice to a different aspect of Venetian culture, the mainland villa tradition. The Brenta Canal isn't merely a transportation route; it's a cultural corridor showcasing how the Republic's wealthy citizens displayed their prosperity through architectural commissions from masters like Andrea Palladio.

Itinerary: Venice to Padua Villa Cruise

Morning: Venice Departure (8:30-9:00 a.m.)

The journey begins at the Venetian waterfront of San Marco or Venice's Sette Martiri near the Gardens, where you'll board a comfortable motorized vessel resembling the historic burchielli. As the boat pulls away from Venice, you'll enjoy a unique farewell view of the floating city receding into the lagoon.

After crossing a small portion of the Venetian Lagoon, the boat enters the mouth of the Brenta Canal. The guide will explain how this waterway was engineered by the Venetians to control water flow between the mainland and their precious lagoon, while simultaneously creating a prestigious transportation route.

First Stop: Villa Foscari "La Malcontenta" (around 10:00 a.m.)

The first villa visit is to one of Andrea Palladio's most celebrated masterpieces, Villa Foscari, nicknamed "La Malcontenta." As you approach from the water, the perfectly proportioned façade comes into view, demonstrating Palladio's genius for harmonious classical design.

Go inside and learn how these villas were so much more than country houses. The frescoed interiors by Battista Franco and Giambattista Zelotti transform the practical rooms into scenes from mythology and allegory. The guide will explain how these decorations weren't merely beautiful but conveyed political messages about the owners' education, taste, and position in society.

The villa's curious nickname, "La Malcontenta" (the discontented woman) comes from a legend about a Foscari wife who was confined here as punishment for her allegedly improper behavior, a story that offers a glimpse into the social expectations of Venetian nobility.

Navigating the Historic Waterway (11:30 a.m.)

Back aboard the boat, the trip continues along the canal, passing under historic bridges and through a series of functioning locks designed using principles dating back to Leonardo da Vinci. These ingenious water management systems allowed boats to navigate changing water levels between Venice and Padua.

Along the way, the guide will point out numerous other villas lining the shores, explaining their architectural features and the families who commissioned them. Some remain private residences, while others have been converted to municipal buildings, hotels, or museums.

The leisurely pace allows for excellent photography opportunities and a chance to observe how the landscape transitions from lagoon to agricultural mainland. The canal is lined with small towns that historically serviced the grand villas, creating a fascinating glimpse into the relationship between nobility and working communities.

Lunch Break at Oriago (1:00-2:30 p.m.)

The boat docks at the historic riverside village of Oriago for lunch at the aptly named "Il Burchiello" restaurant, a traditional establishment that has been serving travelers along this route for generations.

Lunch options include regional Veneto specialties, particularly fish from the lagoon and seasonal produce from the surrounding countryside, the same agricultural bounty that once supplied the villa kitchens. One can choose between a pre-arranged set menu or ordering à la carte from the restaurant's selection.

The restaurant's riverside location provides an opportunity to stretch your legs with a short stroll along the canal banks after lunch, observing the interaction between waterway and local life that continues today, much as it has for centuries.

Afternoon: Villa Widmann Rezzonico Foscari

Continuing upriver, the next stop is Villa Widmann, representing a different architectural period than Palladio's classical restraint. This 18th-century villa showcases the later Baroque and Rococo influences that swept through Venetian design, creating a fascinating comparison with the earlier Renaissance aesthetics.

Originally built by the Scerimon family, nobility of Persian origin, the villa later passed to the Widmann family who renovated it in the fashionable Rococo style. The interior features delightful frescoed scenes of daily life and charming chinoiserie, the European interpretation of Asian artistic motifs that became tremendously fashionable in the 18th century.

The villa's garden, though smaller than some, exemplifies the changing landscape design philosophies, incorporating both formal Italian elements and English-influenced naturalistic areas. Your guide will explain how these gardens weren't merely decorative, but served as settings for elaborate social gatherings where the elite displayed their refinement.

Crown Jewel: Villa Pisani in Stra (4:30 p.m.)

The final and most grandiose stop is Villa Pisani in Stra, often called the "Queen of the Brenta Villas." With 114 rooms and extensive gardens, this monumental estate was built in the early 18th century to celebrate Alvise Pisani's election as the 114th Doge of Venice.

The scale of Villa Pisani demonstrates how these villas developed from practical country retreats to statements of political power and social prestige. The grand ballroom features an extraordinary ceiling fresco by Giambattista Tiepolo titled "The Glory of the Pisani Family," a masterpiece of illusionistic painting.

Outside, the formal gardens include one of Italy's most famous hedge mazes, elegant pools reflecting the villa's façade, and a fascinating "coffee house" where guests would retire for refreshments after garden strolls. The impressive stables across the garden were designed to resemble another palazzo, creating a theatrical backdrop to the main villa.

The guide will share tales of its famous visitors, including Napoleon Bonaparte, who briefly owned the estate after the fall of the Venetian Republic, and more recently, the infamous meeting between Hitler and Mussolini that took place here in 1934.

Arrival in Padua (6:00-6:30 p.m.)

The boat journey culminates at Portello, the historic river port of Padua, where you'll disembark near the 16th-century Burchiello Staircase, a Renaissance landing designed specifically for these elegant boat journeys.

Here, there is the option to explore Padua's historic center or return to Venice via a convenient train connection (approximately 25 minutes) or by pre-arranged bus transportation.

Practical Information

Duration: Full day (approximately 9 hours)

Starting Point: Venice (San Marco/Giardini)

Ending Point: Padua (with return transport options to Venice)

Best Season: April through October, when villas are open to visitors. Spring offers beautiful garden displays, while September provides pleasant temperatures and fewer crowds.

Booking Information: Reservations are strongly recommended, especially during high season (June to September). Several companies operate very similar itineraries, including Il Burchiello, I Battelli del Brenta, and Veneto Inside. Pricing typically ranges from €80 to 150 per person for the full-day experience, depending on inclusions and season.

Beyond the Experience

The Brenta Canal villa cruise offers more than just sightseeing; it provides insight into the social, political, and artistic expressions of Venetian nobility at the height of the Republic's influence. The villas exist in a fascinating middle ground between practical country estates and ostentatious displays of wealth and culture.

For architecture enthusiasts, the opportunity to see multiple Palladian designs in their intended settings is invaluable. For history lovers, the transition from the Venetian Republic through the Napoleonic occupation and into modern Italy is written in these buildings and landscapes.

CHAPTER TEN

Biennale of Venice

International Film Fest, Art, Architecture, Dance, and More

FestaFusion Biennale

Where: Venice and Lido Island

When: Summer (see events below for more specifics).

Average Festival Temperatures: High 29°C (84°F). Low 17°C (63°F).

Event Website: https://www.labiennale.org/en

The Venice Biennale: A Cultural Powerhouse

Founded in 1895, the Biennale di Venezia (Venice Biennale) has grown into one of the world's most prestigious cultural institutions. What began as a singular International Art Exhibition has expanded to include six major disciplines: Art, Architecture, Cinema (Film), Theatre, Music, and Dance.

These events are spread throughout Venice and the Lido, hosted in iconic locations such as the Giardini, Arsenale, and the Palazzo del Cinema. The Biennale's alternating cycle of Art and Architecture exhibitions is supplemented by annual festivals in the other disciplines, offering a rich calendar of global creativity from spring through autumn.

The Many Components of La Biennale di Venezia

Art Biennale

Where: Giardini, Arsenale, and scattered venues across Venice

When: April to November (even-numbered years)

The original Biennale was launched to promote modern artistic expression beyond national boundaries. The first edition in 1895 drew over 200,000 visitors and featured works from 16 countries. Over time, the Biennale developed into an international art stage, featuring national pavilions, curated exhibitions, and solo installations by world-renowned and emerging artists.

Biennale Art Installation 2020, Guardians

Today, the Art Biennale occupies over 60,000 square meters and hosts dozens of permanent national pavilions in the Giardini, while the Arsenale and city-wide venues expand the experience with immersive installations. Themes range from the political to the poetic, making this a must-visit for art lovers and critics alike.

Architecture Biennale

Where: Like the Art Biennale, the Architecture exhibition takes place in the two primary locations of the Giardini and Arsenale, with national pavilions and thematic exhibitions.

When: May to November (odd-numbered years).

The Venice Architecture Biennale, founded in 1980, is a relatively newer addition to the Biennale family. The first initiative toward an architecture exhibition was taken in 1975 with "A Proposito del Mulino Stucky," curated by Vittorio Gregotti, exploring uses for a neglected industrial building. However, the first official Architecture Biennale wasn't established until 1980.

The exhibition will focus on architecture and an extended sphere integrating art, engineering, biology, data science, and social and political sciences.

Theater Biennale

Where: Venice

When: June to July.

Since becoming an annual event in 1934, the International Theatre Festival has welcomed some of the most respected names in contemporary stagecraft. Directed over the years by artists such as Luca Ronconi and Franco Quadri, it emphasizes avant-garde and experimental performance.

Besides productions, the festival includes training programs like the Biennale College Teatro, a platform that nurtures young theatrical talent through mentorship, workshops, and commissioned works.

Music Biennale

Where: Venice

When: September to October.

The Biennale Musica, or International Festival of Contemporary Music, was established in 1930. From its early focus on classical innovation, it has grown to embrace experimental music, digital sound, electronic composition, and cross-disciplinary collaborations.

Concerts and sound installations span historic theaters, outdoor spaces, and experimental venues. The festival frequently premieres bold new compositions and gives voice to the future of music.

Dance Biennale

Where: Venice

When: July

The youngest addition to the Biennale family, the Dance Festival was founded in 1999 and quickly earned acclaim for its global approach to choreography. It offers a stage for both acclaimed choreographers and rising talents.

Performances highlight everything from traditional ballet to cutting-edge movement arts, while the Biennale College Danza fosters young dancers and choreographers through residencies and masterclasses.

Venice International Film Festival

Where: Lido island in the Venice Lagoon at four major venues, the Palazzo del Cinema, the Palazzo del Casinò, the PalaBiennale, and the Sala Giardino, as well as outdoor areas.

When: Late August, early September for 11 days.

Founded in 1932, the Venice International Film Festival is the world's oldest film festival and remains one of the most respected. Established by Count Giuseppe Volpi during Italy's Fascist era, the early editions were politically influenced, yet they laid the foundation for international cinematic celebration.

The festival's prestige grew after World War II, particularly with the creation of the Golden Lion award in 1949. Today, it showcases films from around the world, including major premieres and independent features.

Held at the Palazzo del Cinema, Palazzo del Casinò, and outdoor venues on the Lido, the festival draws global filmmakers, press, and fans. Red carpet events begin around 6:00 p.m. each evening, turning the Lido into a glamorous cinematic village.

Initiatives like the Biennale College Cinema and Venice Film Market support emerging filmmakers and global film industry collaboration.

Beyond the Official Program

While the Biennale's official events are centered in its principal venues, Venice becomes a city-wide stage during festival seasons. Museums, foundations, private galleries, and artists host exhibitions, panels, and parties timed to coincide with the official calendar.

The Biennale Foundation also played a major role in reviving the Venetian Carnival in 1980 and now organizes the International Kids' Carnival, making the cultural season accessible to all generations.

Across disciplines, the Biennale College platform continues to offer mentorship, residencies, and training programs for young artists, integrating education into the heart of each festival.

A Living Celebration of Global Creativity

More than a collection of events, the Venice Biennale is a living, evolving celebration of global creativity. From cinema and architecture to experimental sound and performance, it invites the world to reflect, engage, and imagine new possibilities. Whether you're a casual visitor or a devoted culture-seeker, the Biennale offers a chance to experience Venice at its most dynamic and inspiring.

CHAPTER ELEVEN

FestaFusion Padua

The City Honors Sant'Antonio with a Month of Festivities

FestaFusion Padua

#1. Festa di Sant'Antonio. The Festa di Sant'Antonio in Padua is a grand, citywide celebration held every June 13 to honor the beloved saint.

#2. Giugno Antoniano. Giugno Antoniano is a month-long celebration in Padua honoring Saint Anthony of Padua, the city's patron saint.

#FestaFusion means two or more festivals happen at around the same time in the same town, so visitors can enjoy multiple events during their visit.

Where: Padua (Padova)

When: June 12-13 Festa di Sant'Antonio. Full month of June for Giugno Antoniano.

Average Festival Temperatures: High 26°C (79°F). Low 15°C (59°F).

Festa Website: https://www.santantonio.org/en

Giugno Antoniano Website: padovacultura.padovanet.it

#FestaFusion: When two festivals collide in the same town around the same time, your journey becomes twice as magical.

Padua: Sacred City of Learning and Devotion

Padua (Padova in Italian) is a city where prayer, philosophy, and pilgrimage have shaped the streets for over two millennia. Located just 40 kilometers west of Venice along the Bacchiglione River, and home to about 210,000 residents, it blends medieval majesty with youthful energy thanks to its university and vibrant piazzas.

We discovered Padua during a family trip from Sirmione to Venice. Arriving by train into a postwar station still bearing scars of WWII bombing, we soon reached the city's historic center. Our visit centered on three extraordinary sites: the Scrovegni Chapel, the Cathedral Baptistry, and the Basilica di Sant'Antonio.

Between visits, we stopped at the iconic Caffè Pedrocchi, a neoclassical cafe known for its tricolor rooms and signature Pedrocchino coffee, a delicious mint-laced drink topped with cream and cocoa. We were so enchanted; we went back again after touring the basilica. No regrets. The pastry case tempted with cornetti, crostate, and delicate petit fours. Sitting in a place that has welcomed intellectuals and artists since 1831 added a layer of timelessness to our day.

Padua is refreshingly walkable and less crowded than nearby Venice. Visitors can enjoy an authentic Italian rhythm while exploring world-class art and architecture. In 2021, Padua earned UNESCO World Heritage status for its 14th-century fresco cycles, including Giotto's masterpieces in the Scrovegni Chapel. Known as Urbs Picta ("Painted City"), Padua remains a living gallery.

Padua traces its roots to the ancient Veneti people, who built a thriving settlement here by the 4th century BC. Under Roman rule, it became Patavium, a prosperous city known for wool, horses, and culture, and the birthplace of the historian Livy. Though sacked during the barbarian invasions, the city recovered and by the 11th century had become a flourishing commune. After a dark period under the brutal Ezzelino da Romano, Padua experienced renewal and founded its great university in 1222. Galileo Galilei taught there for 18 years, refining the scientific method and building the first astronomical telescope. The university's anatomy theater, still standing, was the first of its kind in Europe.

In the 14th century, the Carraresi family rose to power, building walls, palaces, and patronizing the arts. Though their rule ended in 1405 when Padua was absorbed into the Venetian Republic, the city entered a new era of stability and cultural flourishing. The university thrived, establishing the world's first academic botanical garden in 1545. Donatello sculpted the commanding statue of Gattamelata outside the Basilica, while Giotto, Mantegna, and Titian left their mark in chapels and churches. In 1678, Elena Lucrezia Cornaro Piscopia became the first woman in the world to earn a university degree, graduating from Padua with a doctorate in philosophy.

Today, Padua's arcaded streets, frescoed chapels, and lively markets continue to enchant. Yet it's the Basilica of Saint Anthony, one of the most visited pilgrimage sites in the world, that draws countless travelers and faithful. Amid its relics, cloisters, and centuries of devotion, Padua continues to inspire as a sacred city where intellect and spirit walk hand in hand.

#1. Feast of St. Anthony: A Celebration of Faith and Tradition

As dawn breaks over Padua on June 13, the medieval city awakens to the pealing of church bells. Streets that normally bustle with university students and locals going about their business transform into pathways of pilgrimage. This is no ordinary day in Padua; it is the Feast of Saint Anthony, when the city honors its beloved patron in a celebration that has continued uninterrupted for nearly eight centuries.

From the earliest hours, pilgrims from across Italy and around the world stream toward the magnificent Basilica di Sant'Antonio, its Byzantine domes and Gothic spires silhouetted against the morning sky. Many have journeyed for days, some fulfilling vows made in moments of crisis, others continuing family traditions that span generations. By mid-morning, the piazza surrounding the basilica becomes a sea of devotees, their faces reflecting both reverence and expectation.

Who Was Saint Anthony of Padua?

Born in 1195 in Lisbon as Fernando Martins de Bulhões, Saint Anthony gave up a life of privilege to join the Augustinian order, dedicating himself to scripture and theology. A turning point came when he encountered the remains of five

Franciscan missionaries martyred in Morocco. Inspired by their sacrifice, he joined the Franciscans, took the name Anthony, and set off to continue their mission.

Illness forced his return, but a storm diverted his ship to Sicily. In Italy, his talents were unexpectedly revealed when he stepped in to preach at an ordination. Word spread quickly. Saint Francis appointed him as a teacher of theology, and Anthony became one of the most beloved preachers of his time. Crowds filled city squares to hear him speak, drawn by his eloquence and compassion.

He died in 1231 at just 36 years old. Canonized less than a year later, Saint Anthony's legacy of faith, humility, and devotion to the poor continues to draw pilgrims from around the world to Padua.

Facade of the Basilica di Sant'Antonio

June 12: The Transit of Saint Anthony

Morning Events:

8:30 a.m.

Procession

A colorful historical procession of 150 people in medieval costumes begins from Piazzale Azzurri d'Italia in the Arcella district of Padua, following the path that would have been taken when the saint's body was transported.

9:30 a.m.

Procession at Sanctuary dell'Arcella

The procession reaches the Sanctuary dell'Arcella, the church that preserves the room where Saint Anthony died. Upon arrival, church bells throughout the city ring in concert, creating a moving soundscape that resonates across Padua.

Throughout the day, special prayer services and masses are held at both the Sanctuary dell'Arcella and the Basilica of Saint Anthony, where pilgrims gather to prepare for the next day's feast.

10:00 a.m.

Infiorata (Floral Carpet Festival)

On the eve of Saint Anthony's feast day, Piazza del Santo, the square in front of the Basilica di Sant'Antonio, is transformed into a vibrant mosaic of floral artwork. This tradition, known as the Infiorata, is a beloved annual event in Padua, bringing together local artists, volunteers, and pilgrims in a unique and reverent artistic offering.

The process begins around 10:00 a.m., when outlines for the designs are sketched directly onto the pavement. Using petals, seeds, colored sawdust, and natural materials, artists begin filling in the designs, featuring religious imagery, symbols of Saint Anthony, or Franciscan themes.

Throughout the morning and afternoon, visitors are invited to observe and sometimes assist in carefully assembling the carpets. The work continues into the late afternoon, with most of the pieces completed by 5:00 p.m., just in time for the evening events and vigils at the basilica.

The floral carpets remain in place through the evening, creating a breathtaking foreground for the June 13 procession and serving as a visible expression of the city's devotion. This combination of artistry, community participation, and faith makes the Infiorata one of the most colorful and symbolic moments of the festival.

June 13: The Feast Day of Saint Anthony

5:30 a.m. - 10:30 p.m.

Basilica Open to Pilgrims

The Basilica remains open continuously to accommodate the thousands of pilgrims who visit throughout the day.

Basilica of St. Anthony

Evening

The Grand Procession

The highlight of the celebration is the solemn procession through the historic center of Padua, carrying Saint Anthony's relics. The reliquary and other relics are carried on an ornate platform adorned with fresh flowers. On the evening of June 13, Padua's historic center becomes the stage for a profound expression of faith and community: the Grand Procession honoring Saint Anthony.

As twilight descends, the massive bronze doors of the Basilica di Sant'Antonio swing open, and a hush falls over the crowd that has gathered throughout the day. Altar servers bearing processional crosses and flickering candles lead the way, followed by white-robed priests and brown-habited Franciscan friars.

The highlight comes as the saint's sacred relics emerge. Carried on ornate platforms trimmed with fresh flowers, the reliquaries containing Saint Anthony's incorrupt tongue and vocal cords glisten in the evening light, powerful reminders of the saint whose preaching once moved thousands to repentance and conversion.

The procession moves at a solemn pace through Padua's medieval streets, making its way through some of the city's most iconic locations. It begins in Piazza del Santo, directly in front of the basilica, and continues down Via del Santo and Via San Francesco, both lined with historic buildings and balconies draped in red cloth. From there, it weaves through Canton del Gallo, Via Roma, and Via Umberto I, where locals and visitors shower rose petals from above as the relics pass below.

Special Festival Food
Bread of St. Anthony

This tradition involves small loaves of bread distributed on St. Anthony's Feast Day that symbolize the saint's generosity in feeding the hungry. Throughout Italy, these bread rolls vary in style. Some are light and brioche-like with sugar and rum, others have anisette for a slight sweetness, while some are simple crusty loaves or contain fennel seeds and black pepper.

The custom of St. Anthony's Bread dates back to 1263 when, according to tradition, a mother whose child had drowned called upon St. Anthony for help, promising to donate the child's weight in grain to the poor if her child was restored to life. When her prayer was answered, this practice of giving food alms in thanksgiving for St. Anthony's intercession began.

In Italian communities, bakers produce extra bread rolls specifically for the feast day. These rolls are purchased and given to friends, family, and neighbors as offerings of thanksgiving for prayers answered by St. Anthony.

#2. Antonian June Festival

Entire month of June

Dates: Entire Month of June

Padua's month-long celebration of its beloved patron saint, known as Giugno Antoniano, blends religious devotion, cultural programming, and community spirit. From solemn pilgrimages and sacred music to museum openings and art exhibitions, the festival honors Saint Anthony's legacy through a rich array of events.

Week 1: Pilgrimages and Spiritual Preparation

The festival begins in late May with La Notte dei Santuari (May 31), a nighttime pilgrimage from the Church of the Good Shepherd to the Sanctuary of Saint Anthony in Arcella, ending with a candlelit vigil. On June 1, the Pellegrinaggio Antoniano della Pace leads pilgrims from Camposampiero to the Basilica di Sant'Antonio, promoting peace and reconciliation through shared prayer and testimony. From June 2 to 12, the Tredicina, a beloved thirteen-day cycle of themed Masses, draws thousands to the basilica for daily liturgies focused on different communities and spiritual intentions.

Week 2: See Festa di Sant'Antonio Events (June 12–13)

As the saint's feast approaches, devotion deepens with processions, the Infiorata floral carpet, special Masses, and the Grand Procession on June 13, the high point of the month's religious observances.

Week 3: Reflection and Cultural Enrichment

Following the feast day, Padua offers guided tours of the Basilica's cloisters, the Scoletta del Santo, and the Oratory of Saint George, highlighting sacred art and architecture. Evenings feature concerts of sacred and classical music performed by choirs, orchestras, and soloists in evocative settings near the basilica. Conferences and lectures by theologians and scholars explore Saint Anthony's enduring relevance in today's world.

Week 4: Civic Spirit and Closing Celebrations

The final week embraces art and community. Exhibitions at venues like Palazzo della Ragione and the Musei Civici agli Eremitani showcase sacred and contemporary works centered on pilgrimage and faith. Across Padua, parishes and neighborhoods host charity dinners, theatrical performances, and workshops in celebration of Saint Anthony's message of service and unity. The festival concludes with a grand open-air concert, gathering citizens and pilgrims for one last tribute to their cherished saint.

Free Museum Access

From June 8 to 13, visitors enjoy free entry to key cultural institutions, including Palazzo della Ragione, Palazzo Zuckermann, and the Museo del Risorgimento, underscoring the festival's commitment to spiritual and civic enrichment.

Walking Tour of Padua

Padua is best explored over two days to fully appreciate its religious treasures, Renaissance art, scholarly landmarks, and vibrant historic center. This walking tour is organized to minimize backtracking and maximize time at each site.

Day 1: The Sacred Heart of Padua

#1. Basilica di Sant'Antonio (Basilica of Saint Anthony)

This monumental basilica is the spiritual heart of the city. Built after Saint Anthony's death in 1231 AD and consecrated in 1310, it combines Romanesque, Gothic, Byzantine, and Islamic elements in a harmonious and awe-inspiring whole. Pilgrims come from all over the world to visit the Chapel of the Tomb, where the saint's body rests within the Arca of St. Anthony, a richly sculpted marble shrine.

We visited this sacred space, and it was a deeply spiritual experience. Standing before the arca, surrounded by carved scenes of miracles and hope, was incredibly moving. You could feel the prayers in the air, left behind by generations of visitors. The art surrounding the tomb is just as powerful as the devotion it inspires, with exquisite Renaissance reliefs depicting some of the saint's most famous miracles.

On an interesting side note, the Chapel of St. Anthony has a 24-hour webcam that watches the Arc of St. Anthony. I wanted to share the link in case you want to see how crowded it is at any time:

https://www.santantonio.org/en/content/chapel-saint-anthony-live-cam

The relics of Saint Anthony, symbols of his preaching and spiritual legacy, are kept in the Chapel of the Relics close by. Together, these spaces form a pilgrimage within a pilgrimage, an emotional encounter with the saint who continues to speak to hearts centuries after his passing.

The high altar, created by Donatello, is one of the most important sculptural ensembles of the Renaissance. It includes lifelike bronze statues of saints, elegant reliefs, and a dynamic Crucifixion scene. Outside, in Piazza del Santo, stands Donatello's equestrian statue of Gattamelata, the first monumental bronze equestrian statue cast since antiquity, celebrating the Renaissance revival of classical art.

Behind the basilica, a series of medieval cloisters offers a peaceful retreat for visitors. I love a cloister. I'm always seeking them out. There's something deeply moving about walking the same corridors that monks or sisters once walked centuries ago, in silence or prayer. This one is especially dear to me, not just for its calm atmosphere but because it offers lovely views of the basilica's domes, rising above the tiled roofs like a quiet reminder of the sacred space within.

Cloister of the Basilica

In springtime, the Cloister of the Magnolia is beautiful, its central garden blooming in contrast to the stone arcades that surround it. The entire space provides a moment of quiet reflection, just steps from the bustling Piazza del Santo.

Within the complex, you'll also find a well-curated bookshop and religious gift store, filled with books on Saint Anthony's life, devotional objects, rosaries, and thoughtful art reproductions that connect visitors more deeply to the basilica's history and message.

The secondary webcam for the Basilica faces the facade. Here is the link:

https://www.skylinewebcams.com/en/webcam/italia/veneto/padova/padova-basilica-di-sant-antonio.html

#2. Scuola del Santo

This 15th-century confraternity hall next to the basilica contains beautiful frescoes by a young Titian, painted in 1511, which depict miracles of the saint with a dramatic use of light, color, and realism. The paintings are significant not only for their religious themes but also as early examples of Titian's emerging mastery.

#3. Oratorio di San Giorgio (Oratory of Saint George)

Directly across from the basilica, this Gothic oratory was built by the Lupi family in 1376 and features vivid frescoes by Altichiero da Zevio, a follower of Giotto. The cycles depict scenes from the lives of Christ, Saint George, and Saint Catherine with vibrant color and Gothic elegance.

#4. Piazza del Santo

This wide and scenic square connects the basilica and adjacent chapels. During the Festa di Sant'Antonio in June, the square is filled with pilgrims, processions, and open-air liturgies. The lively yet reverent atmosphere makes this a great place to pause and reflect.

#5. Prato della Valle

One of the largest squares in Europe, Prato della Valle is a vast elliptical space encircled by 78 statues and a canal, with a green island in the center called Isola

Memmia. It's a favorite place for locals and a hub for weekend markets, seasonal fairs, and public celebrations.

#6. Basilica di Santa Giustina

At the southern edge of Prato della Valle, this massive 16th-century basilica is dedicated to Saint Giustina, one of Padua's early Christian martyrs. It houses the relics of both Saint Giustina and Saint Luke the Evangelist. The interior is expansive, filled with side chapels, domes, and a serene, solemn atmosphere. The basilica is vast, serene, and a hidden jewel for lovers of sacred art and architecture.

#7. Botanical Garden of Padua (Orto Botanico)

Founded in 1545, this is the world's oldest academic botanical garden still in its original location. Created for cultivating medicinal plants by medical students, it now holds over 7,000 species and includes themed gardens, ancient trees, and innovative greenhouses. It is a UNESCO World Heritage Site and a beautiful intersection of science, history, and nature.

Day 2: Art, History, and the Heart of the City

Focus: Renaissance art, university life, markets, and medieval civic pride

#1. Cappella degli Scrovegni (Scrovegni Chapel)

Begin your tour at one of the most important masterpieces in Italy: the Cappella degli Scrovegni. Commissioned by Enrico Scrovegni and built between 1300 and 1303, the chapel was intended as both a private oratory and a penitential offering, as the Scrovegni family had grown wealthy through moneylending, a sin in medieval Christian thought. Enrico hoped to ensure his family's salvation through this remarkable act of patronage.

The chapel was frescoed by Giotto di Bondone in 1303–1305, marking a pivotal moment in Western art. Giotto's 38 fresco panels narrate the lives of the Virgin Mary and Christ, laid out in three registers that wrap around the interior. The images are vivid, emotional, and revolutionary in their use of naturalism, perspective, and expressive human figures. One of the most famous scenes is the Lamentation over the Dead Christ, where Mary and the disciples mourn Jesus in a moment of intimate, visible sorrow. The ceiling is a starry sky that draws your gaze heavenward, while the Last Judgment on the west wall confronts visitors with salvation and damnation.

The frescoes are fragile, so entry is restricted to small, timed groups. It's advisable to book well in advance, especially during festival periods.

Website:

https://www.cappelladegliscrovegni.it/index.php/en/information/biglietti-e-ri duzioni

#2. Chiesa degli Eremitani (Church of the Hermits)

Just beside the Scrovegni Chapel, this Romanesque-Gothic church was heavily damaged in WWII, but it keeps important architectural elements and several fresco fragments by Andrea Mantegna. Originally home to the Ovetari Chapel, it is now a solemn sight of both artistic heritage and wartime memory. The church still features Gothic architecture, painted wooden ceilings, 14th-century tombs, and surviving frescoes from the 14th and 15th centuries. It also serves as a poignant memorial to wartime losses and the resilience of the Padua community.

#3. University of Padua–Palazzo Bo

The historic seat of the University of Padua, founded in 1222. Inside, you can see Galileo's lecture hall, coats of arms of former students, and the world's first anatomical theater, built in 1594. A guided tour is highly recommended to access all parts of the complex. The university played a major role in the development of Renaissance science, medicine, and philosophy.

#4. Caffè Pedrocchi

Built in 1831 and famously known as the "Café without Doors," this neoclassical building was once a 24-hour gathering place for revolutionaries and students. Try the signature Pedrocchi coffee, flavored with mint cream and cocoa. Its upstairs rooms now house the Risorgimento Museum, and its interior still feels like a 19th-century salon.

#5. Piazza delle Erbe and Piazza della Frutta

These adjacent market squares have been in use since the Middle Ages and are still bustling with stalls, shops, and cafes. They are surrounded by historical buildings, and their vibrancy reflects the daily life of Paduans. They are great places to explore for fresh produce, cheese, and artisan gifts.

#6. Palazzo della Ragione

Overlooking the market square, this 13th-century civic hall features a massive wooden roof and interior frescoes representing the signs of the zodiac, trades, and medieval life. Once the seat of Padua's law courts, it remains a grand symbol of the city's independence and civic pride. The upper hall, called the Salone, is vast and richly painted.

#7. Padua Cathedral (Duomo)

The current cathedral of Padua, redesigned in the 16th century, is an elegant example of Renaissance architecture. While its interior is relatively restrained, its importance lies in its history as the city's Episcopal seat and its proximity to a true artistic jewel: the Baptistery of San Giovanni Battista, located just beside the cathedral.

#8. Cathedral Baptistry

Inside the baptistery, visitors encounter one of the greatest fresco cycles of the 14th century, painted by Giusto de' Menabuoi around 1375. The central feature is the magnificent Paradise Dome, which depicts Christ Pantocrator enthroned at the center, surrounded by concentric circles of angels, apostles, prophets, martyrs, and saints. Below him stands the Virgin Mary, arms open in intercession, ringed by musicians and holy figures in a golden halo of eternal communion.

These frescoes are not just decorative; they depict a visual theology of salvation history. Along the walls, Giusto's paintings depicted scenes from the Old and New Testaments, culminating in a striking Last Judgment and a powerful Harrowing of Hell, where Christ rescues souls from the underworld. At the base of the dome, circular panels depict the Evangelists and early Church Fathers, anchoring the vision of heaven in sacred tradition.

This immersive visual experience, filled with vibrant color, storytelling, and divine order, offers a profound spiritual reflection and serves as a dramatic conclusion to your journey through Padua's sacred and cultural heritage.

Logistics

Train: Padua is a major railway hub in northern Italy, served by high-speed (Frecciarossa, Italo) and regional trains. The Padova Centrale station connects directly to Venice (30–35 minutes), Verona (45–50 minutes), Bologna (1 hour), Milan (2 hours), and Florence (1 hour 40 minutes). From the train station, it's about a 15-minute walk or a short tram ride to the historic center and the Basilica of Saint Anthony.

Bus: Local and regional bus service in Padua is provided by Busitalia Veneto, offering convenient routes throughout the city and to surrounding towns. During major festivals like the Festa di Sant'Antonio, additional service is often added. Tickets can be purchased at tabacchi shops, vending machines, or via mobile apps. The SITA bus station, next to the train station, provides regional connections to cities such as Vicenza, Treviso, and Venice.

Car: Padua is easily reached by car via the A4 (Milan-Venice) and A13 (Padua-Bologna) motorways. However, much of the centro storico is a ZTL (Zona a Traffico Limitato), and driving in the center is restricted to residents and permitted vehicles. Visitors arriving by car should plan to park outside the ZTL and walk or use public transport to explore the historic sites.

Parking: There are several paid public parking lots and garages located just outside Padua's historic center. Options include Parcheggio Piazza Rabin on Via Giosuè Carducci (convenient for visiting the Basilica of Saint Anthony), Parcheggio Padova Centro on Via Trieste (near the pedestrian center and shopping area), and Parcheggio Cavalletto on Via Giotto, 2 (close to the university area and Piazza Garibaldi). Rates are typically charged hourly or daily, and most parking facilities support digital payment systems or app-based options.

Restaurant Recommendations

Ristorante al Santo. Address: Via del Santo, 147

Located just steps from the basilica, Ristorante al Santo offers traditional Paduan cuisine in a warm, inviting atmosphere. Known for its homemade pastas and local specialties, it's an excellent spot for a meal before or after visiting the basilica.

The restaurant is especially popular during festival time, with easy access to the procession route.

Pizzeria Al Borgo. Address: Via Beato Luca Belludi, 56

A favorite among locals and visitors alike, Pizzeria Al Borgo serves a variety of delicious pizzas and Italian dishes. Its proximity to the basilica makes it a convenient choice for festival-goers seeking a casual and satisfying dining experience. The service is friendly, and the atmosphere is lively, especially on festival evenings.

Caffè Gattamelata. Address: Piazza del Santo, 5

Situated directly on the square facing the basilica, Caffè Gattamelata is perfect for a quick coffee, light lunch, or aperitivo. Its outdoor seating provides a front-row view of the festival's activities, allowing you to dine amidst the vibrant sounds and energy of the Feast of Saint Anthony.

Accommodation

Hotel Casa del Pellegrino. Address: Via Melchiorre Cesarotti, 21

This hotel is next to the basilica, offering pilgrims and visitors comfortable accommodations with modern amenities. Because of its ideal location, you'll have easy access to all the June 13th festival events, making it perfect for those wanting to be at the center of the fun.

Hotel Donatello. Address: Via del Santo, 102

Overlooking the basilica's square, Hotel Donatello offers elegant rooms with classic decor and a welcoming atmosphere. Guests can enjoy views of the procession from their windows, immersing themselves in the festival's spirit without leaving the comfort of the hotel.

Hotel Giotto. Address: Piazzale Pontecorvo, 33

Just a short walk from the basilica, Hotel Giotto combines modern comfort with a historic setting. Its location along the main pilgrimage and procession route makes it an excellent choice for travelers who wish to attend the religious events, explore the city on foot, and return easily for rest between celebrations.

Day Trips: Nearby Sites, Cities, and Towns

Abano Terme. 12 kilometers (7.5 miles) from Padua. Abano Terme, nestled at the base of the Euganean Hills, has been famous since Roman times for its mineral-rich thermal waters and healing muds. Its name comes from the Greek à ponos, meaning "without pain," and reflects the town's longstanding association with wellness and rejuvenation. The ancient Romans developed it as a curative center, and today it remains one of Europe's premier spa destinations.

Visitors can unwind in lush parks like Parco Urbano Termale or explore historical landmarks such as Montirone Hill and San Lorenzo Cathedral. Many grand Liberty-style hotels still offer traditional spa treatments. The 18th-century Museo Villa Bassi hosts art exhibitions, rounding out a relaxing day focused on health, tranquility, and culture.

Mantua (Mantova). 45 kilometers (28 miles) from Verona. Surrounded by three lakes formed by the Mincio River, Mantua is a Renaissance gem that flourished under the Gonzaga dynasty, earning UNESCO World Heritage status. The city boasts grand architecture, including the vast Ducal Palace with its frescoed Camera degli Sposi by Andrea Mantegna, and the Basilica of Sant'Andrea, designed by Alberti to house a sacred relic.

Just beyond the center lies Palazzo Te, a playful masterpiece of Mannerist art with Giulio Romano's stunning frescoes. With elegant piazzas, a lively weekend market, and specialties like pumpkin tortelli and sbrisolona, Mantua is a refined and richly artistic escape, ideal for lovers of history, architecture, and cuisine.

Monselice. 23 kilometers (14 miles) from Padua. Monselice rises from the Euganean plain like a medieval stronghold, with a layered history dating to Roman times. Its strategic location made it a fortified town under various rulers, including the Lombards, Venetians, and Holy Roman Empire. Cobbled streets and stone gates preserve the town's medieval character.

The Sanctuary of the Seven Churches, modeled after the seven basilicas of Rome, leads pilgrims up the hill to the Villa Duodo. Along the way, chapels and terraces offer views of the countryside. Below, the Castello di Monselice reveals medieval armories and Renaissance interiors, making this an interesting visit for history lovers and spiritual travelers alike.

Arquà Petrarca. 30 kilometers (18.6 miles) from Padua. Set among the scenic Euganean Hills, Arquà Petrarca is one of Italy's loveliest medieval villages, named for the poet Francesco Petrarca (Petrarch), who spent his final years here. His tomb stands near the Church of Santa Maria Assunta and remains a pilgrimage site for literature enthusiasts and humanist scholars.

The village retains its stone alleys, quiet rhythm, and views of olive groves and terraced hills. Visitors can explore Petrarch's house, now a museum, and sample local specialties like brodo di giuggiole, a jujube liqueur. It's a peaceful, evocative place steeped in poetry, history, and rustic elegance.

Padua Festivals and Sagre Throughout the Year

Festa della Donna / International Women's Day

March 8

Though celebrated throughout Italy, Padua marks this day with floral markets, art exhibits, and events held by the University of Padua, highlighting women's achievements. Locals give sprigs of mimosa flowers to honor the women in their lives. Some museums offer free admission to women for the day.

Settimana Santa (Holy Week)

March or April, week before Easter (varies)

Padua observes Holy Week with processions, solemn liturgies, and events centered at the Basilica di Sant'Antonio and the Duomo. The most moving is the Good Friday procession, which winds through the historic center with participants carrying crosses and statues of the Passion. Churches remain open for adoration and confession, and traditional sacred music fills the piazzas.

Festa della Repubblica

June 2

Italy's national holiday is observed with official ceremonies in Prato della Valle, including a flag-raising, civic speeches, and military bands. While not specific to Padua, the city's main piazzas often host concerts and cultural events. It's a festive atmosphere and an opportunity to enjoy the early summer in the city.

Festa di Santa Giustina

October 7

Celebrated at the Basilica di Santa Giustina, this feast honors Padua's early Christian martyr, beheaded in AD 304 under the Roman Emperor Diocletian. A special Mass is held, followed by a day of quiet devotion. While less known than the feast of Saint Anthony, it is meaningful to locals, especially those in the Prato della Valle and Santa Giustina neighborhoods.

Padua Jazz Fest

Mid-November

The Padova Jazz Festival is a celebrated annual music event held in the historic city of Padua, Italy, showcasing a diverse lineup of internationally renowned jazz musicians and rising stars. Founded in 1998, the festival spans several days each November, offering concerts in iconic venues such as Teatro Verdi, Caffè Pedrocchi, and the Sala dei Giganti.

With its rich blend of classic and contemporary jazz, the festival embraces a wide spectrum of styles, from swing and bebop to avant-garde and fusion. Beyond performances, it often includes lectures, jam sessions, and cultural events, creating an immersive experience for jazz enthusiasts in one of Veneto's most artistic cities.

https://www.padovajazz.com/festival/

Natale a Padova (Christmas in Padua)

December 8–January 6

The Christmas season begins on the Feast of the Immaculate Conception (December 8) and lasts through Epiphany. With holiday lights, Christmas markets, and open-air concerts, the historic center sparkles. The Piazza Capitaniato and Piazza delle Erbe host artisans selling crafts, food, and gifts. Churches, especially the Basilica of Saint Anthony, feature Nativity scenes and Advent events.

Epiphany is celebrated on January 6 with La Befana, the witch who brings gifts to children, and some neighborhoods host bonfires and family activities.

CHAPTER TWELVE

Immersion Experience: Pilgrimage

A path of devotion and discovery

The Cammino of Saint Anthony of Padua

A cammino (Italian for "walk" or "path") is more than a hike; it is a pilgrimage, cultural immersion, and often, personal growth. Italians have long embraced these pilgrimage routes to reconnect with faith, tradition, and the natural beauty of their homeland. Whether taken as a religious vow or as a slower way to travel and reflect, these ancient trails are deeply woven into the fabric of Italian identity.

One of the most significant pilgrimage walks in the Veneto region is the Cammino of St. Anthony, a route that traces moments in the life of Saint Anthony of Padua, one of the most venerated saints in the Catholic world. Though his name is tied to Padua, he was born in Lisbon, Portugal, and lived a life of missionary zeal across Europe before dying in Arcella, just outside Padua, in 1231.

Even if you're not yet sure whether a pilgrimage walk is right for you, I hope this introduction to the Cammino di Sant'Antonio gives you a sense of the rich opportunities it offers, both for spiritual reflection and immersive travel through Italy's northeast.

Full Route

The Cammino di Sant'Antonio offers multiple route options. The best-known is the Padova–La Verna route, which spans approximately 430 kilometers (267 miles) and typically takes around 21 days to complete on foot. It links Padua, the city of Saint Anthony's ministry and final resting place, with La Verna in Tuscany, where Saint Francis of Assisi received the stigmata. This route symbolically connects two of Italy's greatest saints, Anthony and Francis, who were contemporaries and members of the Franciscan order.

Route Two

A shorter, more accessible version of the cammino, known as the Cammino Antoniano del Nord, begins at the Santuario di Montepaolo in Emilia-Romagna and ends at the Basilica di Sant'Antonio in Padua. This 110-kilometer (68-mile) route can be walked in 5–7 days and offers a beautiful introduction to the region's countryside, dotted with small churches and Franciscan hermitages.

Route Three

Another route, the Cammino da Camposampiero a Padova, is only 25 kilometers (15 miles), an easy one-day pilgrimage that traces Saint Anthony's final journey in life. This shorter path is ideal for those seeking a more accessible spiritual experience or for families and older travelers.

History and Spiritual Significance

Saint Anthony of Padua was a brilliant theologian and powerful preacher. After joining the Franciscan order, he became known for his deep knowledge of Scripture, his devotion to the poor, and the many miracles attributed to him both during and after his life.

The Cammino di Sant'Antonio retraces key moments of his mission, especially his ultimate days, culminating at the Basilica of Saint Anthony in Padua, a majestic place of pilgrimage visited by millions annually. His tomb remains one of the most important Catholic pilgrimage destinations in Europe.

The idea behind this pilgrimage is not just to walk in the saint's physical footsteps but to follow his spiritual legacy, one of charity, humility, and service.

Stages (Short Route Example: Camposampiero to Padua)

This one-day route is ideal for visitors to the Veneto who want a taste of the pilgrimage without undertaking a full multi-day walk. The key stops include:

Santuario del Noce

Start at the sanctuary where Saint Anthony lived for a time and where, under a walnut tree (noce), he preached to crowds of followers. The site has preserved the chapel and the wooden tree trunk and is surrounded by peaceful gardens.

Tencarola

Walking through small Veneto towns and quiet countryside, pilgrims pass chapels and fields once worked by monks. Many pilgrims stop here for rest and prayer.

Arcella

Before reaching central Padua, the route passes through Arcella, where Saint Anthony died. Today, the Santuario dell'Arcella stands on the site, marking the moment when his life of service came to an end.

Basilica di Sant'Antonio

The pilgrimage culminates at the Basilica of Saint Anthony, one of the most important pilgrimage churches in the world. Inside, pilgrims visit the saint's tomb, the Chapel of the Relics, and the cloisters, reflecting on the life and miracles of the beloved saint. For more about Padua's festivals, see the FestaFusion Padua Chapter (Chapter 11)

What to Expect on the Walk

The Cammino di Sant'Antonio, in any of its forms, is suitable for a wide range of walkers, from experienced trekkers to day pilgrims. The trails are undefinedwell-marked with the Tau cross and other signage. Paths pass through gentle rolling hills, forests, farmland, and historic towns, allowing for a slow, contemplative walk that invites both prayer and rest.

Best Times to Walk: Spring and fall offer the most comfortable temperatures. Summer can be hot in the lowlands, while winter can bring snow in the hill regions.

Accommodations

Ostelli del Pellegrino: In many towns along the route, simple hostels welcome pilgrims with a credential. These are often run by religious orders or local associations.

Monasteries and Convents: Some spiritual retreats offer a place to stay in the form of monastery guesthouses, often for a donation.

Hotels and B&Bs: Along the more traveled parts of the route, especially near Padua, pilgrims can find agriturismo, family-run inns, and small hotels for greater comfort.

Maps and Credentials

Pilgrims can request a Credentiale del Pellegrino, which can be stamped at various stops along the way and presented at the Basilica. Maps and apps are available through the Cammino di Sant'Antonio official site and associated pilgrimage organizations. These tools offer GPS-guided stages, lodging options, and spiritual reflections to accompany your journey.

Why Do Italians Walk Cammini?

Religious Pilgrimage: Historically, cammini were a fundamental aspect of Christian pilgrimage. Italians (like many other Europeans) walked these paths as acts of faith, penance, or devotion. The idea of pilgrimage is central in Christianity, and Italy, with its many saints, shrines, and relics, offers many opportunities for such spiritual journeys. Walking to a sacred site was a way to purify the soul, seek miracles, or express gratitude to God or a particular saint.

Historical Tradition: Italy's history is rich with ancient roads, trade routes, and paths that connected cities, towns, and remote villages. Many of the modern hikes follow these ancient routes, preserving not only the physical paths but also the cultural traditions of the areas. Walking a cammino is, in a way, a journey back in time, offering an intimate experience of historical Italy. Italians have a deep sense of pride in their heritage, and walking these paths allows them to reconnect with their past.

Personal and Spiritual Growth: In recent decades, these hikes have become popular as a form of personal exploration. Many Italians (and visitors) walk these routes not only for religious reasons but also to seek personal transformation, solitude, or mindfulness. Walking a long-distance route provides time for introspection, reflection, and a break from the fast pace of modern life.

Connection with Nature: Italy's walks often pass through some of the country's most beautiful natural landscapes, from the rolling hills of Tuscany to the rugged mountains of Sicily. For many Italians, walking a cammino is a way to immerse themselves in the natural beauty of their homeland. The routes often take hikers through national parks, protected areas, and remote villages that they would otherwise never experience.

Social and Community Bonding: While many walk cammini alone, there is a strong sense of community among pilgrims. Walks provide opportunities to meet other travelers, share stories, and form friendships. Italians, who value social connections and community life, often find the walking experience as much about the people they meet as the places they visit.

Health and Well-being: Walking has long been associated with good health, and Italians have embraced this aspect of walking to stay active and physically fit. Many walks provide a blend of physical challenge and relaxation, offering the benefits of exercise while allowing for moments of spiritual or cultural enrichment.

Eco-Tourism and Slow Travel: Cammini are aligned with the growing global trend of slow travel and eco-tourism, which emphasizes deeper, more sustainable connections with places visited. Italians are drawn to the idea of exploring their country on foot, engaging with local communities, and supporting small, rural economies along the way.

CHAPTER THIRTEEN

Venice's Light Festival

Gratitude, Gondolas, and Fireworks at Redentore

Festa del Redentore

Where: Venice, primarily on the Giudecca Canal and St. Mark's Basin

When: Third weekend in July.

Average Festival Temperatures: High 30°C (86°F). Low 22°C (72°F).

Festival of the Redeemer

The Festa del Redentore (Feast of the Redeemer) is one of Venice's most heartfelt and historic celebrations, born out of devotion and thanksgiving. In 1576, Venice was ravaged by a deadly outbreak of the plague. In desperation, the Venetian Senate made a vow to build a magnificent church in honor of Christ the Redeemer (Il Redentore) if the city was spared. When the plague lifted, the promise was fulfilled.

Designed by Andrea Palladio, the Church of the Redentore on the island of Giudecca became a symbol of salvation and resilience. Every year since 1577, Venetians have gathered to give thanks with a floating votive bridge, candlelit boats, and a sky filled with fireworks. While deeply religious in origin, the modern Redentore is also a time of celebration, food, music, and community, an expression of Venetian joy and memory.

When I speak with friends who live in Venice, they always say this is their most treasured festival. While Carnival may be the most famous and certainly the most photographed, it also draws huge tourist crowds and they avoid it. Redentore, by contrast, still feels like it belongs to the Venetians themselves. There's a sense of connection, of shared tradition, that makes this summer night truly special.

Redentore Church

Festival Events

Third Friday in July

Evening

Preparations and Community Dinners

In the days leading up to the festival, Venetians decorate their boats and terraces along the Giudecca Canal with colorful lanterns and festive banners. Throughout the city, neighborhoods come alive with preparations as long communal tables are set up for informal dinners. On the night of the celebration, locals gather with friends and family to share food, laughter, and stories, often staying out late under the stars. It's a moment of togetherness that blends tradition with the joy of summer nights on the water.

Third Saturday in July: Main Day of Celebration

7:00 p.m.

Opening of the Floating Bridge

A 330-meter (1082-foot) pontoon bridge is constructed to connect Zattere to the Church of the Redentore on Giudecca. The bridge opens with a blessing and a solemn votive procession, as pilgrims cross to attend Mass.

9:00 p.m.

Boat Gatherings and Floating Feasts

As evening falls on the night of Redentore, St. Mark's Basin and the Giudecca Canal transform into a floating city of celebration. Hundreds of boats, from tiny wooden sandoli to elegant bragozzi and sleek motorboats, gather in the lagoon's wide expanse, their decks strung with lights, paper lanterns, and flags fluttering in the summer breeze. For many Venetians, the water is where Redentore truly comes to life.

Festa del Redentore

As the sky deepens from lavender to indigo, the lagoon glows. Floating candles and paper lanterns are gently placed on the water, their flickering flames forming rivers of light that drift between the boats. The reflections of masts, rigging, and colored lamps shimmer across the surface, creating a dreamlike scene that feels as ancient as it is celebratory.

11:30 p.m.

Fireworks Spectacular (Fuochi del Redentore)

One of the most famous fireworks displays in all of Italy, the Fuochi del Redentore lights up the sky over St. Mark's Basin in a dazzling celebration. The show lasts around 45 minutes and draws thousands of spectators to the banks of the Riva degli Schiavoni, the Zattere promenade, and the beaches of the Lido. As bursts of color explode above, their reflections shimmer across the water and dance over the domes of Venice, creating a breathtaking spectacle that celebrates survival, beauty, and unity.

Third Sunday: Regatta and Religious Services

4:00 p.m.

Redentore Regatta (Regate del Redentore)

One highlight of the Festa del Redentore is the Regata del Redentore, a dazzling display of traditional Venetian rowing held on the Giudecca Canal. This waterway, which separates the main island of Venice from the long island of Giudecca, becomes the stage for a beloved and time-honored competition that dates back centuries.

As the sun begins its descent over the lagoon and the city prepares for the night's fireworks, crowds gather along the canal's edge, lining the fondamenta, the wide stone walkways that run beside the water, and leaning from balconies to cheer on the rowers. The regata is not just a race; it is a living expression of Venetian heritage, where strength, skill, and centuries-old maritime tradition converge in the form of sleek wooden boats and powerful oarsmen.

The event features a full program of races, including youth (junior) and adult (senior) divisions, with male and female athletes competing in various boat classes. The most iconic of these are the gondolini, narrow racing gondolas that glide across the water with speed and elegance, and the pupparini, smaller and more maneuverable boats originally designed for lagoon navigation.

Boats of the Regatta

Dressed in traditional regatta attire, rowers stand upright as they row, using the voga alla veneta technique, an elegant, forward-facing style of rowing unique to Venice. The intensity of the competition grows as the races progress, culminating in a thrilling sprint as boats surge toward the finish line near the Chiesa del Redentore, their brightly painted hulls reflecting in the golden light of the canal.

7:00 p.m.

Mass at the Church of the Redentore

A solemn and beautiful service is held at the Redentore Church, attended by locals and clergy. The event closes with music, bells, and personal moments of reflection.

Travel Tips

Book Early: Hotels along the Giudecca and the Riva are in high demand. Book balconies or waterfront tables months in advance if you want prime firework views.

Arrive Early for Fireworks: Locals often claim their boat spots or waterfront benches hours in advance. Bring water, snacks, and a fan.

Walk the Bridge: If you're in Venice on Saturday evening, don't miss the opportunity to walk across the floating votive bridge, it's only open once a year.

CHAPTER FOURTEEN

FestaFusion Bassano

From Floating Stages to Racing Rafts

FestaFusion Bassano del Grappa

#1. **Summer Opera Festival Veneto.** (Operaestate Festival Veneto). An acclaimed, multi-disciplinary summer arts festival that transforms Bassano del Grappa into a cultural stage, featuring opera, dance, theater, music, and cinema in open-air historic venues.

#2. **River Raft Race. (Palio delle Zattere).** A playful July river race where teams on homemade rafts float down the Brenta, reviving Bassano's lumber-trading traditions with medieval flair, music, and street festivities.

Where: Bassano del Grappa and Valstagna

When: Opera Festiva July / August. Palio on the last weekend of July.

Average Temperatures: High 30°C (86°F). Low 19°C (66°F).

Event Website: https://www.operaestate.it/it/

#FestaFusion: When two festivals collide in the same town around the same time, your journey becomes twice as magical.

Bassano del Grappa: A River Town of Resilience and Renaissance

Nestled at the foot of the Asiago Plateau in northern Veneto, Bassano del Grappa lies along the Brenta River, surrounded by the Venetian Prealps. With a population of 43,000, it balances urban energy with small-town charm.

Originally a Roman municipium called Bassianum, it flourished along the Via Claudia Augusta, as evidenced by milestones, bridge foundations, and a 2nd-century merchant's stele. After the fall of Rome, Bassano stood between Lombard duchies and Byzantine outposts. The Lombards fortified the hilltop, and Bishop San Bassiano, whose relics rest beneath the cathedral, established the diocese in the 8th century. This era fostered a resilient civic identity rooted in faith and frontier life.

By the 12th century, Bassano had self-governing walls and a timber-based economy powered by riverside mills. In 1404, it joined the Venetian Republic, exporting fish, ceramics, and famously, grappa. Palladio's iconic 1569 wooden bridge unified the two riverbanks and became a Renaissance symbol.

Napoleonic upheavals and Austrian rule followed until Italy's unification in 1866. The town industrialized with wool mills and locomotive factories, while distilleries like Nardini and Poli elevated grappa to global fame. Despite wartime damage, thoughtful restoration preserved its medieval core and bridge, securing Bassano's place as a living testament to northern Italy's layered history.

#1. Summer Opera Festival Veneto

Founded in the early 1980s, Operaestate Festival Veneto has evolved into one of Italy's premier summer arts festivals. Created to celebrate opera in open-air settings, the festival quickly expanded to include dance, theater, contemporary music, and film. It now draws internationally renowned artists, emerging talent, and curious travelers who gather in Bassano del Grappa's historic squares, gardens, and villas. With a mission to make the performing arts accessible and community-based, the festival has become a hallmark of the Brenta Valley's cultural calendar.

During the festival weeks, typically running from late June through August, the entire town becomes a stage. Local restaurants extend their terraces, artisan shops stay open late, and the evening passeggiata takes on a theatrical quality as festival-goers in elegant attire mingle with locals in the lamp-lit streets. The festival's commitment to accessibility means that many performances are free, transforming art appreciation from an elite pursuit into a communal celebration that reflects the democratic spirit of Italian piazza culture.

Visit the event website for specifics: https://www.operaestate.it/it/

#2. Palio Raft Race

Rooted in the rich timber heritage of the Brenta Valley, the Palio delle Zattere revives centuries-old traditions of river rafting that once linked the forests of the Veneto to the floating city of Venice. Established in the late 20th century to honor this legacy, the event has grown into one of the most spirited and authentic historical reenactments in northern Italy. Held each summer in Valstagna, the Palio is a fierce yet festive race of handcrafted timber rafts, called zattere, navigated by costumed crews from nine rival districts. It's more than a race; it's a celebration of endurance, craftsmanship, and regional pride.

Local artisans and residents line the banks in traditional dress, musicians fill the air with folk melodies, and the town's streets echo with laughter and rivalry. The river, once a highway for commerce, becomes a stage for storytelling, where past and present collide in splashes and cheers.

As the rafts surge through the rapids toward victory, spectators cheer from old stone bridges and riverfront cafes, sipping spritzes and soaking up the ambiance. The Palio's community-driven spirit is palpable, bridging generations through shared memories and spirited competition. It's a uniquely Italian blend of athleticism and theatricality, anchoring Valstagna's identity to its river, its people, and its enduring story.

Walking Tour of Bassano del Grappa

#1. Ponte degli Alpini (Ponte Vecchio)
The town's iconic covered wooden bridge designed by Andrea Palladio in 1569.

e designed by Andrea Palladio in 1569. Marvel at its truss-structure silhouette over the Brenta River and admire how it's been rebuilt and restored through floods and wars.

#2. Piazza Libertà

Bassano's main square, framed by the Loggia del Comune (15th century) and the clock tower. Sip an espresso at one of the cafés while admiring the arcaded façades and the town hall's frescoes.

Piazza Liberta

#3. Museo Civico (City Museum)

Housed in the 14th-century Palazzo Pretorio, this museum displays local art, archaeology, and the story of the Grappa distilleries, an ideal dive into Bassano's cultural roots.

#4. Museo della Ceramica (Ceramics Museum)

In the ornate 18th-century Palazzo Sturm, explore a collection of locally produced pottery and learn how Bassano ceramics influenced Venetian styles.

#5. Orto Botanico "La Serre"

Behind Palazzo Sturm, this botanical garden hosts Mediterranean and alpine plants,perfect for a shaded interlude and a glimpse of regional flora.

#6. Museo Poli Grappa

Step inside a converted distillery to trace the history of Italy's most famous clear spirit. Tastings available at the end will illustrate why "grappa" and Bassano are inseparable.

#7. Duomo di San Bassiano and Baptistry

Conclude your visit at the Duomo di San Bassiano, the spiritual heart of Bassano del Grappa. The cathedral stands on the site of an earlier paleochristian church dating back to the 8th century, though the present structure reflects a blend of Romanesque and Gothic styles, with later Renaissance and Baroque additions.

The façade, though relatively simple compared to Venice's grand churches, exudes a dignified elegance with stone detailing that hints at its medieval origins.

Inside, the cathedral houses valuable artworks, including altarpieces and frescoes by prominent Veneto artists. Most importantly, it holds the relics of Saint Bassianus (San Bassiano), the town's patron saint, who was a 4th-century bishop known for his piety and leadership. His tomb has long been a place of local veneration.

Adjacent to the Duomo stands the octagonal Baptistry, a striking structure dating from the medieval period. Within, you can still see fragments of 15th-century frescoes that once adorned its walls, offering a glimpse into the artistic devotion of the period. The baptistery's simple geometry and aged frescoes contrast beautifully with the more ornate details found inside the cathedral.

Logistics

Train: Bassano del Grappa is easily accessible by train. Direct regional trains run frequently from Venice Santa Lucia and Venice Mestre (approximately 1 hour 20 minutes). There are also connections from Padua, Vicenza, and Treviso. The train station (Stazione di Bassano del Grappa) is located just a 10-minute walk from the historic center.

Bus: Several bus companies provide services to Bassano del Grappa from surrounding cities and regional hubs. SVT (Società Vicentina Trasporti) operates routes connecting Bassano with Vicenza and smaller towns in the province.

Parking: Several parking options are available near the historic center: Parcheggio Le Piazze (Via Cristoforo Colombo) is a large lot about a 10-minute walk from the Ponte Vecchio and city center. Parcheggio Prato Santa Caterina is a convenient location near the old town. Parcheggio Gerhard Rodax is also near the center, accessible for longer stays.

Restaurant Recommendations

Ristorante Birraria Ottone. Address: Via Giacomo Matteotti, 48/50

Near the historic center, Ristorante Birraria Ottone has been a Bassano institution since the 1800s. The elegant yet welcoming dining rooms feature historic décor that reflects the restaurant's long heritage. The menu includes classic dishes from the Veneto region such as baccalà alla vicentina, risottos, and polenta, alongside house specialties. Birraria Ottone also offers its own artisanal beers, a nod to its origins as a brewery-restaurant.

Pizzeria Salernitana. Address: Via Ognissanti, 57

A beloved spot for casual dining, Pizzeria Salernitana is known for its wood-fired pizzas with perfectly crisp crusts and generous toppings. The menu includes both classic favorites, like Margherita and Diavola, as well as creative seasonal combinations. The atmosphere is friendly and relaxed, making it a superb choice for families, groups, or anyone craving authentic Italian pizza at reasonable prices. They also offer a selection of fresh salads, appetizers, and local wines.

Accommodation

Hotel Al Castello. Address: Via Lazzaro Bonamigo, 19

Ideally located just a short walk from the historic center and the iconic Ponte Vecchio, Hotel Al Castello offers comfortable accommodations in a charming, traditional setting. The hotel features well-appointed rooms with classic décor, modern amenities, and some rooms offering views toward the old town.

Bonotto Hotel Belvedere. Address: Viale delle Fosse, 3

A refined choice for travelers seeking comfort and a touch of elegance, Bonotto Hotel Belvedere combines historic charm with modern conveniences. Set in a stately building just a few minute walk from the historic center, the hotel offers spacious rooms with stylish furnishings and a warm, inviting ambiance.

Hotel Victoria. Address: Viale Armando Diaz, 33

Hotel Victoria offers a comfortable stay just outside the historic center, within easy walking distance to Bassano's principal attractions and the train station. The hotel features clean, modern rooms with all essential amenities, making it a practical choice for both short and extended stays.

Day Trip Options: Nearby Sites, Cities, and Towns

Asolo. 29 kilometers (18 miles) from Bassano. Known as "the city of one hundred horizons," Asolo crowns a gentle hill scattered with medieval towers and Renaissance villas. Begin at the Rocca, the ancient fortress whose lookout terrace frames panoramic countryside vistas.

Meander through the historic center to see the 15th-century Palazzo della Ragione, whose loggia once hosted town assemblies, then duck into the Cathedral of Santa Maria Assunta to admire its frescoed chapels. Art lovers can visit the small Museo Civico for works by long-time resident Queen Cornaro della Regina. Cap your visit with a sit-down at a café on Piazza Garibaldi, savoring locally produced extra virgin olive oil drizzled over fresh bread.

Monte Grappa. From Bassano, 23 kilometers (11 miles). Monte Grappa dominates the skyline above Bassano and offers both history and high-alpine scenery. Drive or bike the winding road through chestnut forests up to the Sacrario Militare di Monte Grappa, the solemn First World War memorial that holds the remains of some 12,0000 soldiers.

From its panoramic terrace, you can scan the Venetian plain, the Dolomites and even the Adriatic on a clear day. Nearby, open-air exhibits display restored artillery pieces and dug-in trenches. For a longer outing, follow marked trails to one of the mountain lodges, where you can refuel with canederli dumplings and rich mountain broths before descending back to Bassano.

Bassano Festivals and Sagre Throughout the Year

Fiera di San Bassiano (Medieval Fair)

January 19

This centuries-old fair honors Bassano's patron saint, San Bassiano. The celebration includes a solemn Mass in the cathedral, processions, and a large street fair throughout the historic center with vendors selling sweets, roasted chestnuts, and local crafts. The aroma of frittelle and vin brulè fills the air as the town comes alive with music and stalls.

Carnevale di Bassano

February (dates vary based on the liturgical calendar)

Bassano del Grappa celebrates Carnival with costumed parades, masquerade parties, and children's activities across the city. Piazza Libertà and the bridge become lively gathering points, and the local community organizes theatrical performances and contests for the best masks.

Festa della Liberazione (Liberation Day)

April 25

On Italy's Liberation Day, Bassano commemorates its WWII resistance history with civic ceremonies, concerts, and reenactments. Memorials are placed at key locations, and flowers are brought to the Ponte degli Alpini, a symbol of resilience and identity for the town.

Bassano Fotografia Festival (Photography Festival)

September to November (biennial)

This major cultural event takes place every two years, bringing exhibitions by international and Italian photographers to galleries and public spaces throughout the city. The historic streets and museums become open-air photo galleries, drawing creatives and visitors from across the country.

Festa della Madonna della Salute (Madonna of Good Health)

November 21

A devotional festival celebrated with a candlelight procession to the Church of San Vito, where prayers are offered for health and protection. Locals also enjoy seasonal treats and a small fair near the church. It's one of the more intimate but deeply rooted traditions in the town.

Mercatini di Natale e Villaggio di Babbo Natale (Christmas Markets)

December

Bassano transforms into a charming holiday village during Advent, with wooden stalls filling the main piazzas, selling artisan gifts, mulled wine, and Alpine specialties. The Christmas village includes Santa's House for children, light displays, and weekend events like carol singing and theatrical performances.

CHAPTER FIFTEEN

FestaFusion Lake Garda

Malcesine Music & Garda Jazz

FestaFusion Lake Garda

#1. Malcesine Music Festival: Set against the scenic backdrop of Lake Garda and the medieval Scaliger Castle, the Malcesine Music Festival brings summer nights to life with open-air concerts featuring jazz, rock, pop, and soul in the town's piazzas and lakeside gardens.

#2. Garda Jazz Festival: The Garda Jazz Festival transforms the northern lake towns into a jazz lover's paradise each summer, with world-class performances in historic piazzas, theaters, and scenic open-air venues from Riva del Garda to Arco and beyond.

Where: Lake Garda

When: July / August

Average Festival Temperatures: High: 28°C (82°F). Low: 17°C (63°F).

Malcesine Music Event Website:

https://www.visitmalcesine.com/en/malcesine-music-festival-2

Garda Jazz Event Website:

https://www.gardatrentino.it/en/events/garda-jazz-festival_8924

#FestaFusion: When two festivals collide in the same area around the same time, your journey becomes twice as magical.

#1. Malcesine Music

Picture Perfect Malcesine

Malcesine is a picturesque town on the eastern shore of Lake Garda, in the province of Verona. Nestled between the lake's deep blue waters and the steep slopes of Monte Baldo, the town enjoys a dramatic setting that combines alpine elevation with Mediterranean charm. Its historic center is dominated by the well preserved Castello Scaligero, a fortress with origins dating back to the Lombards and later expanded by the Scaligeri in the 13th century. Over the centuries, Malcesine came under Venetian, French, and Austrian rule before becoming part of Italy in the 19th century.

Today, Malcesine has a population of around 3,500 residents, but its numbers swell in summer due to its popularity with international visitors. The town's geography makes it a magnet for outdoor enthusiasts, offering windsurfing, sailing, and lake swimming and cable car access to hiking and paragliding trails on Monte Baldo. The combination of natural beauty, medieval architecture, and cultural events like the music festival has secured Malcesine's place as one of Lake Garda's most beloved destinations.

Malcesine Music

Malcesine transforms into a vibrant musical stage each summer, with free live performances spanning genres from jazz, blues, funky, soul, and rock to pop and hip hop. Held across several nights in the historic old town and the lakeside Padre Mario Casella gardens, the festival offers a relaxed open air concert experience. Throughout July and into August, a variety of local and national artists bring lively rhythms to this charming lakeside setting.

Whether you're wandering through cobbled alleys or enjoying the evening breeze by the water, the festival blends the atmospheric backdrop of Malcesine, complete with views of the Scaliger Castle and lake, with the energy of live music, making it a delightful addition to any summer trip in the Garda region.

The Malcesine Music Festival delivers a vibrant, multi-genre musical experience with:

- **Street Concerts:** Roaming bands, pop, blues, funk, soul, hip-hop, and rock, perform along routes through the historic center and lakeside public gardens.

- **Garden Concerts:** Evening performances held in the Giardini "Padre Mario Casella," offering intimate outdoor shows under the stars.

- **Jazz-on-a-Boat:** Unique jazz concerts aboard the historic sailing ship Siora Veronica, docked in the harbor.

- **Multi-date Summer Series**: The festival takes place across several summer evenings, with performances in June, July, August, and September.

- **Free Admission**: Most events are open to the public at no cost, making it an accessible and inviting celebration for locals and visitors alike.

Walking Tour of Malcesine

#1. Castello Scaligero

Start the tour at Malcesine's iconic landmark, the Castello Scaligero, perched on a rocky spur above the lake. Originally built by the Lombards and later expanded by the Scaligeri family in the 13th century, the castle features crenellated towers, panoramic terraces, and a small museum dedicated to the natural history of Lake Garda and German poet Johann Wolfgang von Goethe, who visited in 1786. Climb the tower for sweeping views over the rooftops, lake, and Monte Baldo.

My husband and I enjoyed the incredible water and town views from the upper castle fortifications while my son and his friend parasailed off the top of Monte

Baldo. Malcesine's diverse offerings were perfectly captured by the contrast of our calm history tour and their thrilling adventure above.

#2. Palazzo dei Capitani

Head down toward the lakeside promenade to reach the Palazzo dei Capitani, a late Gothic-Venetian palace once used by the Venetian military governors of the area. Set directly on the water with a loggia facing the lake, the building dates to the 14th century and is surrounded by palm trees and gardens. Today it hosts cultural events and exhibitions, and its serene setting makes it a lovely photo stop.

#3. Via Capitanato and the Old Port

Stroll along Via Capitanato, a picturesque street lined with pastel facades, artisan shops, and small cafes. It leads you to the Vecchio Porto, the old port where fishing boats once docked. This area remains lively with outdoor dining and offers postcard-worthy views of the lake and harbor. It's a perfect place for a coffee or gelato break by the water.

#4. Chiesa di Santo Stefano

Climb gently uphill from the port area to visit the Church of Saint Stephen, Malcesine's main parish church. Originally Romanesque, it was rebuilt in the Baroque style in the 18th century. Inside you'll find ornate altars, frescoes, and a beautifully decorated apse. The church sits on a small rise, giving visitors a peaceful vantage point over the rooftops of the town.

#5. Funivia Malcesine-Monte Baldo Station

End the walk at the cable car station for Monte Baldo, located just 10 minutes uphill from the town center. Even if you're not taking the ride, the modern station is worth seeing for its sleek design and the dramatic views of the cliffs above. If time allows, take the 10-minute rotating cable car ride up to Monte Baldo's trails, alpine meadows, and breathtaking lookouts. It's one of the most dramatic ascents in the region.

Malcesine Restaurant Recommendations

Ristorante La Pace. Address: Via Casella, 1

Overlooking the lake and just steps from the Scaliger Castle, Ristorante La Pace offers panoramic views and a romantic setting ideal for lunch or dinner. Known for its warm hospitality and rich culinary tradition, the menu highlights northern Italian favorites like risotto with lake perch, homemade pastas, and fresh-caught fish.

Ristorante Al Corsaro. Address: Via Paina, 17

Located near the base of the castle with a stunning lakefront terrace, Ristorante Al Corsaro blends fine dining with relaxed elegance. The menu emphasizes quality ingredients with an emphasis on fresh seafood, grilled meats, and classic Italian dishes with a modern twist.

Vecchia Malcesine. Address: Via Pisort, 6

Holding a Michelin star, Vecchia Malcesine is a standout for gourmet travelers seeking an inventive and artistic approach to Italian cuisine. With views over the lake and impeccable service, it's an unforgettable culinary experience and a celebration of creativity in a historic town.

Malcesine Accommodation

Hotel Castello Lake Front. Address: Via Paina 21

Perched at the foot of Scaliger Castle with its own private pebble beach, Hotel Castello Lake Front offers contemporary-chic rooms (most with balconies), an on-site restaurant and bar, parking, and a serene lakeside terrace, ideal for romantic or family stays.

Hotel Luna Rossa. Address: Via Paina, 6

Close to Lake Garda and the medieval old town, this 3-star adults-only hotel features a seasonal outdoor pool, garden and terrace, plus 27 rooms, a sundeck, friendly service, free parking, and a peaceful, intimate atmosphere.

Hotel Lago di Garda. Address: Piazza Vittorio Emanuele, 1

In the historic center right by the waterfront, Hotel Lago di Garda is a charming 3-star property with 11 rooms (some with balconies or lake views), a rooftop terrace with sweeping panoramas, plus an on-site Veneto restaurant and shared lounge.

Lake Garda Views

#2. Garda Jazz Festival

Rivo del Garda: Gateway to the Northern Lake

Riva del Garda, affectionately known simply as Riva, is a vibrant lakeside town located at the northern tip of Lake Garda. Framed by dramatic cliffs, olive groves, and the crystalline waters of Italy's largest lake, Riva del Garda stands at the meeting point between Mediterranean softness and Alpine ruggedness, making it one of the most geographically striking towns in the entire Lake Garda basin.

Nestled at 70 meters (230 feet) above sea level, the town is backed by towering peaks such as Monte Rocchetta and Monte Brione, with steep mountains rising almost vertically from the lakeshore. The landscape allows for both lake activities and mountain sports within walking distance. Riva del Garda is also the second-largest town on Lake Garda (after Desenzano), with a population of around 17,000 residents, though its numbers swell significantly in summer with tourists from across Europe.

In the Middle Ages, Riva emerged as a strategic stronghold, particularly prized for its position at the crossroads of northern trade routes between Trento, Verona, and Brescia. It became part of the Bishopric of Trento, and later fell under the rule of the Scaligeri of Verona, the Visconti of Milan, and eventually the Republic of Venice. The imposing Rocca di Riva, a lakeside fortress built in the 12th century and remodeled by the Venetians, stands as a symbol of the town's defensive past.

In the 19th century, Riva became part of the Austro-Hungarian Empire and remained so until 1918, when it was incorporated into the Kingdom of Italy after World War I. Evidence of Austrian influence is still visible today in the town's orderly architecture and lakeside promenades.

Garda Jazz Festival

The Garda Jazz Festival is a renowned annual event that brings the vibrant sounds of jazz to the picturesque northern shores of Lake Garda. Established in 2000 as a continuation of the earlier "Torbole Jazz" festival, it has since evolved into one of Italy's most significant jazz festivals, drawing both national and international artists to its stages.

The Garda Jazz Festival offers a diverse program that includes:

Open-air concerts: Performances set against the stunning backdrop of Lake Garda's natural beauty.

Jazz Cafés: Intimate sessions in local bars and venues, promoting emerging talent from Northern Italy.

Workshops and seminars: Educational opportunities for jazz enthusiasts and musicians.

Special events: Unique performances, such as tributes to jazz legends and thematic concerts.

Event Locations

The festival moves around, with events in pretty towns in Garda Trentino.

Riva del Garda: The main hub, featuring concerts at venues like the Congress Centre and Parco Lido.

Arco: Known for its historic castle, which serves as a dramatic setting for performances.

Nago-Torbole: Offers lakeside venues that enhance the musical experience.

The Garda Jazz Festival is organized by the Alto Garda Music School (SMAG) with support from local municipalities and cultural institutions. While many events are free to the public, some require ticket purchases, especially for performances in prominent venues. Attendees are encouraged to check the official festival website for detailed schedules, ticketing information, and any updates regarding event locations or times.

Walking Tour Rivo del Garda

#1. Piazza III Novembre & Torre Apponale

This lively square is the heart of Riva del Garda's historic center, lined with colorful Renaissance and Venetian buildings. At its center stands Torre Apponale, a 34-meter (112-foot) medieval watchtower from the 13th century. You can climb its 165 steps for a panoramic view of the rooftops and Lake Garda. The piazza is a perfect starting point for your tour and often hosts markets, festivals, and music events.

#2. La Rocca di Riva (Museo Alto Garda – MAG)

A quick stroll from the piazza, this 12th-century lakeside fortress now houses the town's archaeological and art museum. The Rocca, once a military stronghold, was renovated by the Venetians and later the Austrians. Visit to explore local history, medieval frescoes, and paintings by 19th-century Italian artists. The museum also offers a peaceful inner courtyard and lake views.

#3. Chiesa dell'Inviolata (Church of the Inviolata)

Continue for 5–7 minutes uphill to reach this Baroque gem built in 1603, considered the most beautiful church in Riva. The octagonal interior is richly decorated with stucco, gilded wood, and paintings, including works attributed to Palma il Giovane. Despite its small size, it offers a dramatic artistic contrast to the medieval and neoclassical structures nearby.

#4. Porta San Michele and the Medieval Walls

Walk a few minutes north to find Porta San Michele, one of the surviving gates of the old medieval walls. These remnants give you a glimpse of Riva's defensive history, especially its role as a border town under Venetian, Austro-Hungarian, and Italian control. The gate stands as a quiet historic photo spot.

#5. Palazzo Pretorio & Loggia Pretoriana

Return toward the lakeshore and stop at this 14th-century palace, once the seat of the local podestà (governor). Its loggia, arcades, and fresco fragments tell the story of Riva's importance in the Middle Ages and Renaissance. Nearby inscriptions recall edicts and events in Riva's civic life over the centuries.

#6. Lungolago Promenade

End your tour with a stroll along the Lake Garda promenade, stretching eastward from the Rocca. This lakefront walkway offers spectacular views of Monte Brione and the cliffs above. Relax at a café, take photos of the sailboats and swans, or simply enjoy the breeze. It's especially magical in the early evening as the sun sets behind the mountains.

Rivo del Garda Restaurant Recommendations

Ristorante al Volt. Address: Via Fiume, 73

Nestled in the heart of Riva del Garda's historic center, Ristorante al Volt is renowned for its elegant ambiance and commitment to regional cuisine. The restaurant's name, "al Volt," refers to the vaulted ceilings that create a cozy yet sophisticated atmosphere.

Pasta Fresca Bistrò. Address: Via Andrea Maffei, 11

Pasta Fresca Bistrò offers a delightful experience for pasta enthusiasts. This charming eatery specializes in freshly made pasta, prepared daily to ensure authenticity and flavor. The open kitchen allows guests to witness the pasta-making process, adding an interactive element to the dining experience.

Ristorante Pizzeria Leon d'Oro. Address: Via Fiume, 28

A staple in Riva del Garda since 1974, Ristorante Pizzeria Leon d'Oro combines tradition with a warm, family-friendly atmosphere. The restaurant offers a diverse menu featuring classic Italian dishes, including a variety of pizzas baked to perfection.

Rivo del Garda Accommodation

Hotel Europa with SkyPool & Panorama. Address: Piazza Catena, 9

This elegant 4-star hotel is located directly on the lakefront in the heart of Riva del Garda. With a spectacular rooftop pool and sun terrace offering panoramic views of Lake Garda and the surrounding mountains, it's a favorite for travelers seeking relaxation and luxury.

Grand Hotel Riva. Address: Piazza Garibaldi 10

The 4-star Grand Hotel Riva is a historic property with modern touches, perfectly in the old town. Inside, you'll find comfortable rooms, a spa, and a rooftop restaurant with stunning views of Lake Garda.

Hotel Portici: Romantik & Wellness. Address: Piazza 3 Novembre, 19

Overlooking the main square and just a few steps from the lake, this charming 4-star romantic hotel is set in a historic palazzo. It blends timeless elegance with modern wellness offerings, including a spa and sauna.

Hotel Canarino. Address: Via Monte Oro, 9

Just 100 meters (about 330 feet) from the shores of Lake Garda, this friendly, family-run 3-star hotel offers great value and a peaceful garden atmosphere. The property features a pool, sun terrace, and wellness area with a hot tub, sauna, and Turkish bath.

Day Trips: Nearby Sites, Cities, and Towns

Linfano. Distance from Riva del Garda: 3 kilometers (1.8 miles). Linfano is a small hamlet that sits quietly between Riva del Garda and the lakeside town of Torbole. Though modest in size, its location near the mouth of the Sarca River and proximity to both lake and mountain make it a great base for nature walks, river trails, and bike rides. Linfano is particularly appreciated for its peaceful atmosphere and panoramic trails, including access to the Sentiero della Pace (Peace Trail) and viewpoints over the northern tip of Lake Garda. It also serves as a transition point between the mountainous terrain of Riva and the breezy, open lakeshore of Torbole. Ideal for travelers seeking a quiet escape immersed in Garda's natural scenery.

Nago-Torbole. 4 kilometers from Rivo (2.5 miles). Nago-Torbole is a picturesque fusion of two villages: Nago, perched above the lake with mountain views, and Torbole, nestled directly on the lakeshore. Historically, Nago has been a fortified lookout since Roman times, and its strategic importance continued through the medieval period under Venetian and Austro-Hungarian rule. You can still see remnants of medieval walls and military posts as you walk through the older part of town.

Don't miss the Belvedere of Nago, a viewpoint offering panoramic lake and mountain vistas, or the Marmitte dei Giganti, deep glacial potholes formed during the Ice Age. In Torbole, visit the Casa del Dazio, a historic customs house by the harbor, and enjoy the quaint piazzas, waterfront cafes, and access to excellent biking paths. A quick visit here feels like stepping into a postcard of Alpine-meets-Mediterranean charm.

Torbole. 3 kilometers (1.8 miles) from Rivo. Ferry: Available (seasonal). Although technically part of Nago-Torbole, Torbole deserves special mention for its distinct lakeside identity. Once a sleepy fishing village, Torbole has transformed into one of Europe's wind sports capitals, drawing windsurfers, sailors, and kitesurfers from around the world thanks to the reliable Ora and Pelér winds. Its stunning lakefront is backed by the cliffs of Monte Baldo, giving it a dramatic visual appeal.

The town's charm lies in its blend of old-world architecture and active outdoor culture. Visitors can enjoy the lakeside promenade, charming cafes, and waterside sculptures. History lovers will enjoy the small Saint Andrea Church, dedicated to the town's patron saint, and the Casa Beust, a well-preserved 18th-century noble residence. For a laid-back half-day trip, Torbole offers magnificent views, breezes, and lakeside serenity, just minutes from Riva.

Lake Garda Festivals and Sagre Throughout the Year

Flicorno d'Oro – European Band Competition

March or April

A true fanfare of talent, Flicorno d'Oro is one of Europe's most prestigious band competitions, bringing together wind orchestras from across the continent. Held at the Palacongressi di Riva, this multi-day event includes competitive performances judged by an international panel, as well as public concerts and parades. Born in the spirit of musical excellence and friendship, it's a feast for fans of brass, percussion, and symphonic wind ensembles. If you're moved by the power of live orchestral music, don't miss this extraordinary showcase.

Bike Festival Riva del Garda

Early May (typically the first weekend)

Get ready to ride! The Bike Festival Riva del Garda is Europe's premier mountain biking event, where adrenaline meets Alpine beauty. Since its launch in the 1990s, this high-energy festival has transformed the town into a mecca for cycling enthusiasts. From the thrilling Bike Marathon to the eMTB Challenge and the family-friendly SCOTT Junior Trophy, it offers events for all skill levels. A massive expo featuring over 350 top cycling brands and a buzzing social scene with live music and lakeside parties make it a must for both riders and fans. Whether you're a pro or just love the energy of outdoor sports, this is where adventure begins.

Malcesine in Fiore

Late May

A vibrant springtime floral festival filling the lakeside square with colorful plant stalls and garden exhibitions.

MusicaRivaFestival

Mid–Late July

For nearly four decades, this festival has enchanted audiences with its blend of classical, contemporary, and international music. Founded in 1985, the festival was created to promote young musical talent and has since hosted stars like Plácido Domingo. Held in atmospheric venues like the Rocca and Church of Inviolata, it offers a rare chance to hear world-class music amid Riva's historic charm. With masterclasses, youth orchestra performances, and gala concerts, this festival is a cultural jewel for lovers of fine music. Visit for the sound of violins echoing off medieval walls and sunsets accompanied by opera.

In Canto sul Garda (Choral Competition)

October

Raise your voice, or at least your appreciation for harmony at In Canto sul Garda, a renowned international choral competition that turns Riva into a global stage for vocal music. Welcoming amateur and semi-professional choirs from across Europe and beyond, this festival celebrates the unifying power of song. Performances range from gospel and jazz to sacred and folk music, set in historic churches and theaters. It's a moving, uplifting event that blends culture, community, and tradition. Come and hear voices from around the world converge in harmony on the shores of Lake Garda.

Immersion Travel Podcast: Lake Garda Series

To enhance your travel experience, tune into my five-part series on Lake Garda. This audio companion dives deeper into the lake's history, regional culture, and seasonal highlights, while offering insider tips for each area. Whether you're planning your itinerary or simply dreaming of Italy, these episodes guide you through the best towns to visit, must-see sites, lakeside activities, scenic hikes, ferry tips, and culinary stops from north to south.

Podcast Links Available from my Video and Podcast Page.

https://katerinaferrara.com/video-podcast/

Each episode is tailored to help you travel smarter and experience the region like a local.

CHAPTER SIXTEEN

Feltre's Fierce Palio and Proud Past

Festival of Horses and Honor

Palio di Feltre

Where: Feltre

When: First weekend of August.

Average Festival Temperatures: High: 29°C (84°F). Low: 16°C (61°F).

Website: https://www.paliodifeltre.it/

Feltre: Fortress of the Foothills

Feltre is a historic hill town nestled in the Veneto region of northern Italy, serving as the principal center of the Feltrino area. At an elevation of 325 meters (1,066 feet), it lies at the foot of the Dolomite Mountains, approximately 30 kilometers (18.6 miles) west of Belluno and about 100 kilometers (62 miles) northwest of Venice. The town is positioned near the confluence of the Stizzon and Piave rivers, offering a picturesque setting that bridges alpine and Venetian landscapes.

Feltre has a population of 20,568 residents. The town's geography is characterized by its division into two distinct areas: the historic upper town, perched on a hill and encircled by ancient walls, and the modern lower town, which has evolved into the commercial and industrial hub of the city.

Feltre's origins trace back to Roman times when it was known as Feltria. The town was along the Via Claudia Augusta, a significant Roman road that connected Altinum to Augusta Vindelicum (modern-day Augsburg in Germany). This strategic location facilitated its development into a flourishing municipality, with a robust economy supported by artisans, wool recyclers, and timber merchants.

Following the fall of the Western Roman Empire, Feltre experienced a series of dominations, including the Lombards, the Da Romano family, the Scaligeri of Verona, and eventually the Republic of Venice in 1404. The Venetian period ushered in a renaissance for the town, marked by the construction of new fortifications and the flourishing of arts and architecture.

In 1509, during the conflicts of the League of Cambrai, Feltre suffered significant destruction but was subsequently rebuilt in the characteristic 16th-century Venetian style. The town's resilience was further tested during World War I, when it faced sieges and occupations, yet it preserved its rich cultural heritage.

Palio di Feltre

In the summer heat of 1404, with political storms swirling across the Veneto, the citizens of Feltre made a momentous decision. Tired of shifting alliances and the instability of local rulers, they pledged their loyalty to the powerful and flourishing Republic of Venice. The gesture was not only strategic but deeply symbolic, securing their town's future while weaving it into the fabric of Venetian greatness.

To mark the occasion, Feltre erupted in celebration. There were games, races, music, and feasts in the streets. Among the most beloved of these festivities was the Palio, a thrilling horse race that quickly became an annual tradition. Four contrade, or city districts, Castello, Duomo, Santo Stefano, and Port'Oria, each fielded champions to compete for honor, prestige, and a hand-painted banner known as il palio. Rivalries flared, drums rolled, and knights thundered past cheering crowds, while flag-throwers, musicians, and performers filled the piazza with Renaissance splendor.

For centuries, the Palio di Feltre brought the town together in a vivid celebration of identity and pride. But like many historic traditions, it faded with time. By the 1800s, the race had all but disappeared, a victim of modernity and changing tastes.

Then, in 1979, Feltre's spirit came galloping back. Driven by passionate locals and historians, the Palio was reborn, not as a simple race, but as a fully immersive medieval festival. Costumes were stitched by hand. Trumpets blared once more from stone balconies. The contrade, still alive with neighborhood pride, took up their banners and their challenges.

Today, the Palio di Feltre is one of the Veneto's grandest historical reenactments. For four magical days each August, Feltre transforms into a living page from the past. Visitors walk medieval streets alive with vendors, jugglers, knights, and noblewomen. The grand finale, a bareback horse race in Piazza Maggiore, sends hearts pounding as riders career around the square, dust flying, the crowd roaring.

Festival Events

Thursday

Opening Ceremony and Procession

Opening Ceremony and Historical Presentation in Piazza Maggiore. The four contrade are introduced before the public, the newly painted palio banner is revealed, and a costumed reenactment retells the story of Feltre's 1404 allegiance to Venice.

Friday

Concerts, Performances and Dancing

The evening continues with live medieval music, flag performances, and dance reenactments in the old town squares. The historic center glows with torchlight and costumed characters.

Saturday

Medieval Market

The Mercatino Medievale, a lively medieval market, fills the city center. Visitors can meet blacksmiths, calligraphers, weavers, and food vendors offering traditional crafts and recipes.

8:30 p.m.

Night Procession Begins

The Corteo Storico Notturno begins. Hundreds in authentic costume march through the streets by torchlight, accompanied by drummers, flag throwers, and knights on horseback. The nighttime parade brings the entire historic center of Feltre to life with pageantry.

Sunday

Medieval Market

The Mercatino Medievale continues with full activity throughout the day. The streets remain alive with reenactors, food stalls, and artisans demonstrating their crafts.

5:30 p.m.

Corteo Storico in Procession

Corteo Storico, the grand historical parade, features over five hundred participants. Nobles, clergy, knights, flag bearers, and musicians walk together in full procession toward Piazza Maggiore.

6:30 p.m.

Corsa del Palio- the Race Starts

As the sun dips behind Feltre's rooftops and the final drumbeats of the parade fade into the evening air, all eyes turn to Piazza Maggiore. This is the moment everyone has been waiting for. The crowd surges forward. Balconies overflow with spectators waving their district's colors. The air hums with tension. It is time for the Corsa del Palio, the bareback horse race that crowns the festival and ignites the spirit of the city like nothing else.

Months of training have been undertaken by the four contrade: Castello, Duomo, Santo Stefano, and Port'Oria. Each has chosen a rider, tested for courage, strength, and control. There are no saddles and no reins, only balance, grit, and raw power. This race is unlike any other.

A trumpet pierces the silence. The horses, carrying their riders dressed in the colors of their contrada, enter the square with solemn pride. Piazza Maggiore, usually a peaceful place for daily life, has been transformed into a tight, high-stakes racetrack. Barriers line the course. The crowd presses in from all sides. Even the stones beneath seem to hold their breath.

Then, at the signal, they are off. Hooves thunder through the narrow course. The track is short but challenging, with sharp corners and tight turns that demand total control and courage. The crowd roars with excitement. Banners wave. Dust rises. It is a rush of movement, muscle, sweat, and determination.

There are no second chances. One lap, one intense burst of speed decides everything.

And then, in a flash, it is over. The winning rider crosses the finish line and is lifted high in triumph by jubilant supporters. Cheers, tears, laughter, and chants erupt in the piazza. The victorious team claims the palio banner, the most coveted prize of the year, and the reward for months of dedication and neighborhood pride.

9:00 p.m.

Final Events

Final celebrations fill the evening with open-air food tastings, costumed performances, medieval dances, and joyous crowds gathered under the stars.

Walking Tour of Feltre

#1. Porta Imperiale (Imperial Gate)

This 16th-century gateway is the ceremonial entrance into Feltre's historic core. Built under Venetian rule, the gate proudly displays the Lion of Saint Mark, symbolizing the town's allegiance to the Republic of Venice. Passing through this gate, you step directly into Feltre's Renaissance world.

#2. Piazza Maggiore (Main Square)

Piazza Maggiore

This elegant piazza is the heart of the festival and the soul of Feltre. Framed by arcaded Renaissance palaces and adorned with frescoed facades, the square hosts civic life, markets, and the thrilling bareback race during the Palio. Key buildings include the Palazzo della Ragione and Palazzo Guarnieri, testaments to Feltre's 16th-century golden age.

#3. Teatro de la Sena (Sena Theater)

This 18th-century jewel is often called a "small La Fenice" for its ornate design. Commissioned by local nobility and designed by Antonio Galli Bibiena, the theater still hosts performances and is open for guided visits. It reflects Feltre's strong cultural and artistic legacy.

#4. Cattedrale di San Pietro Apostolo (Cathedral of Saint Peter the Apostle)

This majestic cathedral stands on the site of an ancient Roman temple and represents centuries of religious devotion. The current structure, largely rebuilt in the 16th century, houses precious artworks, including canvases by Pietro Marescalchi and a Renaissance-style high altar.

The real treasure lies below: a crypt dating back to the 6th century, where early Christian remains and sarcophagi connect visitors to Feltre's spiritual roots. The bell tower, added in the 18th century, rises as a beacon above the town's skyline.

#5. Castello di Alboino e Torre dell'Orologio (Castle of Alboino and Clock Tower)

Just behind the cathedral, follow the steep path to the ruins of the Castello di Alboino, named after the Lombard king who once dominated northern Italy. Though the original fortress was destroyed and rebuilt over centuries, its layout and imposing walls still evoke Feltre's medieval past.

The highlight is the Torre dell'Orologio, a striking clock tower with battlements and sweeping views of the Valbelluna and surrounding peaks. From here, you can see the full sweep of the town's layout, the Dolomite mountains in the distance, and the valley that has shaped Feltre's history.

#6. Via Mezzaterra

Descend back toward town along this graceful, fresco-lined street. Via Mezzaterra is one of Feltre's most atmospheric routes, once home to wealthy merchants and patricians. The façades tell their own stories through painted symbols, coats of arms, and decorative windows. This is the place to slow down, take photos, and browse small artisan shops or cafés tucked into ancient archways.

#7. Galleria d'Arte Moderna Carlo Rizzarda (Carlo Rizzarda Gallery of Modern Art)

Conclude your walking tour at this refined museum, housed in a stately early 20th-century palazzo. The gallery features wrought iron masterpieces by Feltre-born Carlo Rizzarda, along with a curated collection of modern art, decorative arts, and rare furniture. The villa's original interiors add a warm, refined atmosphere, blending modern design with Feltre's historic charm.

Logistics

Train: Feltre is served by a small but well-connected train station on the Padova–Calalzo line. Regular regional trains (Regionale Trenitalia) run from Padua, Belluno, and Montebelluna, with connections to major hubs like Venice and Treviso. From Padua, the journey takes about 1 hour and 45 minutes. The station is about a 10-minute walk from the historic center. Taxis are occasionally available at the station, but pre-booking is recommended for late arrivals.

Bus: Feltre is connected by Dolomiti Bus, the main regional operator in the Belluno province. Buses run frequently from Belluno, Mel, and nearby villages, with additional lines available during festivals and summer months. The principal bus stop is near the train station and close to the town's pedestrian zone. During the Palio, extra shuttle services are often organized between nearby towns and the festival area.

Car: Feltre is accessible by car from all directions. From Venice or Padua, follow the A27 motorway north to Treviso Nord, then continue on the SS50 toward Feltre. From Trento, take the SS47 south to the SS50 junction. The drive through the foothills is scenic, especially approaching from the east via the Piave Valley. Roads are well maintained, but be cautious in the winter months because of potential snow at higher elevations.

Parking: There is ample parking just outside the historic center, particularly along Viale Farra, Via Montelungo, and Viale della Vittoria. These areas are within walking distance of Piazza Maggiore. Feltre's ZTL (Zona a Traffico Limitato) restricts non-resident vehicle access within the core centro storico, especially during festival weekends.

Restaurant Recommendations

Aurora. Address: Via Garibaldi 68

Just steps from the Concattedrale di San Pietro Apostolo, Aurora offers a cheerful and contemporary dining room with colorful furnishings and soft lighting. The carefully prepared cuisine includes Italian and regional meat and fish specialties with a light, modern twist.

Ristorante San Fermo. Address: Via San Fermo 30

At the foot of Monte Tomatico, Ristorante San Fermo is surrounded by the natural beauty of the Feltrine peaks, just steps from the Dolomiti Bellunesi National Park. The restaurant features various dining rooms suitable for celebrations and an expansive outdoor terrace offering panoramic views of Feltre.

Al Tabià – Pizzeria e Griglieria. Address: Via Culiada 181

Al Tabià offers a cozy atmosphere with rustic decor, serving a variety of pizzas and grilled specialties. The restaurant is known for its friendly service and quality dishes, making it a popular choice among locals and visitors alike.

Accommodation

For this event, I recommend staying for three or four nights in town.

Corte Garibaldi. Address: Via Giuseppe Garibaldi, 6

In the center of Feltre, this recently renovated building offers all modern comforts along with private parking. Corte Garibaldi offers all the beauty of historic homes with modern comforts and the tranquility of the countryside, right in the city center. The bed-and-breakfast is within walking distance of many attractions, including the Catholic church "Cattedrale di San Pietro Apostolo" and Porta Imperiale.

Hotel Doriguzzi. Address: Viale Piave 2

In a central yet quiet area, Hotel Doriguzzi offers rooms and suites equipped with minibars. Guests can enjoy free private parking and a garage for bikes and motorbikes.

Hotel Ristorante La Casona. Address: Via Segusini 17

One kilometer from the city center, Hotel Ristorante La Casona offers comfortable accommodations with an on-site restaurant. The hotel is known for its family-friendly atmosphere and countryside charm.

Day Trip Options: Nearby Sites, Cities, and Towns

Castello di Zumelle. 23 kilometers (13 miles) from Feltre. Near the village of Mel, the Castello di Zumelle is one of the best-preserved medieval castles in the region. Originally built by the Lombards in the 7th century and later fortified by the Franks and Venetians, the castle sits atop a wooded hill overlooking the Valbelluna. Visitors can explore the keep, towers, and drawbridge, while kids will enjoy the reenactments and medieval games often held on site. There is also a panoramic café and a forest trail leading from the base of the hill.

Mel (Borgo Valbelluna). 22 kilometers (12 miles) from Feltre. Mel is a picturesque village and officially one of Italy's Borghi più Belli. Known for its cobblestone streets, noble villas, and peaceful vibe, the town was historically a cultural and administrative center in the Valbelluna. Highlights include Palazzo delle Contesse, now home to an archaeological museum with finds from the Iron Age necropolis, and the charming central piazza with its well-preserved fountain and civic buildings.

Feltre Festivals and Sagre Throughout the Year

Festa della Candelora

February 2

Celebrated at the Santuario dei Santi Vittore e Corona, this ancient religious feast marks the Presentation of the Lord and the purification of Mary. Traditionally, locals climb to the sanctuary for Mass and to light candles as a symbol of light and hope. The event has a spiritual and folkloric atmosphere, often accompanied by small market stalls near the sanctuary.

Pasqua e Processione del Cristo Morto

Good Friday (date varies, March or April)

Feltre marks Holy Week with solemn religious services, culminating in the Processione del Cristo Morto on Good Friday. A statue of the dead Christ is carried through the candlelit streets, accompanied by participants in hooded robes and silent onlookers, creating a moving and mystical atmosphere.

Sagra di San Vittore

May 8 (or the closest Sunday)

Held at the sanctuary of Saints Vittore and Corona, patron saints of Feltre, this sagra combines a religious procession with a festive outdoor gathering. After Mass, local families picnic on the surrounding lawns. Traditional foods and regional wines are offered by vendors, and music performances often accompany the day.

https://www.sagrasanvittore.it/informazioni/

Fiera dell'Ottavario di Pentecoste

Late May or early June (7 days after Pentecost Sunday)

This centuries-old fair dates back to the Venetian Republic. Originally a religious market held after Pentecost, it has evolved into a large spring fair that includes antiques stalls, local crafts, food vendors, and entertainment. It spreads through Feltre's historic center and draws visitors from the entire province.

Sagra di Farra

Mid-August (around Ferragosto)

Held in the hamlet of Farra within the municipality of Feltre, this sagra includes local food stands, traditional dishes, music, and games. It's a beloved community event with dancing, outdoor dinners, and family activities, reflecting Feltre's rural and communal spirit.

Sagra di Villabruna

Late September

Another village celebration within the Feltre area, this sagra features homemade dishes like polenta e pastin, grilled meats, and local wines. It usually includes games, live music, and a relaxed, festive rural setting that offers an authentic taste of the Belluno countryside.

CHAPTER SEVENTEEN

The Culinary Legacy of Valli del Pausubio

Salami Festival

Sagra della Sorpressa

Where: Valli del Pasubio

When: August 9-15

Average Festival Temperatures: High 26°C (79°F). Low 16°C (61°F).

Valli di Pasubio: In the Valley of the Mountain

Nestled in the verdant valleys of northern Italy, Valli del Pasubio traces its roots to Roman times, when the expanding empire brought infrastructure, trade, and administrative systems to this mountainous region. Though small, the settlement was drawn into the Roman world, leaving lasting marks on its cultural identity.

Through the Middle Ages, while much of Italy grappled with shifting power and papal influence, Valli del Pasubio remained a quiet community shaped by its landscape. Forestry and farming formed the backbone of daily life, with knowledge and traditions passed from generation to generation. Sheltered by the mountains, the rhythms of life continued largely unchanged, even as empires rose and fell beyond the peaks.

The town's defining moment came during the First World War, when it stood on the frontline between Italian and Austrian forces. It was here that Italian engineers carved the famous Strada delle 52 Gallerie, the Road of 52 Tunnels, into the rock. Designed to move troops and supplies out of enemy view, this extraordinary military road remains a powerful symbol of ingenuity and endurance.

Today, with just over 3,000 residents, Valli del Pasubio may be small, but it continues to welcome those drawn to its unique blend of history and alpine beauty. Hikers exploring the tunnels or climbing the dramatic peaks become part of a centuries-old story, one shaped by resilience, nature, and quiet strength.

Sagra della Sopressa: A Festival of Tradition

The Sagra della Sopressa of Valli del Pasubio has deep roots in local tradition, dating back several decades as a celebration of the region's prized culinary heritage. This festival emerged in the 1970s when local producers sought to showcase their artisanal cured meats and preserve traditional production methods that had been passed down through generations.

Sopressa is a distinctive type of salami native to the Veneto region, particularly cherished in the mountainous areas around Vicenza. Unlike many mass-produced salamis, authentic Sopressa from Valli del Pasubio is made following time-honored techniques using select cuts of pork, carefully seasoned with a blend of salt, pepper, and other spices that vary slightly from family to family. The meat is then stuffed into natural casings and aged for several months in the unique microclimate of local cellars, where the cool mountain air imparts distinctive flavors.

Festival Events

Opening Day: August 9

5:30

Opening Ceremony

The festival commences with an opening ceremony in the town square, featuring speeches from local officials and a traditional blessing of the salami. At 6:00 p.m., the gastronomic stands open, offering visitors the chance to sample Sopressa paired with local wines, cheeses, and polenta.

8:30

Folk Music

The first evening concludes with local folk music performances.

Weekend Events

The first weekend features expanded activities, including cooking demonstrations beginning at 4:00 p.m. where local chefs showcase traditional recipes using Sopressa. Children's workshops run from 3:00-5:00 p.m., teaching younger visitors about food traditions through hands-on activities. Evening entertainment includes regional dance performances at 7:30 p.m. and contemporary music concerts starting at 9:00 p.m.

Weekday Activities

Midweek events focus on education and tradition, with guided tours of local production facilities available by reservation at 10:00 a.m. and 3:00 p.m. daily. A historical exhibition on the evolution of Sopressa production is open from 11:00 a.m. to 7:00 p.m. in the town hall. Evening talks by food historians and producers occur at 6:30 p.m., followed by more casual musical entertainment starting at 8:00 p.m.

Competition Day: August 14

The penultimate day features the highly anticipated competition to crown the year's best Sopressa. In the afternoon, a blind tasting takes place as a panel of expert judges evaluates each entry based on appearance, aroma, texture, and flavor. Producers submit their finest creations, representing months of careful aging and meticulous preparation. In the evening, the winners are announced during an awards ceremony that confers significant prestige on the victorious producers.

Final Celebration on Ferragosto: August 15

Food, Dance, Fireworks

The festival culminates on August 15 with a grand feast beginning around midday. This ultimate day coincides with Ferragosto, a major Italian holiday, and draws the largest crowds of the event. Special menus highlight creative interpretations of traditional dishes, all centered around Sopressa. In the late afternoon, lively folk dancing begins, filling the streets with music and movement. As night falls, a spectacular fireworks display lights up the sky above the Pasubio mountains, marking the grand finale of the celebration.

Beyond the festivities, the Sagra provides crucial economic support for local producers, creating a valuable market for premium artisanal products that command higher prices than mass-produced alternatives. Many small-scale producers generate a significant portion of their annual income during the festival, both through direct sales and by forming connections with distributors and restaurants.

For visitors, the Sagra offers an authentic immersion into the living traditions of rural Italian life, where food, community, and celebration remain deeply intertwined with the rhythms of mountain life in the Veneto region.

Walking Tour of Valli del Pausubio

#1. Piazza del Municipio

Begin the tour at the heart of Valli del Pasubio, where the elegant town hall stands as a testament to local governance and community pride. Dating back to the early 20th century, this building survived the tumultuous period of World War I when much of the region was damaged in fighting. The square offers a perfect orientation point, with mountain views framing the stone building, and serves as a gathering place during local festivals and civic events.

#2. Chiesa di San Antonio Abate (St. Anthony the Abbot)

Just a short walk from the main square, this parish church dedicated to Saint Anthony Abbot showcases the religious heritage of Valli del Pasubio. The current structure, rebuilt after World War I damage, features a simple but dignified façade typical of mountain churches in the Veneto region. Inside, visitors can admire local religious art, including wooden sculptures and paintings depicting the patron saint, while the bell tower provides a vertical accent to the town's skyline that has called the faithful to worship for generations.

#3. Monumento ai Caduti

This solemn war memorial honors the local soldiers who perished during the World Wars, particularly the First World War, which dramatically impacted Valli del Pasubio and the surrounding mountains. Erected in the interwar period, the monument features a stone obelisk with inscribed names of the fallen, serving as a poignant reminder of the sacrifices made by the community.

The site is moving given the town's proximity to the fierce mountain fighting along what was once the Austro-Italian front line, where thousands of young men perished in harsh alpine conditions.

#4. Fontana Storica

This historic fountain has served as a practical water source and social gathering spot for centuries in Valli del Pasubio. Carved from local stone, the fountain basin bears the marks of countless water vessels that have been filled here by generations of townsfolk before modern plumbing reached mountain homes.

The continuous flow of fresh mountain water symbolizes the natural abundance of the area, while the worn edges of the stonework tell stories of daily life, gossip shared, and community bonds formed around this essential resource.

#5. Contrada Bariola

Wander through this well-preserved neighborhood to experience the traditional mountain architecture that has characterized Valli del Pasubio for centuries. The stone houses with wooden balconies and steep roofs designed to shed heavy winter snow represent the practical adaptation to alpine living conditions. Many structures date back to the 18th and 19th centuries, having been carefully maintained or restored to preserve their authentic character while still serving as family homes for locals who continue mountain traditions in a modern context.

a#6. Museo della Grande Guerra

Housed in a restored historic building, this small but meaningful museum documents the profound impact of World War I on Valli del Pasubio and the surrounding Pasubio massif. The collection includes military artifacts, photographs, maps, and personal items that bring to life the harsh realities faced by both soldiers and civilians during the mountain warfare that raged here between 1915 and 1918.

Exhibits particularly focus on the engineering marvel of the Strada delle 52 Gallerie (Road of 52 Tunnels) constructed during the war, providing context for those planning to hike this famous route that begins near the town.

#7. Malga Bariola

Conclude the tour at this malga, a traditional alpine dairy farm on the outskirts of town, where visitors can connect with the agricultural heritage that has sustained Valli del Pasubio for centuries. The stone structures have been used for generations as summer quarters for dairy cattle grazing in high pastures, where farmers produced the region's renowned cheeses using age-old techniques.

Today, the restored malga offers visitors the opportunity to sample authentic mountain products, including cheese and the town's famous sopressa salami, connecting the culinary traditions of the past with a contemporary appreciation for artisanal food production.

Logistics

Train: Valli del Pasubio does not have its own rail station. The nearest is Schio Stazione, on the Vicenza–Schio regional line. Schio is about 10 kilometers (6 miles) from Valli del Pasubio.

Bus: The main operator is Società Vicentina Trasporti S.r.l. (SVT), which runs the hourly B312 service between Schio Autostazione and Valli del Pasubio.

Car: A little over an hour from Venice.

Parking: Parking near Valli del Pasubio is convenient and scenic, with several options depending on your needs. One of the most picturesque and traveler-friendly spots is the Maso Molino parking area at 36030 Valli del Pasubio. Nestled beside a charming local inn and a babbling stream, this free lot offers a peaceful setting and is open year-round.

Restaurant Recommendations

Ristorante Rifugio Balasso. Address: Via Balasso 1

A rustic mountain refuge at the foot of the Pasubio massif, beloved by hikers and alpine rescuers alike. Expect generous portions of traditional fare, polenta with mushrooms, grilled meats, hearty soups, served in a cozy, wood-lined dining room. The recent renovation added lodge rooms and a sauna, making it perfect for an overnight stay after exploring the Piccole Dolomiti.

Albergo Ristorante da Carla Failela. Address: Via Piazza Alta 26

Family-owned since 1952, "da Carla" promotes genuine Venetian cooking with organic, kilometer-zero ingredients. Don't miss their Sunday night gnocchi special, four freshly made varieties served continuously, or local charcuterie, malga cheeses, and grilled meats.

Accommodation

For Sagre, an overnight stay is unnecessary. Often these towns are small, and I don't recommend staying for the sagra unless you want to enjoy some hiking in the area.

Locanda Belvedere. Address: Via Roma, 26

3 stars. Family-run by the Sberze family for nearly a century, this classic Italian locanda offers 12 spacious, wood-lined rooms equipped with private bathrooms, hairdryers, LCD TVs, air conditioning, safes, and optional cots for children. The on-site restaurant and pizzeria serve traditional Veneto dishes, seasonal specialties, local game, and wood-fired pizzas, as well as personalized menus for dietary needs. Nestled at the foot of Monte Pasubio with panoramic views of the Piccole Dolomiti, it's an ideal base for hikers, motorcyclists, and nature lovers. Complimentary on-site parking is available.

Day Trip Options: Nearby Sites, Cities, and Towns

Rovereto. 28 kilometers (17 miles) from Valli. Rovereto is a charming city nestled in the Vallagarina valley of Trentino, offering visitors a perfect blend of history, culture, and alpine beauty. Founded in the medieval period, the city flourished under Venetian rule during the 15th century before later becoming part of the Austro-Hungarian Empire, influences that are still visible in its architecture and cultural heritage.

The historic center features elegant palazzi along Via della Terra and Corso Bettini, where visitors can admire Renaissance and Baroque architecture while enjoying the relaxed atmosphere of the city's cafés. Wine lovers will appreciate excursions to nearby vineyards producing the region's notable Marzemino wine, famously mentioned in Mozart's opera "Don Giovanni."

Levico Terme. 42 kilometers (26 miles). Levico Terme is a picturesque spa town in the Valsugana valley, renowned for its thermal waters and Belle Époque charm that dates back to its heyday as a retreat for Austro-Hungarian nobility. The town developed as a popular health resort in the late 19th century when its arsenical ferruginous waters were discovered to have therapeutic properties, leading to the construction of grand hotels and elegant public buildings that still grace the town today.

Website: https://www.termedilevico.it/

The heart of Levico's appeal lies in its historic thermal baths, where visitors can experience treatments using the mineral-rich waters that emerge from deep within the surrounding mountains. The town is embraced by lush parkland, with the magnificent Habsburg Park (Parco degli Asburgo) featuring century-old trees, winding paths, and seasonal flower displays that reflect its imperial past.

Beyond its spa heritage, Levico offers cultural attractions including the Forte delle Benne, a World War I Austrian fortress with panoramic views of the valley, and the nearby Lake Levico with its crystal-clear waters perfect for swimming in the summer months.

The town comes alive during Christmas with its lively markets, while throughout the year, local restaurants serve traditional Trentino cuisine featuring mountain herbs, cheeses, and fresh produce from the surrounding valleys. Levico's accessibility to hiking trails and mountain excursions makes it an ideal base for both relaxation and active exploration.

Trento. 53 kilometers (33 miles). Trento, the elegant capital of the Trentino province, stands as a sophisticated city where Italian and Germanic cultures harmoniously blend, reflecting its unique position at the historical crossroads of Latin and Nordic Europe. Founded as the Roman city of Tridentum in the 1st century BC, its strategic Alpine location made it an important commercial and ecclesiastical center, most famously hosting the Counter-Reformation Council of Trent in the 16th century.

The city's magnificent Piazza Duomo forms its cultural heart, dominated by the Romanesque-Gothic Cathedral of San Vigilio and the elaborately frescoed Palazzo Pretorio, now housing the Diocesan Museum. Nearby stands the imposing Castello del Buonconsiglio, once residence of the prince-bishops who ruled Trento for centuries, featuring remarkable medieval and Renaissance frescos including the famous Cycle of the Months in the Eagle Tower.

We really enjoyed our visit to Trento. The primary sites we had planned to see were the cathedral, with its incredible display of reliquaries, and the castle, which offered sweeping views of the city and mountains beyond. Walking through the cathedral, we were struck not only by the architecture but by the quiet presence of so many sacred relics, each with its own story.

At the castle, the frescoes and towers transported us to another time, and we lingered longer than expected, soaking in both the history and the Alpine air. Trento felt calm and refined, and it gave us a glimpse into a side of Italy often overlooked by travelers heading straight to the lakes or Dolomites.

Valli del Pausubio Festivals and Sagre Throughout the Year

Festa di Sant'Antonio del Pasubio

January 17

Local celebration honoring St. Anthony, with religious services, food stands, and a scenic walk through the neighborhoods ending at the Bariola nativity scene. The festival blends spiritual devotion with conviviality, as families gather to enjoy roasted chestnuts, mulled wine, and a bonfire under the winter sky. It's one of the earliest and most heartfelt events of the year.

La Caretera (Riva di Vallarsa)

Third weekend in July

A folkloric race of non-motorized carts descending through the village streets, a colorful and humorous tradition. Locals design imaginative and often whimsical carts, competing not only for speed but for creativity and flair. The event is followed by music, dancing, and local dishes served in the village square, creating a festive atmosphere.

Festa Contadina a Valli del Pasubio (Farmers' Festival)

Last weekend in September

Rural fair with local produce, traditional food (like handmade gnocchi), agricultural parades, and workshops. The event honors the town's deep farming roots and includes demonstrations of old crafts, exhibitions of vintage tractors, and tastings of cheeses, sopressa, and homemade jams. It's a celebration of land, labor, and community pride.

Fiera di San Luca (Fair)

2nd week of October

Traditional livestock fair in Vallarsa parish, including bovine judging, artisanal stalls, and cultural events. This centuries-old fair has deep roots in the region's mountain farming culture, once serving as a key moment for the trade of cattle before the onset of winter.

Today, it continues as both an agricultural showcase and a vibrant village gathering, featuring regional foods, handmade crafts, live music, and children's games. Farmers, artisans, and visitors from neighboring valleys attend to celebrate rural life and community traditions.

Il Presepe di Bariola (Nativity Display)

December

A picturesque living nativity scene set in the village of Bariola (a frazione of Valli del Pausubio), open all month. Set against the rustic backdrop of this mountain hamlet, the scene includes life-size statues and lovingly recreated village settings with twinkling lights and traditional tools. On certain days, locals dress in costume to perform as shepherds, artisans, and the Holy Family, bringing the display to life.

Visitors stroll through the winding alleys, guided by lanterns, experiencing an atmosphere that evokes both reverence and nostalgia for an earlier, simpler time.

Fall Celebrations

September and October

CHAPTER EIGHTEEN

Venice's Centuries-Old Maritime Marathon

Regata Storica

Regatta Storica di Venezia

Where: Venice

When: First Sunday in September.

Average Festival Temperatures: High: 29°C (84°F). Low: 16°C (61°F).

Event Website: https://www.regatastoricavenezia.it/en/

Venice's Regatta Storica: A Living Legacy on the Grand Canal

In the heart of Venice, where water has always been a highway and a battlefield, the tradition of boat racing is as old as the city itself. While the Regatta Storica was officially established in the 13th century during the Festa delle Marie, competitive rowing had likely existed long before in this seafaring republic, where mastery of the oar meant survival and supremacy.

Venice's regattas were born from victory. As the Republic expanded its influence across the Mediterranean, naval prowess became a source of pride. Boat races served as a public display of strength and skill, celebrating the Republic's dominance in trade and warfare. The very word regatta comes from the Venetian dialect, meaning "contention for mastery", a perfect reflection of the spirit of competition that animated the city's canals.

The first known image of a regatta appears in Jacopo de' Barbari's famous View of Venice (c. 1500). Linguist Giuseppe Tassini suggests the term may also derive from riga, or line, a reference to the rope (spagheto) stretched across the water as a starting point for the race.

From Naval Contest to Civic Pageant

After Venice became part of the Kingdom of Italy in 1866, the regatta shifted from a military showcase to a celebration of civic identity and cultural pride. In 1899, during the city's third International Art Biennale, Mayor Count Filippo Grimani officially renamed the event the Regata Storica.

To honor Venice's storied past, a grand historical procession was added. Gondoliers in elaborate Renaissance costume reenact the return of Queen Caterina Cornaro, the Venetian noblewoman who ruled Cyprus and later ceded it to the Republic. Her symbolic homecoming down the Grand Canal, surrounded by richly decorated vessels, has become one of the most anticipated spectacles of the festival.

Sporting Tradition and Evolution

The races themselves have developed over the centuries. Early regattas featured massive boats rowed by 30 to 50 men, but today's competitions use smaller, sleeker vessels designed for speed and agility. Divided into several events, the regatta now includes youth and adult races, as well as the prestigious gondolini race, Venice's Formula 1 on water.

Remarkably, records show that women took part in rowing competitions as early as 1493, a progressive fact for the era. Though interrupted by Napoleon's conquest in 1797 and later Austrian rule, the regattas resumed in 1825, thanks to persistent local advocacy.

A Festival of Culture and Skill

Today, the Regata Storica blends athletic competition with theatrical pageantry. It remains one of Venice's most beloved annual traditions, drawing thousands of spectators to the Grand Canal. More than a race, it is a celebration of the city's enduring relationship with the water, a vibrant tribute to the Venetian spirit, and a moment when the past and present row together in rhythm.

Festival Events

2:30 p.m.

Regattas Begin

The day's activities actually begin around 2:30 with a series of four categories of regattas: Junior Rower's Regatta, Women Rower's Regatta, Caorlina Regatta, and Gondolino Regatta. All competitors wear historically accurate costumes.

4:00 p.m.

Historical Parade

A spectacular display of traditional sixteenth-century boats and Renaissance costumes.

Court of the Regatta Storica

5:00 p.m.

Youth and Women's Races

Competitions showcasing future Venetian rowing champions.

6:00 p.m.

Regatta of Caorline

The Regatta of the Caorline is one of the most striking and powerful races during the Redentore celebrations. Unlike the solo or duo races in smaller boats, this is a team competition that showcases raw strength, coordination, and camaraderie. The caorlina, a wide and stable traditional Venetian boat once used to transport goods through the lagoon, is rowed by six oarsmen standing upright in perfect sync.

Each team, often representing historic Venetian rowing clubs, must combine physical endurance with seamless cooperation to propel the heavy vessel down the course. As the six oars rise and fall in unison, teammates shout encouragement across the water. The brightly painted hulls shimmer in the sunlight, adding vibrant flashes of color to the spectacle.

This regatta is a true test of stamina, timing, and mastery of the voga alla veneta technique. More than a race, it honors the working-class roots of Venice and celebrates the city's enduring connection to its maritime traditions.

6:30 p.m.

Grand Champions Regatta (Gondolini Race)

As the golden light of early evening settles over the Giudecca Canal, anticipation reaches its peak. This is not just any race, it is the Grand Champions Regatta, the pinnacle of Venetian rowing tradition. A hush falls over the boats lining the canal as the gondolini glide into place at the starting line.

The gondolino is the most refined and agile of all Venetian rowing boats, a sleek and lightweight cousin of the gondola, built purely for racing. It cuts through the water with effortless grace, but it is the rowers, the campioni, who command true admiration. These elite athletes come from generations of Venetian oarsmen, each mastering the voga alla veneta, the city's iconic forward-facing rowing technique.

To win this race is to earn a place in Venice's living history.

At the signal, the boats explode into motion. Oars flash in perfect rhythm, and the crowd erupts in cheers and chants. Every stroke demands flawless technique, deep stamina, and unwavering focus as the rowers navigate the wide and winding Giudecca Canal. Every second counts.

Though the race lasts only a few breathless minutes, its meaning lingers long after the finish line. For Venetians, the Regatta of Champions is more than a competition. It is a tribute to the city's maritime soul, a celebration of tradition, and a reminder that, even in the modern world, Venice continues to move forward on the strength of its past.

When the winning boat crosses the line, applause thunders across the water. The champions are lifted in triumph before a sea of waving flags and joyous spectators. For one unforgettable evening each year, Venice is united in motion, memory, and mastery.

Regatta Route

The historical procession begins in St. Mark's Basin, continues along St. Mark's Canal, passes the Rialto and the Railway Station, then returns through the Grand Canal to Ca' Foscari. For the rowing competitions, the finish line is always at Ca' Foscari, while the starting points vary depending on the race and course length.

Best Viewing Locations

To enjoy the most exciting moments, try these spots:

- Rialto Bridge: A prime location to watch the dramatic race turns

- San Marco Basin: Ideal for seeing the beginning of the historical parade

- Accademia Bridge: Offers views of the central part of the course

For those hoping to experience both the historical parade and all the races, the stretch between Rialto Bridge and Ca' Foscari is best. Arrive early, as this area fills up quickly.

Other Venetian Regattas: Celebrating the Lagoon's Many Voices

While the Regata Storica on the Grand Canal is Venice's most renowned rowing event, a vibrant tradition of local regattas pulses through the lagoon's calendar. These smaller, often more community-focused races offer an intimate look into Venetian life and rowing heritage.

Regata di Mestre

Late April

The Regata di Mestre marks the official start of the Venetian rowing season. Held along the canals near Punta San Giuliano, it features a series of competitive races including youth categories, women's gondole, and men's caorline. As one of the earliest regattas of the year, it sets the tone for the rowing events that follow across the lagoon.

Regatta di Sant'Erasmo

Late May

This scenic regatta takes place on Sant'Erasmo, known as Venice's "vegetable garden." Rowers compete in various categories along the quiet canals and lagoon waters surrounding the island. The event is part of a broader celebration of local culture, drawing island residents and Venetians alike for a festive day on the water.

Regatta of St. Peter in Castello

June 29

Another notable event is the Regatta di San Pietro di Castello, held in honor of Saints Peter and Paul on June 29. This regatta unfolds in the historic Castello district, near the former cathedral of Venice, and features races for young rowers, women's crews, and seasoned veterans. The event is tied to the Festa di San Pietro, which includes food stands, music, and a strong sense of neighborhood pride, honoring one of the city's oldest parish communities.

Regatta of Murano Island

First Sunday in July

In Murano, the island famed for its glassmaking, the Regata di Murano typically takes place in early September, just after the Regata Storica. Rowers race along the island's wide canal, with colorful boats and cheers echoing off furnaces and workshops. This regatta is especially beloved by locals, and the celebrations often spill into spontaneous neighborhood feasts.

Festa della Madonna di Marina di Malamocco (Lido Island)

Second Sunday in July

Seven categories are included in the race, all aligned with traditional Venetian rowing (Voga alla Veneta) styles.

Regatta of Giudecca

Mid-July

Giudecca's regatta often takes place during the weekend of the Festa del Redentore in mid-July, adding a sporting element to one of Venice's most beloved festivals.

Regatta of Pellestrina

Late July or Early August

The long, narrow island of Pellestrina hosts its regatta during the Festa di Santo Stefano, transforming the lagoon into a vibrant corridor of colorful boats and determined rowers.

Regatta of Burano

September (date varies)

The island of Burano hosts a colorful regatta that usually coincides with the Festa della Madonna dell'Apparizione in September. Brightly painted boats compete in narrow canals, with enthusiastic crowds cheering from the bridges and water front.

CHAPTER NINETEEN

Immersion Experience: Mosaics of Venice

The Art of Venetian Mosaics

A **Journey into Venice's Golden Legacy**

Tucked away in the quiet alleys of the Castello district, just a short walk from the grand Basilica of Santi Giovanni e Paolo, lies a small workshop where the ancient art of Venetian mosaics is still practiced with devotion. Far from the crowds of St. Mark's, this studio invites visitors to step into a world of glinting glass, gold leaf, and timeless craftsmanship.

My husband and I experienced this firsthand. Curious and eager, we joined a private workshop, unsure of what to expect but excited to learn. The moment we stepped inside, the scent of wood, the shimmer of tiny tesserae, and the quiet focus of the artisans made it feel like we had entered a sacred space. The workshop was modest in size, yet it held centuries of tradition in every corner.

Mosaics, intricate images formed from tiny pieces of colored glass, stone, or gold, have long been a symbol of Venice's artistic and spiritual identity. Influenced by Byzantine aesthetics and trade connections with the East, Venice became a city where light, faith, and beauty met in shimmering form. Nowhere is this more evident than in the golden mosaics of St. Mark's Basilica, where over 8,000 square meters of glittering tesserae tell stories from the Bible and Venetian history. To understand Venetian mosaics is to understand Venice's desire to dazzle, inspire, and convey power through sacred art.

Here, travelers can become temporary apprentices, learning from artisans who not only create original designs but also restore the city's most precious mosaic treasures, including those inside St. Mark's Basilica. The atmosphere is intimate and unhurried. Bowls of colorful glass catch the light, and well-worn tools lie beside half-finished panels that echo centuries of devotion.

A mosaic work in progress in the lab

As we began, our instructor guided us through both the technique and the history behind the craft. Venetian mosaics are distinguished by their Byzantine influence, a legacy brought back from Constantinople after its conquest in 1204. She explained how the placement of each tessera is never flat, but set at slight angles to reflect light differently. This creates surfaces that shimmer and shift as you move, making the mosaic feel almost alive.

It was both humbling and deeply rewarding to place each tiny piece by hand, learning to trust our eyes, steady our hands, and appreciate the patience behind the process. We left with a small mosaic of our own and a much greater appreciation for the artisans who carry on this golden tradition.

The finished mosaic, small but meaningful, becomes more than a souvenir. It is a reminder of a deeper connection, one built through hands on creation, personal discovery, and a shared respect for Venice's artistic soul.

Materials come from across the world, just as they did when Venice was a maritime powerhouse. Deeply colored smalti glass, polished marble, and precious gold leaf glass are combined to create sacred scenes, geometric patterns, and contemporary interpretations. Participants are introduced to the tools of the craft, nippers, wheeled cutters, hammers, and adhesives all of which require a careful balance of precision and patience.

As we selected our simple designs, such as a symbol of Venice, an abstract pattern, or a small religious motif, we began to appreciate the difficulty behind what appears effortless. Cutting the glass into usable shapes, placing each piece in the correct position, and understanding how the light will reflect across the surface are lessons in both technique and artistic sensitivity.

Though the experience may last only a few hours, the connection it creates is profound. Participants gain not only an appreciation for the labor behind Venice's most iconic art, but also insight into the spirit of the artisans who preserve it. These craftspeople are not merely artists, they are stewards of a tradition that stretches back over a thousand years.

The finished mosaic, small but meaningful, becomes more than a souvenir. It is a reminder of a deeper connection, one built through hands-on creation, personal discovery, and a shared respect for Venice's artistic soul.

Practical Information

Experience: Venetian Mosaic Workshop

Duration: Approximately 3-4 hours

Reservation Information:
Booking in advance is essential as these workshops accommodate very small groups (sometimes just 2-4 people) to ensure personalized instruction. Many mosaic studios in Venice offer similar experiences, but for the most authentic connection to traditional techniques, look for artisans who also work on restoration projects for the city's historic buildings.

CHAPTER TWENTY

Murano in Molten Color

The Island's Glass Festival

Venice Glass Week

Where: Murano, Venice Lagoon

When: Mid-September

Average Festival Temperatures: High: 25°C (77°F). Low: 17°C (63°F).

Event Website: https://theveniceglassweek.com/en/

Discover Murano: Island of Fire, Craft, and Crystal

Murano is a small island group just north of Venice, connected by bridges and canals and famous across the world for its centuries-old tradition of glassmaking. Though technically made up of seven islets, it is often referred to as one island and is home to around 4,500 residents. Easily reached by vaporetto (water bus) from Venice in about 15–20 minutes, Murano offers a quieter, artisan-focused counterpart to its more crowded neighbor.

Originally settled by the Romans, Murano became an important port by the Middle Ages. In 1291, the Venetian Republic ordered all glassmakers to relocate their furnaces to Murano, fearing fire hazards within densely packed Venice. This marked the beginning of Murano's ascent as the epicenter of artistic glass in Europe.

By the 14th century, Murano's glassmakers were not only crafting goblets and chandeliers but were also perfecting crystal-clear glass, multicolored millefiori, and aventurine (glass with metallic sparkles). Their techniques were so valuable that craftsmen were once forbidden to leave the island to protect trade secrets. Over time, Murano glass became synonymous with luxury, used by royalty and aristocracy across Europe.

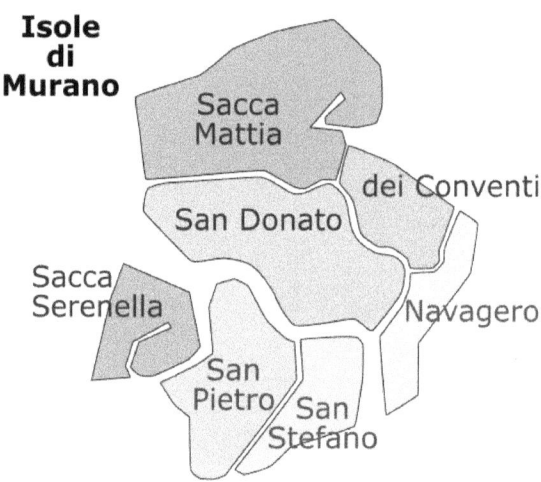

Murano, a collection of small Islands

A Celebration of Light and Fire: The Murano Glass Festival

The annual Festival of Glass (Festa del Vetro) celebrates this legacy each September with a week-long series of events that combine history, innovation, and spectacle. Known in Italian as the Venice Glass Week, the celebration extends across Venice and its islands, but Murano is the beating heart of the event.

The festival features open-furnace demonstrations, art exhibits, and installations across the island's canals, churches, and museums. Local glassmasters, known as maestri vetrai, open their studios to the public, allowing visitors to witness the alchemy of sand and fire transformed into shimmering works of art. Many of the demonstrations happen inside traditional glass furnaces (fornaci), some of which have been operating for generations.

Highlights include:

Night of Glass (La Notte del Vetro): A magical evening when Murano stays open late with live glassblowing shows, canal-side bars, music, and fireworks that light up the island. Studios and galleries welcome guests into their normally closed workshops for rare behind-the-scenes experiences.

Outdoor Installations and Exhibitions: Sculptures and installations made entirely of glass are set up in public spaces such as Campo San Donato, turning the town itself into a walking gallery.

Glassblowing Workshops: Visitors can try their hand at shaping molten glass under the guidance of seasoned artisans, gaining an appreciation for the skill required.

Museum of Glass (Museo del Vetro): During the festival, this already exceptional museum located in the 17th-century Palazzo Giustinian hosts special exhibitions on ancient Roman glass, modern innovation, and the evolution of Murano's style over time.

Floating Glass Art: Several events showcase artworks displayed on floating barges and along the canals, creating a surreal fusion of fire-born beauty and water.

Walking Tour of Murano

#1. Murano Faro (Murano Lighthouse)
Start your walk at the Murano Faro vaporetto stop. This striking white lighthouse stands at the southern edge of the island and has guided vessels through the Venetian Lagoon since the 1910s. It marks your gateway into Murano and offers a picturesque view of the lagoon and the nearby islands of San Michele and Venice.

#2. Chiesa di San Pietro Martire

From the lighthouse, walk northeast along the Fondamenta until you reach the Church of San Pietro Martire. Originally built in the 14th century and rebuilt after a fire in the 1500s, this church is notable for its calm interior and impressive artworks, including paintings by Giovanni Bellini and Veronese. The wooden ceiling and simple brick façade reflect the restrained elegance of Murano's religious architecture.

#3. Museo del Vetro (Glass Museum)

Continue along the canal to reach the Glass Museum in the grand 17th-century Palazzo Giustinian. This is the historical and cultural heart of Murano. The museum traces glassmaking from ancient Roman times to contemporary masterpieces. Highlights include delicate millefiori vases, early baroque chandeliers, and experimental modern glass sculptures. The museum also offers insight into the tools and techniques of the master glassblowers.

Murano Faro

#4. Campo Santo Stefano and the Comet Glass Star

Head north to Campo Santo Stefano, a lively square filled with shops and glass studios. At the center stands the iconic Comet Glass Star, a dramatic modern sculpture made of hundreds of blue glass spikes. This plaza is a perfect place to pause at a café and browse the many small galleries and workshops lining the square.

#5. Chiesa di Santa Maria e San Donato

This remarkable church is one of the most treasured religious buildings in the entire Venetian Lagoon, and a jewel of early Christian and Byzantine architecture. It stands as a testament to Murano's religious, artistic, and cultural history.

Originally founded in the 7th century, the church was rebuilt in its current form during the 12th century, when Murano was flourishing thanks to its trade and growing importance as a glassmaking hub. The most striking feature of the church is its Byzantine-style mosaic floor, laid in 1140, which survives remarkably intact. Crafted from marble, porphyry red marble, and glass tesserae in intricate geometric and floral patterns, the floor evokes comparisons to the opulent mosaic pavements of Ravenna and Constantinople. It is considered one of the finest medieval mosaic floors in Italy.

The church's façade is simple and austere, made of warm-colored brick, but walk around to the apse on the lagoon side and you'll be rewarded with one of the most beautiful views in Murano: a semi-circular apse adorned with elegant blind arches, slender columns, and decorative marble inlays. It's a prime example of Venetian-Byzantine design merging with Romanesque solidity.

Chiesa di Santa Maria e San Donato

Inside, the church is bathed in light, with three naves divided by classical columns and a high wooden ceiling. The main altar is flanked by columns with Corinthian capitals, and in a small chapel behind the altar are the relics of San Donato, the patron saint of the church. According to local tradition, the bones of a dragon slain by San Donato are also displayed here, hanging on the wall behind the altar, one of Murano's unique and beloved curiosities.

Though less grand than Venice's Basilica di San Marco, Santa Maria e San Donato is deeply atmospheric and profoundly spiritual. It represents a sacred and artistic continuity that has shaped the island for over a thousand years. Entry is free, though donations are appreciated, and respectful silence is encouraged inside.

#6. Fornace Open Studio Visit (choose one nearby)
Around the church, you'll find several traditional glass furnaces offering live demonstrations. Two notable studios often open to the public are Barovier & Toso and Gino Mazzuccato. Watch molten glass shaped with breath, tools, and fire into vases, goblets, or elaborate sculptures. Some studios allow visitors to try simple glass-shaping with assistance.

Gino Mazzuccato: Founded in 1958, his workshop became internationally known for preserving traditional techniques while also embracing innovative design. The Mazzuccato family has long been associated with intricate chandeliers and art glass.

Barovier & Toso: One of the oldest glassmaking companies in the world, with roots tracing back to 1295. The Barovier family merged with the Toso family in 1936, creating a brand that symbolizes the highest quality in Murano craftsmanship, especially in luxury lighting and artistic pieces.

#7. Fondamenta Venier and Boutique Shopping
Finish your walk along the Fondamenta Venier, a canal-side promenade lined with boutique glass shops. This is the place to find handmade jewelry, ornaments, and home decor. Prices vary widely, but most shops label authentic Murano pieces, and many ship internationally.

The Art at Gino's Studio

Logistics: Getting to Murano by Vaporetto

Murano is easily reached from Venice via the vaporetto, Venice's public waterbus system, operated by ACTV. The island lies just north of the principal city and is served by several vaporetto lines that run frequently throughout the day.

From Venice's Fondamente Nove stop, take Line 4.1 or 4.2, which circle the city in opposite directions and both stop at Murano Colonna, the island's main landing point. The journey takes approximately 10–15 minutes. You can also reach Murano from Piazzale Roma or Santa Lucia train station by taking Line 3, a direct route with fewer stops, which brings you to Murano in about 20 minutes.

Murano has multiple vaporetto stops, including Murano Faro, Murano Venier, Murano Museo, and Murano Navagero. Most visitors disembark at Murano Colonna or Murano Museo, which are ideal for exploring the glass museum, the main churches, and the studio workshops.

Vaporetto tickets can be purchased at ACTV kiosks, ticket machines, or online, and must be validated before boarding. A single ticket is valid for 75 minutes, allowing transfers between lines. For travelers planning multiple trips around the lagoon, including visits to Burano and Torcello, the ACTV day passes (valid for 24, 48, or 72 hours) offer excellent value and convenience.

Restaurant Recommendations

La Perla Ai Bisatei. Address: Campo San Bernardo 5/6

A favorite among locals, La Perla Ai Bisatei is known for its authentic Venetian seafood dishes served in a lively, casual setting. The menu features classics like spaghetti alle vongole and mixed fried seafood, all offered at reasonable prices. The atmosphere is welcoming and unpretentious, making it a magnificent spot for a traditional meal in the heart of Murano.

Trattoria Busa alla Torre da Lele. Address: Campo Santo Stefano 3

Near the iconic clock tower, this trattoria offers charming courtyard dining. It's a popular place to enjoy fresh seafood and Venetian specialties, including bigoli with bottarga and grilled calamari. The setting is relaxed, with friendly service and views of the town's vibrant central square.

Osteria Acquastanca. Address: Fondamenta Manin 48

Osteria Acquastanca is a cozy and refined spot with a creative approach to traditional Venetian flavors. The menu changes seasonally and features dishes like squid ink pasta or handmade gnocchi with local vegetables. The interior is stylish yet intimate, ideal for a leisurely lunch or dinner after exploring Murano's glass studios and museums.

Accommodation

Hyatt Centric Murano Venice. Address: Riva Longa 49
Set in a former glass factory along Murano's main canal, this four-star hotel blends modern luxury with industrial charm. Rooms are sleek and spacious, some with canal views or private patios. The hotel offers a private water taxi to and from Venice Marco Polo Airport and features a wellness center, stylish bar, and courtyard restaurant.

NH Collection Venezia Murano Villa. Address: Fondamenta Andrea Navagero 29

Located inside a converted glasswork factory, this stylish four-star hotel offers contemporary rooms and suites with floor-to-ceiling windows and lagoon views. The on-site restaurant serves local Venetian cuisine, and guests enjoy proximity to the Murano Museo vaporetto stop. It's ideal for couples seeking modern comfort in a peaceful setting.

Ca' dei Giuspini. Address: Calle del Cimitero 7

For a more personal and budget-friendly option, this charming guesthouse offers cozy rooms with Venetian-style furnishings just a short walk from Murano Faro. Family-run and welcoming, Ca' dei Giuspini provides a peaceful base with easy access to local shops, studios, and restaurants.

Day Trips: Nearby Sites, Cities, and Towns

See Chapter 21, Immersion Experience: Islands of the lagoon.

Murano Festivals Throughout the Year

Festa della Traslazione di San Donato (Feast of the arrival of St. Donato)

August 7

Step into Murano's sacred past with the Festa della Traslazione di San Donato. This powerful celebration marks the arrival of the saint's relics and the legendary "dragon bones" to the island's basilica in 1125. Experience the reverence of a centuries-old tradition that continues to inspire awe today.

Natale di Vetro (Christmas of Glass)

Early December to New Year's, opening on December 5 (St. Nicholas Day)

A month-long celebration honoring Murano's glassmaking heritage. Festivities begin with a St. Nicholas mass at Chiesa di San Pietro Martire, followed by artisan workshops, exhibitions, a dazzling "Tunnel of Lights" installation of glass chandeliers, the "Glassworks Regatta" on the Grand Canal, and special "Furnace Food" dinners prepared in glass furnaces.

CHAPTER TWENTY-ONE

Immersion Experience: Islands of the Lagoon

The Islands beyond Venice

A **Private Boat Journey Beyond the Grand Canal**

The true Venice reveals itself not only in the winding streets of the historic center, but in the wide embrace of the lagoon that surrounds it. As the morning mist begins to lift, a polished wooden water taxi glides across the quiet canals, heading toward the outlying islands, each a world unto itself, rich in character, history, and tradition.

This journey is designed to follow the natural rhythm of the lagoon. Avoiding the midday rush, the route begins with Murano, famed for its blazing glass furnaces. From there, it continues to the silent sanctuary of San Francesco del Deserto, then to the vibrant colors and lacework of Burano for lunch. In the afternoon, the path leads to the ancient stones of Torcello and ends with a quiet reflection on San Michele, the cemetery island.

We experienced this route with family and friends during one of our visits, and it remains one of the most memorable ways to encounter the spirit of Venice beyond the city's more familiar streets.

Led by a Venetian captain, often someone whose family has lived and worked on these waters for generations, travelers experience more than sightseeing. This is a voyage into Venice's living heritage, a tapestry woven from art, faith, craftsmanship, and memory.

Murano: Island of Fire and Glass

Our first destination emerges from the lagoon just a quick ride north of Venice, Murano, the legendary island of glassmakers. Since 1291, when the Venetian Republic ordered all furnaces moved here because of fire risks in the densely packed city, Murano has been synonymous with the transformative art of turning sand into transparent treasures.

What to see in Murano

See Chapter 20, Murano in Molton Color

San Francesco del Deserto: Sanctuary of Silence

Back on the boat, we cruise eastward through the lagoon's central basin toward a tiny island many visitors never discover. San Francesco del Deserto appears as little more than a cluster of cypress trees rising from the water, their vertical lines stretching skyward like natural bell towers.

"Saint Francis stayed here in 1220," Marco explains as we approach. "He was returning from the Holy Land and found this place a perfect retreat for prayer."

The island is home to a small community of Franciscan friars who welcome respectful visitors to their sanctuary. As we disembark, the profound silence is immediately noticeable, a stark contrast to busy Murano. A robed brother greets us and offers to show us around the monastery.

The cypress-lined paths, meticulously maintained gardens, and simple cloisters create an atmosphere of tranquility that feels suspended in time. In the small church, our guide shows us relics associated with St. Francis, including the stone where tradition says he preached to the birds. Whether factual or legendary, the story perfectly captures the island's harmonious relationship with nature.

We speak in hushed tones, respecting the contemplative atmosphere. The brother explains that only a handful of friars live here now, continuing a tradition of prayer and simplicity that has persisted through plagues, wars, and the rise and fall of the Venetian Republic.

Before departing, we sit briefly in the garden overlooking the lagoon. The view hasn't changed for centuries; water, sky, and distant islands merging in a palette of blues and greens. I understand why Francis chose this place, and why the brothers maintain their presence despite the challenges of island life.

Walking Tour of San Francesco del Deserto

#1: Entrance Wharf and Cypress Alley
The approach through tall cypress trees creates an immediate sense of entering a sacred space. Notice how the trees act as a natural windbreak, protecting the monastery gardens.

#2: The Cloisters
Two peaceful cloisters form the heart of the monastery, with ancient wellheads and carefully tended plants. The older cloister dates back to the 13th century.

#3: The Church
Simple and modest, the church houses several treasures, including a beautiful wooden crucifix and paintings depicting the life of St. Francis.

#4: The Rear Garden
End your visit with a moment in the garden that overlooks the lagoon. This view has inspired spiritual contemplation for eight centuries.

Burano: A Canvas of Colors

From monastic simplicity, we journey to exuberant expression. Burano announces itself from a distance, a kaleidoscope of brightly colored houses rising from the northern lagoon like a mirage. As we approach, the reflections of pinks, blues, yellows, and greens dance on the water's surface.

"Each color represents a unique family," Marco tells us. "Fishermen returning in the fog could recognize their homes. At least, that's what we tell the tourists," he adds with a wink. "Some colors also signified what business was conducted inside; the yellow house might be the baker, the red the butcher."

Whatever the historical truth, the effect is magical. Burano feels like a painting brought to life, each lane revealing new compositions of complementary and contrasting hues. Women sit in doorways working on the island's other famous tradition, intricate lacework that rivals the delicacy of the glassware we saw on Murano.

The leaning bell tower of San Martino church watches over the scene, its tilt a reminder that these islands share Venice's challenges with shifting foundations. Nowhere is time better spent than simply wandering, camera ready, through the residential back canals where laundry flutters between houses in an unintentional echo of the colorful buildings.

Houses of Burano

Top Sights in Burano

#1: Via Galuppi
The main street is lined with lace shops, bakeries selling traditional bussolai (butter cookies), and cafés perfect for people watching. Look for authentic lace demonstrations; true Burano lace takes hours to create even a small piece.

#2: Piazza Baldassare Galuppi
The main square features the Church of San Martino with its leaning campanile and the Lace Museum. The Lace Museum (Museo del Merletto) showcases the

island's heritage with exquisite historical pieces and occasionally features women demonstrating traditional techniques.

#3: Tre Ponti (Three Bridges)
This picturesque spot where three canals meet offers some of the most iconic views of the colorful houses. The perfect place for photographs.

#4: Residential Canals
Venture down quieter side canals like Rio Pontinello to see where locals actually live, away from souvenir shops. Notice the immaculately maintained boats and the pride residents take in their distinctive homes.

Burano Restaurant Recommendations

Al Gatto Nero da Ruggero
Via Giudecca, 88
A beloved institution since 1946, this family-run restaurant specializes in ultra-fresh seafood caught daily in the lagoon. Their famous risotto di gò uses the prized goby fish found in Venetian waters. The spider crab pasta and fritto misto are equally spectacular. While not inexpensive, the quality justifies the price. Reservations essential.

Trattoria da Romano
Via Galuppi, 221
Another Burano classic, famous for its risotto (which they stir with such vigor it develops a creamy texture without added cream). Hemingway was a fan. The seafood antipasti platters offer a taste of multiple lagoon specialties. The walls are covered with paintings by artists who exchanged their work for meals, creating an unintentional gallery of local history. Reservations recommended.

We chose Al Gatto Nero, where we feasted on tender baby artichokes, followed by their legendary risotto. The unhurried pace of island dining gives us time to absorb the atmosphere, fishermen mending nets, tourists photographing every angle, and locals going about their business with the resigned patience of those who share their home with visitors.

Mazzorbo: The Quiet Sister of Burano

Just across a wooden footbridge from the bright colors and bustling crowds of Burano lies Mazzorbo, a peaceful and often overlooked island that offers a slower, more contemplative experience of the Venetian Lagoon.

While Burano dazzles with lace shops and postcard hues, Mazzorbo whispers its story through gardens, vineyards, and ancient stones. Once a thriving community in the early days of the lagoon's settlement, Mazzorbo today is a place of quiet resilience, home to just a few hundred residents and a growing commitment to preserving Venice's rural heritage.

Our visit begins with a stroll through the Venissa estate, a walled vineyard reclaiming an ancient tradition. Here, the rare Dorona grape, once cultivated for the Doges, is grown organically in salty soil and sea air, producing one of Venice's most distinctive wines. The vineyard is a living testament to Mazzorbo's agricultural past and its future as a model for sustainable lagoon life.

Walking the tidy paths, we pass fig trees, artichoke plants, and roses climbing the walls, all framed by the serenity of the canal and the faint sounds of birdsong. The estate also hosts a Michelin-starred restaurant and boutique hotel, where local ingredients and lagoon flavors are elevated into an unforgettable culinary experience.

Beyond Venissa, we follow the canal to the Church of Santa Caterina, the island's most historic landmark. This simple 14th-century church is one of the oldest surviving in the lagoon, with a graceful bell tower that once served as a navigational beacon. Inside, a quiet hush hangs in the air, broken only by the echo of our footsteps on the worn stone floor.

Unlike the tourist-heavy islands nearby, Mazzorbo encourages slowness. We linger on the waterfront promenade, watching boats pass and the sun play off the water. There's space here for thought, for breath, for something timeless.

What to Explore in Mazzorbo

#1: Ponte Longo (Long Bridge)

This wooden pedestrian bridge connects Burano and Mazzorbo, offering views of boats, vineyards, and daily life on the water. It's the ideal vantage point for photographers and flâneurs alike.

#2: Venissa Estate and Vineyard

Surrounded by medieval walls, this estate combines winemaking, agriculture, and fine dining in a restored space that honors lagoon traditions.

#3: Church of Santa Caterina

Possibly dating back to the 13th or 14th century, this church features a rare wooden ceiling and one of the oldest bells in the lagoon, cast in 1318.

#4: Lagoon Promenade and Gardens

A peaceful walk along Mazzorbo's canals and green spaces allows for quiet reflection and a rare glimpse of Venetian rural life.

Mazzerbo Restaurant Recommendation

Trattoria alla Maddelena. Address: Fondamenta di Santa Caterina, 7/b

Located just steps from the Mazzorbo vaporetto stop, Trattoria alla Maddalena offers a peaceful dining experience far from the crowds of Venice. Set along the quiet canal with outdoor seating, the restaurant provides lovely views of passing boats and the pastoral charm of the island. It's an ideal spot to relax and enjoy the slower rhythms of lagoon life.

The menu focuses on traditional Venetian cuisine, with a strong emphasis on fresh fish and seasonal vegetables. Signature dishes include risotto with lagoon herbs, grilled cuttlefish, and house-made pasta with clams or crab. The wine list features a selection of regional labels, including bottles from nearby Venissa's Dorona vineyard.

Torcello, the Original Island of Venice

After lunch, we cruise to perhaps the most historically significant island in the lagoon. Torcello, now home to just a handful of residents, was once a thriving center with a population of 20,000 before malaria and the rise of Venice proper led to its decline.

Approaching by water, Torcello appears almost wild, with overgrown fields and scattered ruins hinting at its lost grandeur. The island's treasures require a short walk along a canal from the boat landing, past artisan shops and the famous Locanda Cipriani, where Hemingway once stayed.

Our destination is the Cathedral of Santa Maria Assunta, a magnificent testament to Torcello's former importance. Founded in 639 AD, this ancient church predates St. Mark's Basilica by centuries and represents the earliest significant Christian monument in the lagoon.

As we enter, the interior seems deceptively simple until our eyes adjust to the dim light. Then, the western wall reveals its treasure, an enormous, awe-inspiring Byzantine mosaic of the Last Judgment dating from the 11th century. Christ sits in judgment as angels trumpet and demons drag sinners to their fate in vivid, golden detail.

Adjacent to the cathedral stands the circular Church of Santa Fosca, a perfect example of Byzantine Venetian architecture. Together, these buildings and the ancient throne known as "Attila's Chair" (though it has no actual connection to the Hun leader) create a deeply atmospheric ensemble that transports visitors to the lagoon's earliest Christian settlements.

Landmarks of Torcello

#1: Devil's Bridge (Ponte del Diavolo)
This ancient humpbacked bridge has no railings, a typical feature of early Venetian bridges. Local legends suggest various supernatural explanations for its name.

#2: Church of Santa Fosca
This elegantly simple circular church creates a perfect architectural complement to the grander cathedral beside it. Note the beautiful portico and harmonious proportions.

#3: Cathedral of Santa Maria Assunta
The interior contains some of the most important mosaics in the Venetian

lagoon. Beyond the famous Last Judgment, look for the delicate 11th-century mosaic of the Virgin and Child in the apse.

Santa Maria Assunta

#4: Archaeological Museum

Housed in the former Palazzo del Consiglio, this small museum contains artifacts that trace Torcello's history from the Roman era through its medieval apex. The garden offers peaceful lagoon views.

San Michele: Island of Rest

As the afternoon light begins to soften, we make our final stop at San Michele, Venice's cemetery island. The imposing brick walls and cypress trees that surround this sacred ground are visible from much of Venice proper, a constant memento mori for the living city.

"Many visitors find this stop too melancholy," Marco comments as we approach. "But Venetians see it differently. Death has always been part of our city's story, from the plague monuments to the funeral gondolas. San Michele is beautiful, peaceful."

He's right. As we pass through the monumental entrance designed by Mauro Codussi in the 15th century, the cemetery reveals itself as a contemplative garden, meticulously maintained and filled with artistic funerary monuments. Famous residents include composers Igor Stravinsky and Ezra Pound, ballet impresario Sergei Diaghilev, and countless generations of Venetians.

We wander respectfully through the different sections, noting how even in death, the city maintains its cosmopolitan character; there are Orthodox, Protestant, and Catholic areas, reflecting Venice's long history as a crossroads of cultures.

The island has a serene beauty, with paths lined by cypress trees leading between sections filled with flowers and personal mementos left by mourning families. Far from being macabre, San Michele offers a dignified space for reflection on mortality in a city where the passage of time is palpable in every weathered stone.

"We should leave before they close the gates," Marco reminds us gently. "Legend says spirits from San Michele sometimes follow visitors back to Venice after dark," he adds with a theatrical whisper. "We wouldn't want any uninvited passengers on our return journey."

Points of Interest on San Michele

#1: Church of San Michele in Isola
The first Renaissance church in Venice, with its elegant façade by Mauro Codussi marks a transition from Gothic to Classical styles in Venetian architecture.

#2: Foreign Sections
The Protestant and Orthodox sections house tombs of famous expatriates who made Venice their home, including poets, composers, and artists.

#3: Military Memorial
A sobering section dedicated to fallen soldiers, with rows of identical white crosses reminiscent of military cemeteries worldwide.

#4: Modern Section
Unlike the elaborate older monuments, contemporary Venetian burials are marked by simple plaques organized in neat walls; space on the island is limited, and after 10 or 12 years, remains are typically moved to an ossuary to make room for new burials.

Returning to Venice

As the boat glides back across the lagoon, the skyline of Venice rises in golden light. The day's journey reveals far more than scenic beauty, it brings to life the layered identity of the lagoon: the artistry of Murano, the serenity of San Francesco, the cheerful spirit of Burano, the deep history of Torcello, and the solemn dignity of San Michele.

These islands, each with its own voice, together tell the story of Venice, its innovation, devotion, resilience, and grace. Long after the crowds fade from the Piazza San Marco, the quiet currents of the lagoon continue to sustain the soul of the city.

Passing fishermen casting nets using techniques unchanged for centuries, the boat nears the Grand Canal. "Venice is not just monuments," the captain often says. "The lagoon gives us everything. When you understand the islands, you understand Venice."

As travelers step ashore once more, what they carry with them is not just a day of exploration, but a deeper connection to the spirit of La Serenissima, one more lasting than any souvenir.

Islands of the Venice Lagoon

CHAPTER TWENTY-TWO

Sip, Stroll, and Celebrate in Bardolino

Grape and Wine Festival

Festa dell'Uva e del Vino

Where: Bardolino

When: Last weekend of September / First weekend of October.

Average Festival Temperatures: High 24°C (75°F). Low 12°C (54°F).

Bardolino: A Lakeside Town Steeped in Wine and History

Bardolino, a picturesque town, is on Lake Garda's eastern shore in the province of Verona. It lies at an elevation of approximately 130 meters (426 feet) above sea level, embraced by gently rolling hills, olive groves, cypress trees, and, most famously, vineyards. The area's temperate climate and fertile glacial soil have made it ideal for cultivating grapes since ancient times.

I absolutely love Lake Garda. Its blend of natural beauty, cultural depth, and historic lakeside towns is unmatched. In fact, I've devoted an entire 5-part podcast series to Lago di Garda on my Immersion Travel Podcast, covering towns like Bardolino, Sirmione, Garda, and more. You can listen on Apple Podcasts or Spotify, with quick links available at https://katerinaferrara.com/video-podcast/

Bardolino's roots stretch back to the Bronze Age, as evidenced by archaeological finds in the lakebed and nearby hills. It later became a Roman settlement strategically located along trade and military routes, with several Roman villas and road markers discovered in the area. The name "Bardolino" likely derives from the Latin bardus or bardus-linus, possibly indicating a land grant or villa estate.

During the Middle Ages, Bardolino became part of the vast holdings of the Scaligeri family, who fortified the town with walls and towers, remnants of which still mark the old town center. In the 15th century, it came under the rule of the Republic of Venice, which supported the development of fishing, olive oil, and viticulture, establishing Bardolino as a small but thriving lakeside economy. Churches such as the Romanesque San Severo and San Zeno, dating from the 8th to 12th centuries, bear witness to the town's early religious and cultural significance.

In the 19th century, Bardolino gained fame as a destination for health and leisure tourism. Wealthy Austrians and Germans visited the lake for its clean air and beauty, and at the same time, Bardolino wine was bottled and exported, bringing new recognition to the town's viticultural traditions. In the modern era, Bardolino wine received DOC (Denominazione di Origine Controllata) status in 1968 and DOCG (Denominazione di Origine Controllata e Garantita) status for Bardolino Superiore in 2001.

Today, Bardolino is home to approximately 7,000 residents and attracts visitors year-round, especially during its vibrant festivals and harvest season. With scenic lakefront promenades, bustling cafés, and historic churches, the town blends cultural richness, natural beauty, and culinary excellence, making it one of Lake Garda's most beloved destinations.

Bardolino Wine Festival (Festa dell'Uva e del Vino)

The Festa dell'Uva e del Vino is Bardolino's most anticipated annual event, a celebration of the grape harvest and the town's long winemaking heritage. Founded in the early 20th century, the festival has grown into one of the largest wine events in the Veneto region. It brings together local wineries, food producers, artists, and musicians for nine days of lakeside festivities.

The heart of the celebration is the lakefront promenade, where wooden stalls are set up, offering tastings of Bardolino wines, including the famed Bardolino Classico, Chiaretto rosé, and sparkling Spumante. Each stall is run by a local vineyard, and visitors can purchase a souvenir glass to sample a variety of labels as they walk along the scenic shoreline.

Each evening, the town comes alive with live music, folk dance performances, and cultural parades. Local restaurants and trattorias prepare special menus highlighting traditional Veronese dishes and wine pairings, while chefs give public demonstrations of regional recipes. Throughout the week, Bardolino's piazzas and waterfront host fireworks displays, art shows, and family-friendly activities like grape-stomping contests and wine-themed games.

The Grape Parade

The highlight of the festival is often the "grape parade", where elaborately decorated floats roll through town in celebration of the harvest. In keeping with tradition, some locals dress in historic winemaker costumes, and musicians and dancers from across the Veneto add festive energy to the streets.

Whether you're a wine enthusiast or simply love cultural immersion, the Bardolino Wine Festival offers a joyful, authentic, and delicious way to experience one of Italy's most charming lakeside towns.

Walking Tour of Bardolino

#1. Bardolino Lakeside Promenade and Piazza Matteotti

Begin the tour at the vibrant heart of Bardolino: Piazza Matteotti, the central square lined with cafés, shops, and gelaterie. From here, enjoy a stroll along the lakeside promenade, which curves along the shoreline and offers sweeping views of Lake Garda's calm blue waters, moored sailboats, and distant hills. During the wine festival, this promenade is transformed into the main tasting route, with wooden stalls offering Bardolino DOC and Chiaretto wines.

Panoramic view of Lago di Garda

#2. Chiesa di San Severo

Tucked just east of the promenade, the Church of San Severo is a Romanesque gem with 9th-century origins. Expanded in the 11th and 12th centuries atop an earlier Lombard foundation, it stands as one of Bardolino's most important early Christian landmarks.

Its simple stone façade and tall bell tower give way to a single-nave interior, framed by rounded Romanesque arches. Inside, visitors find remarkable 12th-century frescoes, the oldest in the Lake Garda region, depicting Christ, the Apostles, and scenes from the New Testament.

The crypt below, once part of a Benedictine monastery, adds a mystical atmosphere with its low stone vaults and columns. Quiet and contemplative, it invites reflection and a deeper connection to Bardolino's spiritual heritage.

#3. The Old Town Streets and Wine Shops

Wander through Bardolino's stone-paved alleys, many of which still follow the Roman grid. The streets are full of character, with pastel-painted façades, wrought-iron balconies, and artisan shops selling olive oil, wine, and handmade crafts. Stop in a local enoteca to taste Bardolino Classico or a glass of refreshing Chiaretto rosé, the town's pride and joy.

Bardolino Street View

#4. Chiesa di San Zeno

Just a short walk from the center, the Church of San Zeno is one of Bardolino's oldest landmarks, dating to the 8th or 9th century. Modest in size, it is one of the best-preserved Carolingian churches in northern Italy.

Its architecture reflects early medieval design, with horseshoe-shaped arches and simple stone capitals marking the transition from classical to Romanesque styles. Inside, the single nave and semicircular apse remain unadorned, preserving the purity of early Christian worship spaces.

Subtle carvings of animals, crosses, and geometric patterns hint at the symbolic language of the time. Still used for occasional services, the church offers a quiet, spiritual atmosphere and a glimpse into Bardolino's distant past, just minutes from the bustling lakefront.

#5. Bardolino Wine Museum (Museo del Vino)

Head north along Via Costabella toward the Zeni Winery, home to the Museo del Vino. This museum is run by the Zeni family and provides an engaging overview of Bardolino's winemaking traditions through historic presses, tools, barrels, and guided tastings. It's located slightly uphill, so enjoy the view of vineyards stretching toward the lake as you approach.

#6. Villa Guerrieri and the Olive Oil Museum (optional extension)

If time allows, continue north to visit the Museo dell'Olio, a small museum dedicated to olive oil production, within an old oil mill at Villa Guerrieri. Bardolino's olive oil, like its wine, is a prized product of the local terroir. The museum displays antique grinding stones and presses, with tastings of oil and regional products available.

#7. Porto di Bardolino (The Old Harbor)

Return to the lakefront and walk toward the Porto di Bardolino, the old harbor that once served as a vital point for trade and transport. Lined with colorful boats and shaded benches, it's the perfect place to end your tour. Enjoy an aperitivo at one of the many lakefront cafés while watching the sunset over the water.

Logistics

Train: Bardolino does not have a train station. The nearest train station is in Peschiera del Garda, approximately 13 kilometers (8 miles) south of Bardolino. Peschiera is on the main Milan–Venice line and is well connected to cities like Verona, Milan, Venice, and Bologna. From the station, you can reach Bardolino by bus, taxi, or seasonal lake ferry.

Bus: Public bus service to Bardolino is provided by ATV (Azienda Trasporti Verona). From Verona Porta Nuova station, take ATV bus line 164 or line 185, both of which connect Verona with Garda towns, including Bardolino.

There is also regular bus service from Peschiera del Garda, connecting the train station to Bardolino in about 25–30 minutes.

Ferry: Bardolino is served by Lake Garda's Navigazione Lago di Garda ferry system, offering seasonal ferry routes between towns such as Sirmione, Garda, Lazise, Torri del Benaco, and Desenzano del Garda. Ferries run more frequently from spring to fall, with reduced service in winter. Passenger ferries and a few vehicle ferries (e.g., to Toscolano-Maderno) operate daily during the high season. Tickets can be purchased at the lakefront ferry terminal near Piazza Matteotti or online through Navigazione Lago di Garda.

Car: Bardolino is easily accessible by car from Verona or the A22 and A4 motorways.

The scenic SR249 (Gardesana road) connects Bardolino to other lake towns and offers beautiful lake views along the way.

Parking: During festival periods and in high season, parking in Bardolino can be limited in the town center. However, several public pay lots are available: Parcheggio Via dello Sport–large lot near the town entrance, Parcheggio Piazzale Aldo Moro–convenient for accessing the lakefront, or Parcheggio Via Dante Alighieri–close to the old town and ferry terminal.

Restaurant Recommendations

Taverna da Memo. Address: Piazza Statuto, 15

In the heart of Bardolino's old town, Taverna da Memo serves up traditional Veronese dishes with flair. The outdoor seating in the lively piazza offers a perfect setting to enjoy specialties like homemade bigoli with duck ragù, risotto all'Amarone, and lake fish. The staff is friendly, and the wine list includes excellent Bardolino DOC selections.

La Loggia Rambaldi. Address: Piazza Principe Amedeo, 7

Set in an elegant 16th-century palazzo overlooking the lake, this refined restaurant is known for its romantic atmosphere and creative regional cuisine. Dishes feature seasonal ingredients and fresh lake fish, and the terrace is an ideal spot for dinner at sunset. Don't miss the Chiaretto risotto or their beautifully plated desserts.

Ristorante La Porta. Address: Piazza Statuto, 5

This cozy, family-run restaurant is located just steps from the old harbor. It's known for its friendly service, homemade pasta, and an excellent selection of local wines. Try the grilled lavarello (lake whitefish) or the tagliolini al tartufo, and enjoy the relaxed, welcoming vibe that makes this spot popular with locals.

Accommodation

Hotel Caesius Thermae & Spa Resort. Address: Via Peschiera, 3

This luxurious 4-star wellness resort is located a short walk from the lake and offers thermal pools, a full-service spa, and Ayurvedic treatments. The rooms are elegant and comfortable, and the resort features multiple restaurants, beautiful grounds, and excellent service, perfect for travelers seeking both relaxation and lake access.

Hotel San Pietro. Address: Via Madonnina, 15

Just a few minutes from the historic center and lakeside promenade, Hotel San Pietro offers modern rooms with balconies, a pool, and a panoramic rooftop terrace. The hotel is known for its breakfast buffet and warm hospitality. It's a splendid choice for couples or small groups wanting comfort and convenience in a central location.

Hotel Capri. Address: Via Mirabello, 21

Hotel Capri is a family-run 3-star hotel located close to both the lake and Bardolino's old town. It features comfortable rooms, a well-kept garden with a pool, and a quiet, restful atmosphere. Guests appreciate the helpful staff, clean accommodations, and easy walking distance to restaurants, the harbor, and wine festival events.

Day Trip Options: Nearby Sites, Cities, and Towns

Sirmione. Distance from Bardolino: 35 kilometers (22 miles) by road; reachable by ferry from Bardolino in warmer months (spring–fall). Sirmione is my favorite town on the lake (we stayed at Hotel Sirmione in a fairly small room with views of the lake.)

Perched on a narrow peninsula that juts into the southern end of Lake Garda, Sirmione is one of the most romantic and historic towns on the lake. Known since Roman times as a wellness retreat, Sirmione is famed for its thermal springs, ancient ruins, and fairy-tale charm.

The crown jewel is the Scaliger Castle (Rocca Scaligera), a 13th-century fortress surrounded by a moat and accessible via a drawbridge. You can climb the tower for panoramic lake views. At the far tip of the peninsula lie the Grottoes of Catullus (Grotte di Catullo), the ruins of a vast Roman villa, believed to have belonged to the poet Catullus. Visitors can explore the olive tree–dotted grounds and learn about Roman lakeside life in the attached museum.

Sirmione also offers beautiful lakeside promenades, thermal spas, and gelaterias with flavors as artistic as they are delicious. The town is pedestrian-only in many sections and ideal for a relaxing day trip.

Garda. Distance from Bardolino 4 kilometers (2.5 miles) north along the lakeside promenade; ferry service available between towns during the tourist season

The town of Garda gives the lake its name and is just a short stroll or bike ride from Bardolino. With its colorful harbor, tree-lined waterfront, and casual charm, it's perfect for a half-day visit. Garda is less touristy than Sirmione and keeps a laid-back village atmosphere.

Key sights include the Palazzo dei Capitani, a 14th-century Venetian Gothic palace that once housed the regional governor. Stroll the Lungolago Regina Adelaide, lined with cafes and artisan shops. For hikers, the Rocca di Garda, a hilltop with ruins of a medieval fortress, offers rewarding views of the lake and surrounding hills after a short, scenic climb. The area is also home to vineyards producing Bardolino and Chiaretto wines.

Torre del Benaco. Distance from Bardolino 11 kilometers (7 miles) north; accessible by road or ferry from Bardolino (seasonal).

Nestled beneath Monte Baldo, Torre del Benaco is a picturesque lakeside town known for its ancient port, quiet streets, and Scaliger Castle—a highlight for any visitor. The castle, built in the 14th century by the della Scala family, houses a museum of lake culture, which includes exhibits on olive oil production, fishing traditions, and even a medieval lemon greenhouse (limonaia), beautifully preserved within the castle grounds.

The town has a tranquil feel, with stone alleyways, lakefront terraces, and small art galleries. It's an ideal place to enjoy a slower pace while exploring the cultural legacy of Lake Garda. From here, you can also catch a car ferry across to Toscolano-Maderno on the western shore of the lake, making it a gateway for wider exploration.

Bardolino Festivals and Sagre Throughout the Year

Carnevale di Bardolino

February or early March (varies with Easter)

Bardolino celebrates Carnival with a colorful parade, live music, and traditional Venetian costumes. The town fills with families, children in masks, and festive food stalls offering frittelle, galani, and vin brulé. The event closes with the "maccheronata," a community pasta feast served in Piazza Matteotti, drawing locals and visitors alike.

Palio del Chiaretto (Rosé Wine Festival)

Last weekend of May

This early-summer festival honors Bardolino's famous Chiaretto rosé wine with a three-day celebration along the lakefront. Visitors can sample Chiaretto DOC from multiple producers, paired with local specialties. The promenade is lined with wine stalls, live music stages, and pink-themed decorations in honor of the wine's blush hue. The event includes cooking shows, art displays, and tastings overlooking the lake.

Festa dei Santi Patroni (Feast of the Patron Saints Nicolò and Severo)

June 18

This religious celebration honors Bardolino's patron saints, San Nicolò and San Severo, with a solemn Mass, a procession through town, and an evening concert or fireworks display by the lake. Church bells ring throughout the day, and the historic churches of San Zeno and San Severo become focal points for devotion and local pride.

Bardolino Air Show (Frecce Tricolori)

Held in July or early August (varies by year)

During select summers, Bardolino hosts an aerial demonstration featuring the Frecce Tricolori, Italy's famed air force aerobatic team. Crowds gather along the lakefront to watch the planes perform stunts and formations over the water, trailing smoke in the colors of the Italian flag. The event is accompanied by food stands, music, and family-friendly activities.

San Martino in Cantina (St. Martin's Day Wine Festival)

November 11

On the feast of San Martino, Bardolino opens its wine cellars to celebrate the new wine of the season. This low-key but cherished festival includes tastings of novello (newly fermented wine), small bites, and vineyard tours. It is an intimate, off-season event, perfect for travelers who want to experience Bardolino's wine traditions away from the summer crowds.

CHAPTER TWENTY-THREE

Immersion Experience: Prosecco Hills

Sparkling Landscapes

A **Journey Through Italy's Celebrated Wine Region**

Morning mist clings to the steep, terraced hillsides as a driver winds along narrow roads through the UNESCO-designated Prosecco Hills between Conegliano and Valdobbiadene. The landscape unfolds as a living mosaic of vineyards, stitched carefully into the contours of the land, so precisely maintained they seem drawn by hand.

The unique ciglioni, narrow grass-reinforced terraces, define the hills and earned the region its UNESCO recognition in 2019. A local guide explains that viticulture here is more than an agricultural practice; it is a way of life shaped by the slopes, the soil, and the seasons.

One of the most immersive ways to experience the Prosecco Hills is through a full-day tour that weaves together vineyard visits, regional cuisine, and olive oil tasting. On a recent trip, I joined friends on just such a journey. The experience blends history, craft, and flavor into something unforgettable; an invitation to understand the land not through observation alone, but through taste, tradition, and connection.

Morning: The Soul of Prosecco Production

The day begins at a small, family-owned vineyard near Valdobbiadene, the heart of Prosecco Superiore DOCG. Here, everything is done by hand. Steep hills prevent machinery, and generations of knowledge guide every pruning and harvest. A walk through the rows of Glera grapes reveals how closely growers work with the land, adapting to its demands with care and respect.

Inside the modest production facility, visitors learn how Prosecco gets its signature sparkle using the Martinotti method. Unlike Champagne, where bubbles form in the bottle, Prosecco's second fermentation takes place in stainless steel tanks, preserving its freshness and delicate fruit character.

A guided tasting rounds out the visit, offering a deeper appreciation for the wine's range, from the crisp, dry Brut Nature to the elegant Valdobbiadene Superiore, and the highly prized Cartizze, made from the region's most exclusive vineyards. More than a lesson in wine, it is an introduction to the rituals and everyday joy that Prosecco represents for locals.

Midday: A Culinary Interlude

Lunch at a hillside osteria introduces the flavors that have grown alongside the vines for centuries. Sopressa salami, mountain cheeses, and Treviso radicchio risotto are paired with local wines, and each dish carries a story tied to the land. Baccala mantecato, or creamed salt cod, served on grilled polenta, proves a perfect match for Prosecco's acidity and sparkle.

Between courses, guests are often invited to explore herb gardens, where rosemary, sage, and thyme thrive in the same microclimate that shapes the vines. The connection between food and wine, soil and flavor, becomes unmistakably clear.

Afternoon: Liquid Gold Among the Vines

Later in the day, the tour continues to a family-run olive mill. Though less known than the wine, olive oil here benefits from the same hillside conditions and dedication to tradition. At a small estate, guests see both old stone wheels and modern extraction techniques at work. The result is a fragrant, high-quality oil that tells its own story of struggle and reward.

During the tasting, visitors learn how to warm the oil, sip, and breathe in the aromas to detect the presence of healthy polyphenols and unique flavor profiles. Oils vary from buttery to bold, each shaped by different olive varieties and microclimates. The experience is tactile and sensory, tying this lesser-known product to the land with the same reverence as wine.

Practical Information

Experience: Prosecco Hills Wine & Olive Oil Tour

Duration: Full day (approximately 8 hours).

Best time to visit: Late spring through early fall for ideal weather and vineyard views. September-October to witness the harvest.

Starting point: Tours typically depart from Venice, Treviso, or accommodations within the Prosecco region

Booking Information:
Advanced reservations are essential, especially during high season (June-September). Many tour operators offer both group and private experiences, with private tours providing more flexibility and personalized attention. For the most authentic experience, look for tours that include smaller, family-run vineyards rather than only large commercial operations.

Winter Celebrations

December through February

CHAPTER TWENTY-FOUR

Festa Fusion Belluno

Belluno's Blend of Devotion and Delight

FestaFusion Belluno

#1. Festa di San Martino. Belluno's celebration of its patron saint, San Martino.

#2. Fiera di San Martino. The Fiera di San Martino transforms Belluno into a bustling open-air market, with stalls selling everything from alpine cheeses to handcrafted goods, drawing locals and visitors alike for a festive fall gathering.

Where: Belluno

When: November 11 and the Sunday following November 11.

Average Festival Temperatures: High: 10°C (50°F). Low: 3°C (37°F).

#FestaFusion: When two festivals collide in the same town around the same time, your journey becomes twice as magical.

Belluno: Alpine Beauty with Ancient Roots

Nestled in a wide green basin at the edge of the Dolomite mountains, where dramatic limestone peaks rise like stone cathedrals above forested slopes, Belluno is a town that balances wild natural beauty with centuries of history. With a current population of around 35,000, this gateway to the Dolomites feels both timeless and alive, a perfect blend of mountain village charm and Renaissance elegance.

Long before it became the capital of this alpine province, Belluno was already known to the ancient Veneti, who gave the town its name, Belo-dunum, meaning "splendid hill." When the Romans arrived in the 1st century BC, they formalized its role as a strategic outpost along the road from the Po Valley to the Alpine passes. Belluno thrived as a commercial hub, connecting northern Italy to Noricum (modern Austria) through the Piave River valley, a route still vital to this day.

In the medieval period, Belluno's position made it a desirable prize. It passed from Lombard control to that of the Patriarchs of Aquileia and later became part of the Republic of Venice in the early 15th century. The Venetian era would leave a lasting mark on the town's architecture and economy. Even today, Belluno's historic center echoes with the legacy of the Serenissima, from graceful arcades to Gothic windows with intricate tracery.

Despite its relatively small size, Belluno's identity is immense. The town stretches between the Piave River and the rugged cliffs of the Dolomiti Bellunesi National Park, earning it a UNESCO World Heritage backdrop that changes with the seasons, from snow-draped winter peaks to sunlit summer meadows.

#1. Festa di San Martino

Belluno's Festa di San Martino, held each year on November 11, honors the city's patron saint, San Martino di Tours, a figure celebrated across Europe for his compassion, humility, and military renunciation. But in Belluno, the celebration takes on a distinctively local character, blending religious tradition with small-town warmth and alpine flair.

Who Was Saint Martin?

San Martino (Saint Martin of Tours) was born around AD 316 in what is now Hungary. A Roman soldier turned monk, he is best known for a legendary act of charity: seeing a poor beggar shivering in the cold, Martin cut his cloak in half to share it. That night, he dreamt of Jesus wearing the piece of cloak he had given away. The experience changed him; he left the army, was baptized, and eventually became bishop of Tours in France. His feast day, November 11, became one of the most beloved fall celebrations across Christian Europe.

Saint Martin was named patron saint of Belluno in the early Middle Ages, likely by the 6th or 7th century, when his cult was spreading rapidly through northern Italy. Belluno's cathedral, Duomo di San Martino, has been dedicated to him since at least the 9th century. His themes of protection, generosity, and humility resonated deeply in this mountainous town, where the seasons were harsh and community interdependence was vital. Over the centuries, local devotion grew stronger, culminating in the annual city-wide festival in his honor.

Though pinpointing the exact year is difficult, Belluno's Festa di San Martino has been celebrated for at least 900 years, with formal processions and religious rites recorded as early as the 12th century. As with many Italian patron saint festivals, its origins were likely a small, local observance around the cathedral, which eventually grew to encompass the whole town.

Festival Events

8:00 a.m.

Campane a Festa (Bells Ring throughout the Morning)

Church bells throughout Belluno ring in celebration, calling the town to mark the feast day.

9:00 a.m.

Holy Mass at the Duomo di San Martino

A solemn Mass is celebrated in the cathedral, often presided over by the Bishop of Belluno-Feltre. This Mass includes special prayers for the city and blessings for civic leaders.

10:30 a.m.

Procession of Saint Martin

The statue of St. Martin is carried through the city's historic center, accompanied by clergy, city officials, and sometimes children dressed in Roman and medieval costumes. The route often includes stops for prayers and blessings at key points in the old town.

4:30 p.m.

Belluno Folk Concert or Band Performance

Local musicians gather in the piazza or town theater for traditional folk music and seasonal songs. This includes groups dressed in traditional regional attire.

6:00 p.m.

Evening Vespers and Candlelight Prayer

At the Duomo or the nearby Church of San Rocco, an evening service closes the religious side of the celebration with reflective prayers and soft choral music.

8:00 p.m.

Community Dinner or Cultural Event

The Cena di San Martino (San Martino communal dinner) is held in civic halls or mountain lodges, followed by storytelling, local poetry readings, or musical acts.

#2. Fair of St. Martin

Traditionally held on the first Sunday following November 11th (San Martino's feast day), the fair transforms Belluno's historic center into a vibrant hub of cultural and food festivities.

Event Highlights

Bustling Market Stalls: The city center brims with a diverse array of stalls offering local delicacies, artisanal crafts, flowers, plants, toys, and antiques. A notable feature is the "Cose di Vecchie Case" antique market, which attracts collectors and enthusiasts alike.

Culinary Delights: Visitors can savor traditional treats such as roasted chestnuts and mulled wine. The "Sapori di San Martino" street food village in Piazza Piloni showcases Belluno's local flavors, providing a feast for the senses.

Cultural Exhibitions: The fair features an exhibition of wooden sculptures created during the "Ex Tempore" woodcarving event. These artworks are displayed at Palazzo Fulcis, where attendees can vote for their favorite pieces, engaging the community in celebrating local artistry.

Guided Tours: The Duomo of Belluno offers guided tours of its crypt, where visitors can admire a magnificent 15th-century polyptych. This is a multi-panel altarpiece that features richly detailed scenes from the life of San Martino. Each painted panel illustrates a different moment in the saint's story, serving as both a devotional artwork and a visual narrative masterpiece from the Renaissance period. These tours provide insight into the city's rich religious heritage.

The Fair offers a unique blend of tradition, culture, and community spirit, making it a must-visit event for those seeking an authentic Italian festival experience.

Walking Tour of Belluno

#1. Piazza dei Martiri

Begin your walk in the heart of Belluno at the piazza of the martyrs, the city's main square and traditional gathering place. Once known as Piazza Campedel, it was renamed to honor local partisans who lost their lives during World War II. The wide, elliptical piazza is framed by arcaded buildings with Renaissance and Baroque details, lively cafés, and elegant shops. At its center stands a verdant garden with a monument to the fallen.

On market and festival days, this square becomes the bustling center of Belluno, hosting music, parades, and outdoor dining. From here, you have direct access to many of the city's top landmarks.

#2. Duomo di Belluno (Cathedral of St. Martin)

Just steps away from the piazza lies the Duomo, dedicated to Saint Martin of Tours, Belluno's patron saint. The cathedral's 16th-century Renaissance facade conceals a rich interior filled with works by local artists and Venetian masters. Look for the striking altar dedicated to San Martino and the ornate wooden choir stalls.

Don't miss the crypt below, where medieval fresco fragments and sacred relics offer a glimpse into the city's deep spiritual roots. The bell tower, designed by renowned architect Filippo Juvarra, is one of the most recognizable symbols of Belluno's skyline.

#3. Palazzo dei Rettori

Next to the cathedral, the Rettori Palace stands as a testament to Belluno's time under Venetian rule. Built in the 15th century, it was once the residence of the Venetian governor. Its elegant loggia, Gothic windows, and marble coats of arms represent the city's political prestige. The civic tower attached to the palace offers an impressive clock and panoramic views from nearby streets. This building now serves administrative functions but remains a symbolic cornerstone of Belluno's historical identity.

#4. Porta Dojona and the City Walls

From the palazzo, walk a few minutes to Porta Dojona, one of the ancient gates to the walled city. Dating back to the 14th century and restored in later centuries, the gate stands near the remnants of the medieval city walls, which once protected Belluno from invasions. The gate bears the Lion of St. Mark, Venice's emblem, marking Belluno's importance within the Venetian Republic. The nearby walls offer scenic overlooks of the Piave River and the surrounding Dolomites.

#5. Chiesa di San Rocco (St. Roch)

Continuing your walk through the winding medieval streets, you'll reach the small Church of St. Roch. Built in the early 1500s as a plague chapel, it is now a peaceful sanctuary featuring Renaissance frescoes and a quiet courtyard. Though modest, it's cherished by locals and often used for cultural events and classical music concerts.

#6. Palazzo Fulcis – Civic Museum

Next, head to Palazzo Fulcis, an 18th-century noble residence that houses Belluno's Civic Museum. The palazzo's restored rooms provide an opulent setting for a varied collection that includes medieval religious art, 19th-century landscapes, and archaeological artifacts from the Belluno area. One highlight is the series of wooden sculptures by Andrea Brustolon, known as the "Michelangelo of wood." The museum's temporary exhibits often tie into Belluno's seasonal festivals, making this a dynamic stop on your walk.

#7. Chiesa di Santo Stefano (St. Stephen)

Just a short walk away is the Church of St. Stephen, another architectural and spiritual gem. Built in the 15th century, the church houses impressive Renaissance altarpieces and a beautifully preserved organ. Art lovers will appreciate the altarpiece by Cesare Vecellio, a cousin of Titian, and the quiet atmosphere invites a moment of reflection.

#8. Ponte della Vittoria and the Piave Overlook

To finish your walk, follow the road gently downhill to the Ponte della Vittoria, a bridge crossing the Piave River. From this vantage point, you'll enjoy one of the most striking views of Belluno's position between the Dolomite foothills and the river valley. The surrounding mountains shift color with the time of day, and on a cloudless afternoon, this is the perfect place to reflect on your journey through this underrated Alpine gem.

Restaurant Recommendations

Trattoria da Gino. Address: Via Feltre 120
A beloved local institution, Trattoria da Gino serves traditional Bellunese and Veneto dishes in a cozy, wood-paneled setting. Known for its generous portions and warm hospitality, it's a great place to try homemade pastas, polenta with game, or local cheeses. Reservations are often recommended, especially on weekends.

Osteria del Tiziano. Address: Via Camillo Benso di Cavour, 15
This charming osteria blends rustic charm with refined flavors, offering a rotating menu based on seasonal ingredients. Highlights often include mountain cheeses,

venison, and hearty soups, accompanied by an excellent regional wine list. The setting is intimate and relaxed, with an emphasis on slow food and local traditions.

Ristorante La Bussola. Address: Via Vittorio Veneto 79
La Bussola delivers an elegant dining experience with a focus on fresh, high-quality ingredients and innovative takes on traditional dishes. The menu features both meat and seafood, beautifully presented in a refined yet welcoming atmosphere. It's an ideal spot for a special evening or a long, leisurely lunch.

Accommodation

Albergo Delle Alpi. Address: Via Jacopo Tasso 13
This welcoming 3-star hotel is ideally located in the center of Belluno, just a short walk from both the train and bus stations. Recently renovated, it features modern rooms with sleek furnishings, air conditioning.

Suites Hotel Astor. Address: Piazza dei Martiri 26/E
This stylish 4-star hotel sits directly on Belluno's main piazza and offers elegant, contemporary rooms with sweeping views of the Dolomites and the Piave River. Each suite is uniquely decorated and outfitted with modern amenities, while the hotel's rooftop terrace and wine lounge provide a refined space to relax after a day of sightseeing. Its location in the heart of the old town puts you within steps of Belluno's top attractions.

Albergo Cappello e Cadore. Address: Via Sebastiano Ricci 8
This charming 3-star hotel blends classical architecture with modern comfort. Located just off the main square in a historic building, it features warmly decorated rooms with wooden furnishings that reflect the traditional Alpine style. A generous buffet breakfast is served in a bright, spacious dining room. Its central location is perfect for travelers who want to explore Belluno's historic streets, churches, and shops without needing transportation.

Nearby Sites, Cities, and Towns

Bolzano. 130 kilometers (81 miles) from Belluno. Nestled in a wide Alpine valley where Italian and Austrian influences blend seamlessly, Bolzano is the gateway to South Tyrol and a striking contrast to Belluno's Dolomite backdrop. Historically, a trading hub between northern and southern Europe, Bolzano became part of Italy only after World War I and retains a strong Germanic character.

The town is best known as the home of Ötzi the Iceman, Europe's oldest natural human mummy, on display at the South Tyrol Museum of Archaeology. Its arcaded medieval center is a delight to explore, with elegant pastel-colored buildings, Gothic churches, and bustling piazzas like Waltherplatz. The city is surrounded by mountains and vineyards, and offers easy access to cable cars like the Renon funicular, which climbs to panoramic plateaus and alpine villages. Bolzano is a perfect blend of nature, history, and Tyrolean culture.

We stayed for five nights most recently at the Mavik Suite, hosted by Stay Cooper. The stay included an exquisite breakfast each morning. The spacious suite features full kitchen, incredible views, three beds, two full bathrooms, and a washer, ideal for a comfortable and extended stay in Bolzano. Located just a short walk from the historic center, it offers modern amenities in a quiet yet central location.

https://www.stay-cooper.com/en/bolzano/mavik-lofts/mavik-suite/

Bolzano views

Canale d'Agordo. 43 kilometers (27 miles) from Belluno. Tucked into the Biois Valley at the foot of the Dolomites, Canale d'Agordo is a peaceful Alpine village surrounded by dramatic peaks like the Pale di San Martino and Marmolada. With its wooden chalets, cobbled streets, and rich religious heritage, the town offers a serene contrast to the bustle of larger mountain resorts.

Canale d'Agordo is best known as the birthplace of Pope John Paul I, affectionately called "The Smiling Pope." Visitors can explore his legacy at the Museo Albino Luciani (MUSAL), which showcases his life and work through personal items, photos, and historical exhibits. The town's 17th-century parish church, San Giovanni Battista, features a Baroque tabernacle by Andrea Brustolon and a historic Callido organ once played by the future pope himself.

Nature lovers will find nearby treasures like the Cascate delle Comelle waterfalls and the rugged trails of Val di Gares, offering rewarding hikes through forests and alpine meadows. Whether you're seeking spiritual insight, natural beauty, or a quiet mountain escape, Canale d'Agordo is a hidden gem in the Veneto Dolomites.

Belluno Festivals and Sagre Throughout the Year

Sagra dei Fisciòt (Festival of the Whistles)

Two Sundays before Easter

Dating back to 1716, this beloved spring fair takes over Belluno's historic center with lively stalls and handcrafted whistles, a symbol of joy and the arrival of spring. Visitors are treated to local food, crafts, and festive street performances, creating a colorful and cheerful atmosphere for all ages.

Belluno Photo Festival

Mid-May to early June

This annual celebration of photography brings together local and international artists for a series of exhibitions held in galleries, palaces, and open-air spaces around Belluno. The festival explores diverse themes, ranging from nature and travel to social commentary, through powerful visual storytelling.

Lungardo In Fest

Late May

Held along Via Lungardo, this community festival features live music, pop-up food stands, and entertainment ranging from children's games to late-night dancing. It's a vibrant expression of Belluno's neighborhood life and a splendid chance to experience local culture in an informal, welcoming setting.

Desmontegada (Festival of the Herds' Return)

Late September

Celebrated in the Dolomite valleys near Belluno, this four-day festival honors the return of livestock from alpine pastures. Parades of flower-adorned cows, cheese tastings, and traditional music fill the streets. Events include "Dì del Formai" (Cheese Day), farm visits, and the grand Sunday procession known as La Desmontegada, the largest of its kind in the Alps.

Festa di San Martino (Feast of Saint Martin)

November 11 (with Fiera on the following Sunday)

Belluno's patron saint is honored with solemn mass at the cathedral, followed by the lively Fiera di San Martino. The historic center hosts hundreds of stalls selling crafts, food, and gifts. Highlights include castagnate (roasted chestnuts), street food in Piazza Piloni, antique markets, and guided tours of the Duomo's crypt.

CHAPTER TWENTY-FIVE

Peschiera del Garda: Fortress of Festivity

Faith and Fire over Lake Garda

Festa di San Martino

Where: Peschiera del Garda

When: November 11

Average Festival Temperatures: High: 12°C (54°F). Low: 5°C (41°F).

Peschiera del Garda: A Fortress Town at the Lake's Edge

Where the crystalline waters of Lake Garda narrow into the gentle current of the River Mincio, there stands a town that has guarded Italy's most beautiful lake for over two thousand years. When my family and I arrived in Peschiera on a warm July afternoon, crossing the ancient moat through the castle's grand portico with blooming flowers cascading on both sides, it felt like stepping through a portal between past and present. We spent hours exploring the town's fortresses with their commanding views of the harbor, and as evening approached, we watched a beautiful sunset paint the Roman-looking bridge in golden light.

This star-shaped fortress, home to 11,000 residents, rises from the lake's southernmost point like a crown of weathered stone and flowing water. Its unique geography has made it a prize worth fighting for since Roman legions first recognized the strategic importance of controlling the passage between Lake Garda and the Po Valley. Today, the UNESCO-recognized Venetian fortifications still embrace the historic center in their protective arms, while canals thread through the town like liquid streets reflecting centuries of architectural ambition.

The Romans founded Arilica here, but it was the medieval Scaligeri of Verona who first transformed this lakeside settlement into a veritable fortress, building towers and walls that gave Peschiera its enduring martial character. The Venetians later raised massive ramparts and bastions that still enclose the town, and in the nineteenth century Austrian engineers further fortified it, making it part of the Quadrilatero, a chain of four fortresses with Mantua, Verona, and Legnago guarding Austria's Lombardy-Venetia territory.

Sunset on the Canal inside the Fortress

Walking through this living museum of military architecture, from the medieval Voltoni arches to the mighty fortress walls, visitors can trace the shifting tides of northern Italian power. As evening approaches and golden light shimmers across the canals within the castle walls, watching the sunset paint the Roman-looking bridge in warm hues, it becomes clear why so many empires fought to possess this jewel where lake meets river. Here, surrounded by bridges, piazzas, and the gentle lapping of water against ancient stones, Peschiera remains what it has always been:

a perfect marriage of natural beauty and human ingenuity, where history lives not in museums but in every reflection dancing on the canal's surface.

Feast of St. Martin

When November's crisp air settles over Lake Garda and the first chill hints at winter's approach, Peschiera del Garda awakens to its most cherished celebration. The Feast of San Martino transforms this fortress town into a stage where sacred tradition meets joyful spectacle, drawing locals and visitors into the ancient streets where devotion and community pride have danced together for centuries.

This patronal feast stretches back to medieval times, when the people of Peschiera first placed themselves under Saint Martin's protective care. What began as a simple religious observance has blossomed into the town's most important celebration, weaving together solemn Masses with Venetian-style rowing regattas, market stalls heavy with seasonal treasures, and the spectacular fireworks finale known as the "Fire of the Voltoni" that sets the night sky ablaze.

The fortress setting makes everything magical. Ancient canals become racecourses where oarsmen compete in contests that echo Peschiera's Venetian maritime heritage, while the historic Voltoni bridge serves as both a viewing platform and dramatic backdrop. The air fills with the scent of roasted chestnuts and the crisp notes of local Lugana DOC wines as vendors display their fall bounty beneath stone arches that have witnessed countless generations of celebration.

When darkness falls and fireworks burst above the fortress walls, their reflections shimmer across canal waters like scattered stars, creating moments where past and present merge in brilliant light. The town band's melodies drift through medieval streets while families gather around food stalls, continuing traditions that bind this lakeside community together in gratitude for their patron saint's enduring protection.

Who is Saint Martin?

In the bitter cold of a fourth-century winter, a young Roman soldier named Martin encountered a shivering beggar on the road near Amiens. Without hesitation, he drew his sword and cut his military cloak in half, wrapping the stranger in warm wool before continuing on his way. That night, Christ appeared to Martin in a dream, wearing the very cloak he had shared, speaking words that would transform a soldier into one of Europe's most beloved saints.

Born around 316, Martin of Tours became the living embodiment of Christian charity. After his divine vision, he left military service to embrace monastic life, eventually rising to become Bishop of Tours in France. His reputation for humility, compassion, and miraculous healings spread across the continent, making him one of the first non-martyrs to achieve sainthood and inspiring countless communities to seek his protection.

In Italy, San Martino's feast marks the turning of seasons, when harvest celebrations meet winter preparations in villages across the peninsula. For Peschiera del Garda, his role as patron saint runs deeper than seasonal observance. His example of sharing what one has with those in need resonates through a community that has always understood how fortress walls protect not just buildings, but the bonds between neighbors who choose to care for one another.

Festival Events

November 8

The celebrations begin as the first food and wine stands open in Piazza Battistoni at Porto Centrale. Visitors can sample hearty fall dishes such as risotto al tastasal, bigoli with sardines, grilled meats, roasted chestnuts, and steaming cups of vin brulé. The evening has a welcoming, convivial air as the community gathers to share flavors and mark the start of the patronal feast.

November 9

During the day, local groups and civic organizations present their history and activities, emphasizing the town's strong community spirit. In the afternoon, the festival's most colorful spectacle unfolds on the water with the Palio di San Martino, a Venetian-style rowing regatta along the Canale di Mezzo. The race recalls centuries of connection with Venice and brings crowds of spectators to cheer from the fortress walls and bridges. Afterward, the town band fills the air with lively music as festivities continue in the piazzas, with markets, food stalls, and opportunities to explore the fortress museums and canals by boat.

November 10

In the morning, children take part in the Battesimo della Sella, a symbolic first ride on horseback in the gardens of the Palazzina Storica, a tradition that delights the youngest participants. Cultural events and book presentations often enrich the day, alongside guided tours and open museums. The most solemn moment comes mid-morning with a Mass celebrated in the Church of San Martino, often presided over by the Bishop of Verona, drawing worshippers from across the region. Throughout the day, the streets remain alive with markets, tastings, and music until evening.

November 11: Feast Day of San Martino

The feast day itself is dedicated above all to religious observance and devotion to the town's patron saint. In the afternoon, a solemn Holy Mass is celebrated in the neoclassical parish church of San Martino in Piazza Ferdinando di Savoia. Following the service, a traditional procession honors the saint, with clergy, banners, and townspeople winding their way through the historic streets. The presence of the fortress walls and canals gives this ritual a striking character, as the community gathers both on land and along the water to witness the devotion.

As night falls, anticipation builds for the climactic finale, the Incendio dei Voltoni (the fire of the bridge). This pyro-musical spectacle transforms the Voltoni Bridge and the Canale di Mezzo into a stage of fire and light. Fireworks are launched in synchrony with the music, exploding above the fortress and cascading reflections onto the dark waters below. The effect is breathtaking: the medieval arches glow red and gold, and the surrounding walls seem to shimmer with living flame.

Historic Voltini Bridge Where the Fireworks Take Place

The best vantage points are along the fortress embankments, from the bridges crossing the canals, or even from boats that line the water, where the fireworks appear to fall directly overhead. Locals and visitors stand shoulder to shoulder, their faces illuminated by the bursts of light, as centuries of history seem to come alive in this shared moment of wonder.

Walking Tour of Peschiera del Garda

#1. Porta Verona and the Fortress Walls

The walk begins at Porta Verona, the grand entry gate to the city that stands above the water. Crossing the stone bridge here is unforgettable, as it brings you directly into the star-shaped fortress surrounded by canals. The monumental gate, built during the Venetian period, sets the stage for exploring one of the most striking fortified towns in Italy.

Protective Moat Canal with Fortress Bastions

#2. Piazza Ferdinando di Savoia

Continue into the spacious Piazza Ferdinando di Savoia, often considered the heart of Peschiera. The square is framed by the Church of San Martino, the ancient Roman ruins of Arilica, and elegant historic buildings. This is also where the solemn Mass for the patronal feast connects the past and present.

#3. Ponte dei Voltoni (Voltini Bridge)

From the piazza, walk toward the Ponte dei Voltoni, the five-arched brick bridge built in the sixteenth century by the Venetians. This landmark is iconic during the Feast of San Martino, when the "Fire of the Voltoni" fireworks are launched from it, reflecting across the water. Even outside festival days, the view of the arches over the Canale di Mezzo is breathtaking.

#4. Bastione San Marco and Canals (Fortress Bastions)

Follow the canal-side paths to the Bastione San Marco, one of the fortress's massive bastions. From here you can look out over the waterways and gain a sense of the town's military importance under the Scaligeri, Venetians, and Austrians. The cool stone walls, green spaces, and lapping water create a peaceful yet impressive atmosphere.

Fortress Bastion with Lake Garda behind

#5. Porta Brescia and the Walk Along the Walls

End the tour at Porta Brescia, the western gate of the fortress. From here, you can follow the walkways along the ramparts, with panoramic views over the River Mincio and the surrounding countryside. At sunset, the light across the water and the fortress walls is especially magical, recalling the same scenes that make the Feast of San Martino so memorable.

Logistics

Train: Peschiera del Garda is one of the best connected towns on Lake Garda. The Peschiera del Garda railway station sits just outside the fortress and is on the main Milan to Venice line. High-speed and regional trains stop here frequently, with travel times of about 1 hour to Milan and 15 minutes to Verona.

Bus: The town is linked by regional buses operated by ATV Verona, connecting Peschiera with Verona, Lazise, Bardolino, Garda, and other southern lake towns.

Car: Peschiera is easily reached from the A4 Autostrada, with its own exit. Driving into the historic center is limited, but car parks are located around the fortress perimeter. From Verona, the drive takes about 30 minutes, while from Milan it takes around 1 hour and 30 minutes.

Parking: During major festivals, parking within the historic center is restricted. Designated festival parking areas are set up around town with shuttle buses and pedestrian access to the fortress gates. Arriving early on feast days is recommended to secure a convenient spot.

Restaurant Recommendations

Trattoria al Combattente. Piazza Ferdinando di Savoia, 1

Located right in the historic piazza, this trattoria is a favorite for hearty meals and a lively setting. The menu offers regional specialties such as tortellini in brodo and grilled meats. The view over the square makes it a perfect place to soak in the festival atmosphere.

Ristorante Vecchio Mulino Beach. Località Fornaci

Set on the lakeside, a short walk from the center, this restaurant combines spectacular views with a menu of lake-inspired and regional dishes. Outdoor tables by the water provide an unforgettable dining experience, especially at sunset.

Day Trip Options: Nearby Sites, Cities, and Towns

Lazise. 10 kilometers (6 miles) from Peschiera. One of the most charming lakefront towns on the eastern shore, Lazise is easily reached by ferry from Peschiera. Its medieval walls and lakeside promenade create a storybook setting, while the Scaliger Castle dominates the old town. Stroll through narrow lanes lined with shops and cafés, or enjoy a walk along the lake to see colorful fishing boats bobbing in the harbor.

Bardolino. 13 kilometers (8 miles) from Peschiera. Also accessible by ferry, Bardolino is famed for its vineyards and the wine that bears its name. The lakeside promenade is among the most beautiful on Lake Garda, framed by gardens, palms, and waterfront cafés. The old town is filled with Romanesque churches, inviting trattorie, and shops selling local wines and olive oil.

Verona. 30 kilometers (19 miles) from Peschiera. Verona, the city of Romeo and Juliet, is only about 15 minutes away by train. Known for its Roman Arena, medieval piazzas, and Renaissance palaces, it offers one of the richest cultural experiences in northern Italy. Highlights include Piazza delle Erbe, the Castelvecchio fortress, and Juliet's House, where travelers leave messages of love. Verona is also a UNESCO World Heritage Site for its well-preserved historic center, making it an essential excursion from Lake Garda.

Vicenza. 80 kilometers (50 miles) from Peschiera. Vicenza can be reached in just under an hour by train from Peschiera and is celebrated for its architecture by Andrea Palladio. The elegant Corso Palladio is lined with palaces, while the Teatro Olimpico, one of the first indoor theaters in the world, remains a marvel of Renaissance design.

Festivals and Sagre Throughout the Year

Carnevale di Peschiera del Garda

February or March

Peschiera welcomes Carnival with parades of floats, costumed performers, and bands filling the fortress streets. Children dress up and throw confetti, while food stalls serve fritelle, crostoli, and other seasonal treats.

Palio delle Mura di Peschiera

Summer months

This Venetian-style rowing regatta takes place along the town's canals and fortress walls, echoing the traditions of the Palio di San Martino. Teams from different neighborhoods compete, while the waterfront fills with spectators and music.

CHAPTER TWENTY-SIX

Venice, the Virgin, and the Vow

Celebrating Mary of Mercy

Festa della Madonna della Salute

Where: Venice

When: November 21

Average Festival Temperatures: High: 12°C (54°F). Low: 4°C (39°F).

Event Website: https://basilicasalutevenezia.it/pellegrinaggio-annuale/

Festa della Madonna della Salute

In the autumn of 1630, Venice found itself in the grip of one of the deadliest plagues in its history. The disease had arrived aboard merchant ships and spread rapidly through the city's narrow streets and canals. Within two years, nearly 50,000 people had died, including the Doge, Nicolò Contarini. It was the second major plague to strike the Republic in less than a century.

In desperation, the Venetian Senate turned to divine intervention. On October 22, 1630, the government made a solemn vow to the Virgin Mary: if she would deliver the city from the plague, they would build a church in her honor. She would be invoked as Our Lady of Health.

When the plague finally subsided in 1631, the Republic kept its promise. They chose Punta della Dogana, the prominent spit of land at the entrance to the Grand Canal, as the site of the new church. A public competition was held, and a young architect named Baldassare Longhena, just 26 years old, won with a bold Baroque design that would take nearly fifty years to complete.

The result was the Basilica di Santa Maria della Salute, a monumental expression of Venice's gratitude. Built on a foundation of over one million wooden piles, its vast octagonal dome now rises above the Grand Canal like a beacon of hope and healing. The church's Marian symbolism is woven into every element: the eight-sided floor plan, the star-shaped dome, and the balance of light and space that lifts the gaze heavenward. Inside, masterpieces by Titian and Tintoretto enrich the devotional atmosphere, including Descent of the Holy Ghost and Marriage at Cana.

Francesco Zanin painting of the Festival and Church, 1700's

A Living Tradition

Since its early construction, the church has been the site of a yearly pilgrimage held on November 21, the Feast of the Presentation of the Virgin Mary. The Festa della Madonna della Salute is one of Venice's most cherished and personal religious celebrations. Where Carnival and the Regata Storica offer grandeur and spectacle, the Salute festival is marked by humility, family devotion, and enduring faith.

Each year, thousands of Venetians make the pilgrimage across a temporary votive bridge built for the occasion. The bridge connects Campo Santa Maria del Giglio in San Marco to the steps of the basilica in Dorsoduro. It is one of the most iconic features of the celebration, appearing each November like a ribbon of devotion stretched across the Grand Canal.

Pilgrims come from across the city and nearby islands, many walking barefoot or carrying candles. Entire families participate, from grandparents to young children. They light candles, offer prayers for healing, and give thanks for blessings. For many locals, this tradition is deeply personal, passed down through generations as a testament to faith and family.

Inside the vast basilica, the scent of wax and incense fills the space. The soft flicker of candlelight glows beneath the soaring dome as the faithful pause before the revered Byzantine-style statue of the Madonna and Child. There is a stillness here, an atmosphere of sacred intimacy that envelops all who enter.

Outside, the mood is lighter and more festive. Along the Fondamenta delle Zattere and Campo della Salute, vendors sell candied fruits, roasted chestnuts, fritole, hot chocolate, and small religious souvenirs. Children clutch balloons and caramel apples. The blend of reverence and warmth transforms the neighborhood into a vibrant celebration of both faith and community.

Festival Events

All day, beginning at sunrise

The Votive Bridge across the Grand Canal opens for pilgrims. As dawn breaks over the lagoon, early visitors walk quietly across the bridge to light candles and pray inside the basilica. For many, arriving at sunrise is a cherished family ritual.

7:00 a.m.

Mass

The first Mass is celebrated inside the church, open to early visitors and those seeking quiet reflection. Masses continue hourly throughout the day, with homilies focused on healing, mercy, and the intercession of the Virgin Mary.

10:00 a.m.

Pontifical Mass

A Solemn Pontifical Mass, often presided over by the Patriarch of Venice, takes place, accompanied by sacred music and choral singing. This is the central liturgical event of the day, frequently attended by civic leaders and broadcast on local media.

Midday to Afternoon (12:00–4:00 p.m.)

Pilgrimage to the Bridge

Thousands more visitors arrive, many families with children. Long lines form along the votive bridge and around the basilica as people wait their turn to enter. Street vendors open nearby, selling candied apples, hot chocolate, roasted chestnuts, fritole, and toys.

5:00 p.m.

An evening Mass draws locals returning after work, continuing the rhythm of prayer throughout the day. The votive bridge remains open into the evening to accommodate latecomers.

8:00 p.m.

The final services conclude, but many remain inside the basilica in quiet prayer. The soft glow of candles continues into the night, reflecting the enduring devotion that defines this uniquely Venetian celebration.

Visiting the Basilica di Santa Maria della Salute

The first time we visited the Madonna della Salute church, it wasn't during the famous November festival, but on a warm spring morning. As we crossed the wooden Accademia Bridge and walked along the Grand Canal toward the Punta della Dogana, the church's massive white dome gleamed ahead like a beacon. Approaching the grand staircase, we couldn't help but pause and admire how the building seemed to rise straight from the water, its Baroque curves set against the rippling blue of the lagoon.

Interior

Our first stop was the high altar, directly under the dome. It's impossible to miss the Byzantine-style statue of the Madonna and Child, believed to be miraculous by many Venetians. The altar itself is a marvel: flanked by twisting marble columns, it's crowned with a radiant canopy and surrounded by votive candles. Some flickered quietly, placed there by locals continuing a family tradition of prayers for health and protection.

St. Mark Enthroned by Titian

We took our time exploring the side chapels, each dedicated to different saints and adorned with remarkable paintings. Two works by Titian, St. Mark Enthroned with Saints and The Descent of the Holy Ghost, command attention. I found myself lingering in front of them, not just for the artistry but for the sense of timelessness they conveyed. Generations of Venetians had stood where I stood, asking for the same mercy and protection.

Dome Climb

Then came the climb. We had heard that, on certain days, visitors could ascend to the dome's gallery, and we were lucky, it was open that day. A guide led us to a discreet door in one of the chapels. From there, we began the narrow, winding ascent up stone staircases that gradually revealed the architectural secrets of the church. As we climbed, small windows provided teasing glimpses of the Grand Canal and the rooftops of Dorsoduro beyond.

Finally, we emerged onto the gallery that circles the interior of the dome. Standing there, we could look directly down onto the floor of the church, pilgrims and tourists milling below looked small and quiet in the vast space. But the real reward lay just a few steps higher.

Basilia di Santa Maria della Salute

At the very top, through a final narrow passageway, we stepped out onto the outer gallery. The view was breathtaking. The Grand Canal wound away toward Rialto and San Marco, the Campanile rising prominently across the water. Behind us stretched the lagoon, dotted with boats and distant islands shimmering in the haze. We stood in silence, the only sounds being the wind and the distant hum of vaporetti engines. It felt like Venice itself was laid out at our feet.

Whether during the crowded festival or in the quiet of an ordinary morning, Santa Maria della Salute is more than just a beautiful building. It's a place where the past and present meet, where gratitude and hope are renewed every day by those who step through its doors.

We purchased tickets in advance for the museum, sacristy, and cupola. You can also organize guided visits at this link.

https://basilicasalutevenezia.it/la-basilica/

CHAPTER TWENTY-SEVEN

FestaFusion Cortina

Fashion, Ski Slopes, and Christmas Markets

FestaFusion Cortina

#1. Cortina Fashion Weekend / Start of the Ski Season Festival. Kick off winter in style with runway shows, après-ski parties, and chic alpine vibes at Cortina d'Ampezzo's glamorous fashion and ski festival.

#2. Mercati di Natale. Wander through Veneto's magical Christmas markets filled with artisan gifts, festive lights, mulled wine, and seasonal treats in charming historic settings.

Where: Cortina d'Ampezzo

When: First weekend in December and the Christmas Markets throughout December.

Average Festival Temperatures: High 5°C (41°F). Low: -5°C (23°F).

Website: https://www.cortinafashionweekend.cortinaforus.it/

#FestaFusion: When two festivals collide in the same town around the same time, your journey becomes twice as magical.

Cortina d'Ampezzo: Glamour in the Heart of the Dolomites

Cradled in the soaring peaks of the Dolomites, Cortina d'Ampezzo is the crown jewel of alpine Italy, a town where natural drama meets sophisticated charm. In the province of Belluno, Cortina is surrounded by some of the most breathtaking scenery in the country, with jagged mountains like Tofane, Cristallo, and Croda da Lago forming a cinematic backdrop. At an elevation of 1,224 meters (4,016 feet), this UNESCO World Heritage wonder blends fresh mountain air with luxury living.

Though small, with a population of just 5,600 residents, Cortina boasts a big reputation. It's internationally known for its world-class skiing, stylish boutiques, and rich Olympic legacy, drawing elite travelers, athletes, and creatives for over a century.

But Cortina is far more than its polished surface. Its roots run deep into prehistoric times, when the Veneti and Raetian peoples first settled the alpine basin. Under Roman rule, the area was part of the province of Noricum, a crucial point for trade routes and mountain crossings. Though Cortina never developed into a grand Roman city, its role as a strategic alpine outpost made it a key part of northern Italy's ancient history.

Through the Middle Ages, Cortina found itself under shifting dominions, from the Holy Roman Empire to the Republic of Venice in the 15th century. This alpine enclave became an important stop on high-altitude trade routes, retaining a unique cultural identity thanks to its Ladin heritage and relative isolation.

By the 1800s, word of Cortina's beauty spread. European aristocrats and intellectuals arrived, seeking both refuge and inspiration in its dramatic landscapes. But the town's transformation into an international destination came after the 1956 Winter Olympics, when Cortina dazzled the world and earned its place as Italy's most glamorous mountain resort.

Today, Cortina is once again stepping onto the world stage as it prepares to co-host the 2026 Winter Olympics with Milan (February 6-22, 2026). Visitors come not only for the thrill of skiing or the allure of the designer boutiques, but to experience a town that sits at the crossroads of history, luxury, and alpine wonder.

#1. Cortina Fashion Weekend

Cortina Fashion Weekend is a stylish celebration of mountain life and luxury. It was launched to highlight Cortina's dual identity: both a top-tier winter sports destination and a center of fashion and culture.

Since its early years, the festival has grown to include:

- **Fashion Shows**: Italian and international designers preview their collections, often in unique settings like hotel lobbies or open-air stages

- **Window Art Competitions**: Boutiques on Corso Italia compete for the most creative, winter-themed window displays

- **Après-Ski Events**: Bars and mountain chalets host live music, DJ sets, and champagne toasts

- **Ski Season Preview**: Athletes and teams showcase gear and training for the season ahead

- **Art Exhibits & Performances**: Cultural institutions participate with rotating exhibitions and performances, blending mountain life with the arts

#2. Christmas Markets

As snow begins to blanket the rooftops of Cortina and the jagged peaks of the Dolomites turn winter white, the town transforms into a storybook Alpine village. From early December through the end of the month, Cortina hosts its beloved Mercatini di Natale, or Christmas markets, a festive tradition that captures the spirit of the season in truly magical surroundings.

The heart of the market unfolds along Corso Italia, the town's elegant pedestrian street, where wooden stalls trimmed with pine garlands and fairy lights line the cobblestones. Local artisans sell handcrafted gifts, woolen scarves, hand-carved wooden ornaments, and other treasures that reflect the mountain traditions of the Veneto and Ladin cultures. The air is rich with the scent of cinnamon, roasted chestnuts, and mulled wine, a warm contrast to the crisp mountain cold.

Music fills the town square as carolers sing, live nativity scenes are performed under softly falling snow, and occasional concerts light up the winter nights. Children gather wide-eyed to see Santa Claus, while adults linger over hot beverages and holiday treats, enjoying the laid-back joy that the holidays in Cortina seem to inspire.

Walking Tour of Cortina

#1. Piazza Angelo Dibona
This central square is the symbolic heart of Cortina d'Ampezzo. It features a monument to the Alpine Troops and offers stunning views of the surrounding Dolomite peaks. The square is a popular gathering point and is surrounded by historic buildings and elegant cafés.

#2. Basilica Minore dei Santi Filippo e Giacomo
Just steps from Piazza Venezia, the main square of Cortina d'Ampezzo, stands the town's most important religious site: the Basilica Minore dei Santi Filippo e Giacomo, dedicated to Saint Philip and Saint James the Less. The current structure was built between 1769 and 1775, replacing an earlier medieval church that had become too small for the growing community. The design reflects the late Baroque style, popular in the Dolomites during the 18th century, with an elegant yet welcoming façade.

Inside, the basilica is known for its ornately decorated altars, crafted from local wood and marble. The pastel-colored frescoes, added in the 19th century, depict scenes from the lives of the saints and other biblical narratives, contributing to the serene, uplifting ambiance. Of special note is the high altar, with its fine sculptural details and the altarpiece dedicated to the patron saints.

The church's interior also features precious wooden choir stalls, a richly carved pulpit, and several side chapels, each adorned with devotional art and statuary. The campanile (bell tower), built in 1852, rises high above the town and has become one of Cortina's most recognizable landmarks. Its tall, slender profile is visible from many points in the Ampezzo Valley, and the sound of its bells marks the rhythm of daily life and local festivities.

#3. Corso Italia
Cortina's main pedestrian boulevard is lined with boutiques, luxury shops, and

traditional artisan stores. Strolling along Corso Italia is a must for soaking in the town's fashionable atmosphere. During December, it is transformed into a winter wonderland for the Cortina Fashion Weekend and Christmas markets.

#4. Museo d'Arte Moderna Mario Rimoldi

Located inside Ciasa de ra Regoles, this museum holds an outstanding collection of 20th-century Italian art. It includes paintings by De Chirico, Sironi, Morandi, and other modern masters. It's a surprising find in a mountain town and highlights Cortina's cultural side.

#5. Former Railway Station

Walk to the preserved structure of the old Cortina railway station, once part of the Dolomites Railway. Though trains no longer arrive, the building is a quiet reminder of the town's past. A scenic path, part of the Lunga Via delle Dolomiti, begins here and can be followed for a peaceful walk into the countryside.

Ski Cortina: World-Class Slopes in the Heart of the Dolomites

No winter trip to Cortina is complete without time on the slopes. As part of the legendary Dolomiti Superski network, Cortina offers an alpine experience that is as dramatic and refined as the town itself, unforgettable in both scenery and atmosphere. When December's chill settles in, Cortina d'Ampezzo transforms into a skier's paradise. The resort provides direct access to more than 120 kilometers (75 miles) of runs from town, with 1,200 kilometers (745 miles) across the greater Dolomiti Superski area, all covered by a single ski pass.

Mountains of Cortina d'Ampezzo

Main Ski Areas:

- **Tofana Area**, closest to town with access from the Freccia nel Cielo cable car, is ideal for intermediate and advanced skiers. It features World Cup and Olympic slopes, including the thrilling Olympia delle Tofane. https://www.freccianelcielo.com/en/

- **Faloria-Cristallo-Mietres**, accessible by cable car from the town center (Piazza Roma), offers long, scenic runs and spectacular views. Mietres is quieter and well-suited for families. https://faloriacristallo.it/en/

- **Cinque Torri–Lagazuoi**, a bit farther out but reachable by ski bus or car, is famous for its dramatic beauty and the stunning Lagazuoi Armentarola run, one of the most breathtaking descents in the Alps. https://lagazuoi.it/index_en.php

Ski Pass and Info:

The Dolomiti Superski Pass grants access to all ski areas in the Dolomites; passes are available for daily or weekly use and can be purchased online or in town. https://www.dolomitisuperski.com/it/home

A more localized Skipass Cortina Only is also available for those staying closer to town.

Getting to the Slopes:

You don't need a car in Cortina itself; ski buses and free shuttles efficiently connect the slopes, hotels, and town center. If you're arriving by train or bus from Venice, you can rent skis and purchase passes upon arrival. However, a car can be helpful for reaching more distant areas like Lagazuoi or for connecting to the Alta Badia or Arabba ski zones.

Equipment Rental and Lessons:

Snow Service Cortina is centrally located and offers high-end equipment with online booking. https://www.snowservice.it/

Scuola Sci Cortina provides both private and group lessons for all skill levels. https://scuolascicortina.com/

Key Ski Season Dates:

Opening Weekend aligns with Cortina Fashion Weekend in early December.

Full Ski Season typically runs from late November to mid-April, depending on snowfall.

Peak Periods include Christmas and New Year's, Carnival, and February holidays; advance booking is highly recommended.

Events and Highlights:

World Cup Races take place in January on the Tofana slopes.

Cortina will also co-host the 2026 Winter Olympics alongside Milan, adding even more prestige to its legendary ski terrain.

Logistics

Train: Cortina d'Ampezzo does not have its own train station. The nearest station is Calalzo di Cadore, located approximately 35 kilometers (21 miles) south of Cortina. Travelers can take a train from Venice Santa Lucia to Calalzo di Cadore, followed by a Dolomiti Bus service or taxi to reach Cortina.

Bus: Cortina is accessible via several bus services: Cortina Express offers routes connecting Cortina with Venice, Treviso, and other regional destinations. ATVO provides connections from Venice, Mestre, and Treviso to Cortina d'Ampezzo.

Car: Cortina is accessible by car via the A27 motorway, exiting at Pian di Vedoia, and continuing on the SS51 Alemagna road. From the north, drivers can use the A22 motorway, exiting at Bressanone, and proceeding through Dobbiaco and the SS51.

Parking: Parking options in Cortina include both free and paid areas. Due to ongoing preparations for the 2026 Winter Olympics, some central parking lots may be closed or limited. Alternative parking areas have been established, such as the Acquabona lot, which offers a free shuttle service to the town center.

Restaurant Recommendations

Ai Forni. Address: Via del Mercato 12
A refined restaurant in the town center known for its wood-fired specialties and elegant alpine decor. The menu highlights local ingredients with dishes such as venison, homemade pasta, and grilled meats. Ideal for a cozy yet upscale dining experience.

Villa Oretta. Address: Via Guido Rossa 2
Set in a charming villa with views over the Ampezzo Valley, this family-run restaurant is renowned for combining Ladin traditions with Venetian cuisine. Fresh seafood, risottos, and seasonal dishes are complemented by an extensive wine list.

Ampezzo Pizza. Address: Via Roma 23
A casual and popular spot for pizza lovers, offering a wide selection of wood-fired pizzas in a relaxed setting. Fast service, friendly staff, and a convenient location make it a favorite among both visitors and locals.

Accommodation

Hotel Dolomiti. Address: Corso Italia 202
A traditional, family-run hotel located right on the main pedestrian street. Rooms are comfortable with alpine-style furnishings and mountain views. Known for its warm hospitality and central location, it's an excellent base for exploring the town on foot.

Grand Hotel Savoia. Address: Via Roma 62
This 5-star historic hotel combines elegance and luxury with breathtaking mountain views. Built in 1912, it has hosted royalty and celebrities. The spa, fine dining, and classic interiors make it one of the premier places to stay in the Dolomites.

Hotel Cristallina. Address: Via Campo di Sotto 1
A cozy three-star hotel slightly outside the main pedestrian zone, offering a peaceful atmosphere and warm service. It features wood-beamed ceilings, simple rooms, and easy access to ski lifts and walking trails.

Hotel Olympia. Address: Via Zuel di Sopra 1
A charming budget-friendly option with comfortable rooms and a rustic alpine ambiance. Near the Olympic ski jump area, it's ideal for outdoor enthusiasts looking for convenient access to ski slopes and hiking routes.

Day Trip Options: Nearby Sites, Cities, and Towns

Auronzo di Cadore. Distance from Cortina: 32 kilometers (20 miles). Tucked along the shores of Lake Santa Caterina, Auronzo di Cadore is a postcard-perfect village surrounded by dramatic peaks. It's best known as a base for visiting the Tre Cime di Lavaredo, one of the most iconic mountain formations in the Dolomites.

The town itself offers a relaxing lakefront promenade, a historic center, and mountain trails suitable for every level of hiker. In summer, the lake sparkles with canoes and paddleboats, while in winter, snowshoeing and cross-country skiing take over. It's a scenic and peaceful escape that's easy to reach yet filled with natural beauty.

San Vito di Cadore. Distance from Cortina: 11 kilometers (7 miles). Just a short drive south of Cortina, San Vito di Cadore offers a quieter, family-friendly alternative with equally stunning mountain views. The town is framed by Monte Pelmo and Antelao, and its trails are ideal for relaxed walks or more adventurous hikes. San Vito is also home to small museums and cultural centers that celebrate Ladin traditions.

It's a perfect spot for travelers who want to escape the buzz of Cortina while still enjoying the dramatic scenery and rich alpine culture. In winter, it has its own ski area with gentler slopes, making it ideal for beginners and families.

Cortina Festivals and Sagre Throughout the Year

Sagra d'Ampezzo

First Sunday of July

The summer of village fests begins on the first Sunday of July, with the town fair, in Italian: "Sagra d'Ampezzo," a typical event with stalls all along "Corso Italia," the pedestrian center of Cortina. During the fair representatives of the various districts compete in a series of sporting events, including "the running race of the districts," known with its dialect name "Ra Corsa dei Seštiére," the stump saw and the tug of war.

The event is a moment of celebration and sharing rich in tradition for the Ampezzan population, with the Sestieri (neighborhood districts) setting up food service with various gazebos along Corso Italia.

Una Montagna di Libri (A Mountain of Books)

July (summer edition) & winter edition (December–April)

A two-edition literary festival (summer & winter) hosting author talks, readings, and book presentations in iconic open-air and indoor venues. Started in 2009, it has featured renowned writers like Emmanuel Carrère and Peter Cameron.

Rosadira Festival

Weekend in late August

A unique marriage between nature and lifestyle. Three days of music, art, fashion and design in the magical frame of the Queen of The Dolomites. Dance floors, workshops, sport activities, exhibitions and much more will make an unforgettable experience to live and savor the beauty of nature.

The festival is indeed a creative fusion of music, art, fashion, design, outdoor sports, and workshops set against the dramatic backdrop of the Dolomites. The name comes from L'Enrosadira, the phenomenon where, at dawn and sunset, the peaks of the Dolomites take on a pink coloration.

Fèšta de ra Bàndes (Festival of the Bands)

Last Sunday of August

The Marching Bands Festival of Cortina is also known as "Ra Fèšta de ra Bàndes" in the local dialect or "Festa Delle Bande" in Italian. It is a week of festivities and music where, each evening, there is an open-air concert played by different music bands from the area.

The event ends on the last Sunday of August with a day of festivities in which all the marching bands parade down Corso Italia. "Ra Fèŝta de ra Bàndes" was created in 1977.

Delicious Festival Dolomiti

Last weekend of September

A two-day event featuring sporting competitions, including races and gourmet dishes from Cortina restaurateurs served in the PalaDelicious pavilion, with evening entertainment including music and DJ sets.

CHAPTER TWENTY-EIGHT

Twilight in Treviso

Welcoming the New Year with Fire and Tradition

Brusa la Vecia / Piroea Paroea (Panevin)

Where: Treviso and across the Veneto, including Venice Lagoon islands, Conegliano, San Donà di Piave, and many rural villages

When: Evening of January 5 (Eve of the Epiphany).

Average Festival Temperatures: High 9°C (48°F). Low 0°C (32°F).

Treviso: A Living City of Water, History, and Art

The first time I saw Treviso, I was surprised by the architectural beauty of its narrow streets and canals. This is not Venice, but it doesn't try to be. Here, medieval towers rise above slow-moving waters where herons fish, and Renaissance frescoes peek out from behind ivy-covered walls. It is a quieter city, one that rewards curiosity.

Encircled by its original medieval walls, Treviso is remarkably compact and walkable. Flowing past the city, the Sile and Cagnan rivers mold it, branching into canals under bridges and along homes seemingly rooted in the water.

We first came here as a side trip from Venice, invited by friends for an aperitivo. That evening blossomed into a love affair with Treviso. Now, whenever the crowds in Venice feel overwhelming, we escape to this riverside gem just thirty minutes away by train.

Treviso does not clamor for attention. It reveals itself slowly: a frescoed Madonna on a quiet wall, a courtyard glimpsed through an open door, a watermill still turning in the current. As we have returned over the years, we have come to know its rhythms, where to find the best cicchetti, which café offers the finest people watching, which bakery still sells warm focaccia before noon.

Our friends have introduced us to neighbors, restaurant owners, and shopkeepers who greet us like locals. Treviso has become a kind of secret Italy for us, where the past lives on in the present and where every visit uncovers something new.

Treviso's Canals and Watermill

The Hidden Legacy of Treviso

Treviso's story begins long before the Roman Empire. It was a Venetic and Celtic settlement before becoming the Roman town of Tarvisium in the first century BC. Strategically located near the Via Postumia, it flourished as a regional hub. The Romans laid out a grid of streets, parts of which still shape the historic center today.

By the fifth century AD, Treviso had grown into a bishopric and early Christian stronghold. During the Middle Ages, it became a thriving commune known for its wool production, civic architecture, and artistic culture. Its university, founded in 1263, was one of the earliest in Italy.

In the fourteenth century, Treviso voluntarily came under the protection of the Republic of Venice, becoming one of the mainland terraferma cities. The Venetians fortified the city, built graceful bridges and palaces, and expanded its water management systems. This period also saw the rise of Prosecco viticulture in the surrounding hills.

After Venice's fall in 1797, Treviso passed briefly through Napoleonic hands before becoming part of the Austrian Empire, and finally the Kingdom of Italy in 1866. Though it suffered damage in both World Wars, the city has restored much of its architectural heritage.

Today, Treviso is a prosperous and cultured city of about 85,000 residents. It is home to companies like Benetton, De'Longhi, and Geox, but also remains rich in tradition. Its painted facades, peaceful canals, and lived-in piazzas offer a unique blend of history and daily life without the crowds.

Bread and Wine Festival

The Bread and Wine Festival, known locally as Brusa la Vecia (Burn the Old Woman), is rooted in Italy's ancient past. Long before Christianity, Celtic tribes lit bonfires and burned effigies to purify and appease their deities. Farmers gathered around the flames, singing and shouting good wishes for the year ahead.

Rather than abolish these beloved customs, early Christian leaders adapted them to the liturgical calendar. Some scholars trace Brusa la Vecia to the Roman Saturnalia, originally celebrated around the winter solstice. As the solstice became associated with the birth of Christ, the fire ritual shifted to the eve of the Epiphany, January 5th, when Christians commemorate the arrival of the Magi.

By the Middle Ages, the tradition was fully integrated into Christian celebrations. The burning effigy came to symbolize purification and renewal, a way to cast off the misfortunes of the past year and begin the new one with hope.

The Ceremony: A Dance of Fire and Fortune

At the heart of the celebration stands a towering pyre, built from dry branches, brushwood, and symbolic household discards—items no longer needed, representing what is ready to be left behind. Atop this pile sits la vecia, a puppet-like figure with exaggerated features who embodies the hardships of the past year.

As the fire is lit, families gather in the winter dark, warmed by the flickering light and the scent of burning wood. Children watch in awe as the flames reach upward and sparks spiral into the night sky.

One of the most captivating moments is the prognostico, the reading of the fire. A local vate (bard) observes the direction of the flames and smoke to predict the community's fortune. If the sparks blow east, good things are coming; if west, challenges may lie ahead.

Community Spirit and Local Flavor

The bonfire becomes more than just a symbolic act; it is a shared experience. As la vecia burns, people sip cups of steaming vin brulé (mulled wine), enjoy sandwiches with codeghin (a local sausage), and listen to folk music and humorous rhymes. It is a time to reconnect, laugh, reflect, and look ahead together.

Across the Veneto and neighboring regions, Brusa la Vecia takes slightly different forms. In Treviso and its surroundings, bonfires are lit on the evening of January 5th. Celebrations are held at sites such as Prato della Fiera and Fiera di Sant'Artemio, where official speeches, music, and the main fire begin around 6:00 p.m.

In smaller towns, parish groups and cultural associations preserve deeply local versions of the festival. There, you might hear the prognostico read in dialect or see traditional dances passed down for generations. Whether grand or intimate, each celebration captures the essence of renewal, community, and the enduring power of fire to mark life's turning points.

Festival Events

5:00 p.m.

Held at multiple sites, including Prato della Fiera and Fiera di Sant'Artemio. Events begin at 5:00 p.m., with official speeches and music by 6:00 p.m. A short blessing or traditional song may precede the lighting.

Special Festival Food and Drink
Vin Brule & the Pinza

Vin brulè (pronounced veen broo-LAY) is a traditional hot mulled wine served throughout Italy during winter festivals, particularly during the Epiphany bonfire celebrations in January, such as Panevin, Brusa la Vecia, or Piroea Paroea in Treviso and the Veneto region.

The name comes from the French vin brûlé, meaning "burned wine," and it refers to red wine gently heated with spices, such as cinnamon, cloves, and star anise, and often sweetened with sugar, orange peel, and lemon zest. It is sometimes enhanced with a splash of brandy or grappa.

At these January festivals, vin brulè is traditionally served outdoors around the bonfire, warming hands and spirits as villagers watch the effigy burn and await the reading of the sparks. The drink is a symbol of community warmth, seasonal comfort, and the ushering in of good fortune for the new year.

Pinza is a traditional sweet, dense cake from the Veneto region, especially associated with Epiphany bonfire festivals like Panevin and Brusa la Vecia celebrated on January 5 in Treviso and surrounding towns.

Historically a peasant dessert, Pinza was made in winter using simple, readily available ingredients: cornmeal, flour, dried figs, raisins, nuts, fennel seeds, and a splash of grappa or wine. Modern versions may also include apples, pine nuts, candied orange peel, or even cocoa, but the cake retains its rustic, hearty texture and earthy flavor.

During the festival, Pinza is baked in large round loaves and served in slices around the bonfire, alongside vin brulè (hot mulled wine). The cake symbolizes abundance, the fruits of the land, and the closing of the old year. Its rich, warming character makes it a beloved seasonal treat that brings families and neighbors together on a bitter January night.

8:00 p.m.

The fire usually burns bright until about 8:00 or 8:30 p.m., after which families return home to prepare for the Epiphany morning and the arrival of la Befana, the good witch who brings sweets to children.

Other Notable Bonfire Celebrations in the Veneto

- **Conegliano**: The bonfire near the Piave River is known for its large turnout and strong winds, ideal for spark-watching.

- **Jesolo**: Fireworks and carnival rides add flair to this coastal version.

- **Venetian Lagoon Islands**: On Murano, Burano, and Sant'Erasmo, locals still gather to burn smaller bonfires and make weather predictions over the lagoon.

Walking Tour of Treviso

#1. Duomo di San Pietro Apostolo (Cathedral of Treviso)

Treviso's cathedral, dedicated to Saint Peter the Apostle, stands on the site of an ancient Roman temple. The current structure dates back to the 11th–12th centuries but has undergone many renovations, resulting in a fascinating mix of Romanesque, Renaissance, and Neoclassical elements. The exterior is rather austere, but step inside to discover an elegant nave, peaceful crypt, and side chapels adorned with Renaissance frescoes.

Of special note is the Malchiostro Chapel, which contains a celebrated fresco by Titian, painted in 1517. This Annunciation scene is both dramatic and delicate, with the angel Gabriel rendered in flowing robes and the Virgin Mary appearing startled yet graceful. The chapel also features a refined Renaissance portal by Tullio and Antonio Lombardo. Don't miss the crypt below the main altar. It dates from the early Christian era and holds relics and tombs of Treviso's bishops.

#2. Piazza dei Signori

Treviso's central piazza is a hub of civic life and one of the most atmospheric corners of the city. The square is framed by graceful porticoes, cafes, and historic government buildings. Dominating the square is the Palazzo dei Trecento, a 13th-century brick building that once housed the town council. Though damaged in WWII, it was meticulously restored and now serves as a venue for exhibitions and public events. The piazza often hosts cultural gatherings, markets, and is a favorite spot for locals enjoying a spritz in the afternoon sun.

#3. Palazzo del Podestà and Torre Civica

Next to Piazza dei Signori, the Palazzo del Podestà was once the seat of the Venetian-appointed magistrate. It features stately arches and a dignified clock tower known as the Torre Civica, which rises elegantly above the city skyline. The area beneath the porticoes contains shops and cafes, making this a lively corridor and a historic monument. The buildings speak to Treviso's role under the Serenissima (the Venetian Republic), when it served as an important inland hub.

#4. Chiesa di San Nicolò (Church of St. Nicholas)

This massive Dominican church, located a short walk from the historic center, is one of Treviso's architectural gems. Constructed in the late 13th and early 14th centuries, it was funded in part by local noble families and boasts a rare combination of brick Gothic and Cistercian austerity. The tall nave is lined with enormous cylindrical columns, creating a solemn, monastic atmosphere.

The impressive Chiesa di San Nicolo

The highlight is found in the Sala del Capitolo (Chapter House), which features a cycle of frescoes painted in 1352 by Tommaso da Modena. These include one of the earliest known images of eyeglasses, depicting a monk hunched over a manuscript, glasses perched on his nose. The frescoes are detailed, humanizing, and filled with insight into monastic life in the Middle Ages. The main church also contains a striking wooden crucifix and fresco fragments that hint at its former decorative grandeur. San Nicolò is still an active parish and keeps its contemplative spirit.

#5. Chiesa di Santa Lucia (Church of St. Lucy)

This small church near Via Martiri della Libertà is often overlooked by tourists but beloved by locals. Its origins date back to the 14th century, and while the interior is modest, it houses several devotional artworks and has a hushed, intimate feel. Locals visit to light candles and offer prayers to Saint Lucy, patroness of sight. It's a peaceful place to pause between stops.

#6. Mulino della Pescheria (Water Mill of Treviso)

Just around the corner from the fish market is a beautifully preserved watermill, with a large turning wheel powered by the canal's current. Set against a charming stuccoed building and shaded by leafy trees, it offers a postcard-perfect view of Treviso's watery soul.

The mill represents the city's medieval use of water power for grain and textile production and adds a sense of quiet nostalgia to the walking route. Pause here for a photo or to watch the tranquil ripple of water pass under ancient stone bridges.

#7. Isola della Pescheria (Fish Island)

Tucked between two branches of the Cagnan River, this artificial island is home to Treviso's open-air fish market. The market is busiest in the mornings Tuesday through Saturday, but even outside of those hours, the setting is picturesque. Water flows on all sides, and charming footbridges connect it to the surrounding streets. Swans glide by, and weeping willows dip into the canals, creating one of Treviso's most romantic corners.

#8. Buranelli Canal

From the fish market, stroll north along the canal paths that follow the Canale dei Buranelli. Named after the fishermen and merchants from Burano who lived here during Venetian rule, this stretch is flanked by pastel buildings whose lower façades dip directly into the water. Reflections ripple gently at dusk, making it a favorite spot for photography. During the holidays, lights illuminate the canal, adding to the fairy-tale feel.

#9. Porta San Tomaso

This ornate city gate, built in 1518, once served as the northern entrance to Treviso. It's a magnificent example of Renaissance architecture, with Corinthian columns, relief sculptures, and a prominent sculpture of the Winged Lion of Saint Mark, signaling Treviso's allegiance to Venice.

The gate remains perfectly preserved and is surrounded by open space where the old city walls once stood. From here, you can loop back into the historic center or continue walking along the riverside promenade.

Canal Views Treviso

Logistics

Train: Treviso is served by the Treviso Centrale train station, located just a 10-minute walk from the historic center. Frequent regional trains connect Treviso to Venice Santa Lucia (30–35 minutes), Padua, Udine, and Trieste, making it a convenient base or day trip from nearby cities.

Bus: Local bus services in Treviso are operated by MOM (Mobilità di Marca). Buses run regularly within the city and to nearby towns in the province, including Conegliano, Castelfranco Veneto, and Asolo. There are also airport shuttle buses to Treviso Airport (TSF) and Venice Marco Polo Airport (VCE). Tickets can be purchased at ticket offices, tabacchi shops, and via the MOMUP mobile app.

Car: Treviso is easily accessible by car, with the A27 motorway connecting it to Venice and Belluno. The SS13 and SS53 roads also provide regional connections. While driving is convenient for reaching nearby countryside destinations such as Valdobbiadene or Cison di Valmarino, visitors should note that the historic center of Treviso is a ZTL (limited traffic zone), restricted to non-residents during most of the day.

Parking: For visitors arriving by car, several public parking lots are available just outside the ZTL. The most convenient options include: Park Miani (Via Giovanni Miani, 4), a short walk from the city walls. Piazzale Burchiellati (Viale Burchiellati, near Porta San Tomaso) is ideal for access to the northern gate and historic sights. Park Frà Giocondo (Viale Frà Giocondo, 11) is convenient for reaching Piazza dei Signori and the center. Most parking areas are paid, with hourly or daily rates, and many are equipped with digital meters or app-based payment systems.

Recommended Restaurants

Da Pino Piazza dei Signori. P.za dei Signori, 23

We enjoyed pizza and local specialities at Da Pino in Piazza dei Segnori. They have beautiful outside seating, delightful staff, and delicious food, highly recommended.

Osteria Arman. Address: Via Manzoni, 27

A cozy, family-run restaurant with a traditional tavern feel, Osteria Arman is beloved by locals for its hearty, authentic cuisine. The atmosphere is warm and rustic, with wooden beams and vintage decor. Diners can enjoy regional favorites like risotto al radicchio (Treviso's prized bitter red chicory) or homemade pastas with seasonal sauces. The wine list focuses on local vintages, especially Prosecco and reds from the Veneto.

Antico Portico. Address: Piazzetta Sant'Andrea, 5

Set in an elegant historic building tucked into a quiet square, Antico Portico is known for combining traditional Veneto recipes with modern culinary techniques. The restaurant offers a refined atmosphere that's ideal for a special dinner. Dishes are beautifully plated, and the staff can suggest thoughtful wine pairings from their well-curated list. Favorites include seasonal fish dishes, fresh pasta, and inventive desserts.

Trattoria Toni del Spin. Address: Via Inferiore, 7

A rustic trattoria with a long-standing reputation among locals, Toni del Spin serves hearty Trevigiano dishes that are especially satisfying in winter. The menu highlights polenta, grilled meats, and traditional Venetian stews. The dining room, with its exposed brick and casual, friendly atmosphere, feels like stepping into a beloved neighborhood institution. Reservations are recommended, especially for dinner.

Accomodation

Maison Matilda. Address: Via Riccati, 44

A refined boutique hotel set in a beautifully restored historic mansion, Maison Matilda blends old-world charm with contemporary designer interiors. Each room is uniquely decorated with luxurious fabrics, elegant furnishings, and thoughtful details that create a warm, sophisticated atmosphere.

Hotel Continental. Address: Via Roma, 16

Centrally located 4-star hotel near the train station and major attractions. Spacious rooms and convenient amenities.

Hotel Rovere. Address: Viale Gian Giacomo Felissent, 13

For visitors seeking a peaceful retreat just outside the historic center, Hotel Rovere offers modern accommodations in a quiet residential area. The hotel is known for its excellent service, comfortable, stylish rooms, and a welcoming, family-run atmosphere.

Day Trips: Nearby Sites, Cities, and Towns

Conegliano. 32 kilometers (20 miles) from Treviso. Conegliano is a graceful hill town at the edge of the Dolomites, in the heart of the Prosecco DOCG wine zone. Together with Valdobbiadene, it anchors the celebrated Strada del Prosecco, the first wine road established in Italy. Conegliano is also the birthplace of Cima da Conegliano, a Renaissance painter whose influence can still be seen throughout the city.

Surrounded by terraced vineyards and dotted with frescoed palazzi, Conegliano blends medieval elegance with rustic Veneto charm. The town is ideal for wine tastings, scenic strolls, and sampling local cuisine.

Among the key places to visit is the Castle of Conegliano (Castello di Conegliano). Reachable by a short walk uphill through the park, the castle offers panoramic views of the vineyards and rooftops. Inside, the Civic Museum houses archaeological finds, weapons, manuscripts, and works by local painters, including pieces by Cima da Conegliano.

Strolling along Via XX Settembre, the town's main street often called a "frescoed street," you'll encounter Renaissance and Baroque façades, arcades, and cafés. Look up to see allegorical paintings that once conveyed stories to townspeople who could not read. The Duomo di Santa Maria Annunziata e San Leonardo, adjacent to the Scuola dei Battuti, features a serene interior with Gothic arches and a stunning altarpiece by Cima da Conegliano, painted in 1493.

For wine lovers, Prosecco wine tastings are a highlight. Many small producers offer tastings and cellar tours. Look for Ca' di Rajo, Borgoluce, or Villa Sandi nearby, all known for producing classic Prosecco Superiore DOCG.

Treviso Festivals and Sagre Throughout the Year

Festa di San Valentino

February 14

In many parts of Treviso province, especially in smaller parishes, Saint Valentine's Day is not just for lovers but is celebrated with church services and local fairs. Some towns hold themed markets and evening concerts.

Treviso Carnevale

February or March (dates vary based on Easter)

Treviso's take on Carnival includes parades, costumed entertainers, children's events, and food stands offering traditional treats like frittelle (fried dough balls). Though smaller than Venice's version, it's a festive and family-friendly celebration.

Festa della Liberazione

April 25

Italy's Liberation Day is marked by ceremonies in Treviso's main piazzas, parades by the Carabinieri, and musical events honoring the fall of Fascism and the end of World War II.

Festa di San Liberale (Patron Saint of Treviso)

April 27

San Liberale, a 5th-century bishop and protector of Treviso, is honored with Masses at the Cathedral, a civic procession, and in some years, classical music concerts or historical reenactments. His relics are kept in the Duomo's crypt.

Spring Markets and Flower Festivals

Early May

Held in central Treviso and nearby towns, this multi-day spring market features flowers, regional food tastings, wine stalls, and performances. The city's medieval streets become a lively stage for cultural life and shopping.

Festa della Repubblica

June 2

Italy's Republic Day includes flag-raising ceremonies in front of Treviso's municipal buildings and commemorative events throughout the day. Though more low-key than other festivals, it holds great civic pride.

Jazz Festival

May or June

One of the province's leading summer music events, Marca Jazz features local and international jazz musicians performing in open-air venues, cloisters, and historic palaces. Some events are free and spread across Treviso and nearby towns. https://www.trevisosuonajazz.it/

Suoni di Marca Festival (Music Festival)

Late July to mid-August

A two-week music festival held along the Treviso city walls at Bastioni San Marco. Concerts range from rock to indie, jazz to folk, with street food stands and craft stalls. It's one of the largest music events in the province, drawing thousands.

https://www.suonidimarca.it/

Treviso Comic Book Festival

Late September

This internationally recognized event showcases illustration, graphic novels, and independent comics. The city becomes a living gallery, with exhibitions, workshops, and artist talks across museums, shops, and cafes.

https://www.tcbf.it/24/

Festa della Castagna (Chestnut Festival)

October (weekends)

Several villages in the Treviso hills (such as Combai and Cison di Valmarino) celebrate the chestnut harvest with rustic festivals offering roasted chestnuts, chestnut honey, grappa, and traditional music.

Festa di San Martino (St. Martin)

November 11

This feast day of Saint Martin is widely celebrated in Treviso with processions for children, sweetbreads in the shape of Saint Martin on horseback, and market stalls selling toys, candies, and warm seasonal foods.

Natale a Treviso (Christmas in Treviso)

Early December through January 6

Treviso's historic center becomes a winter wonderland with Christmas lights, artisan markets, choirs, and a skating rink in Piazza dei Signori. Events include concerts, living nativity scenes, and family activities culminating on Epiphany.

CHAPTER TWENTY-NINE

FestaFusion Carnevale di Venezia

Art and Allure

FestaFusion Carnevale di Venezia

Where: Venice

When: Usually February. Begins two Saturdays before Fat Tuesday.

Average Festival Temperatures: High 10°C (50°F). Low 0°C (32°F).

#FestaFusion: Venice Carnevale is not a single celebration but a spectacular series of interconnected festivals and events spanning several weeks.

The History of Carnevale: Venice's Magnificent Masked Festival

The enchanting Venice Carnival traces its origins to the 11th century, emerging from the shadows of medieval Venice when the Serenissima Repubblica (Most Serene Republic) sought diversions during the bleak winter months. What began as a modest street celebration exploded into a magnificent cultural phenomenon during the 18th century, Carnevale's golden age, when Venice glittered as Europe's pleasure capital.

During this era, the Grand Canal transformed into a shimmering parade of ornate gondolas, while palazzos hosted lavish masked balls where candlelight danced across gilded ballrooms. The city became a magnificent theater where reality and fantasy intertwined beneath a confetti sky. Aristocrats spent fortunes on elaborate costumes, competing to create the most spectacular impressions while reveling alongside merchants, artisans, and visitors from across Europe.

The ingenious Venetian masks, crafted by specialized artisans called mascherari, whose guild had strict rules and secret techniques, became powerful symbols of liberation. Behind these intricate disguises of papier mâché, porcelain, and leather, a duchess might dance with a gondolier, forbidden lovers could meet openly, and gambling debts accumulated without immediate consequences. The famous phrase "Buongiorno, Siora Maschera" ("Good day, Masked Lady/Sir") acknowledged this delicious anonymity that pervaded the city for months.

Basilica di San Marco

When Napoleon's troops conquered Venice in 1797, they saw the masks not as innocent revelry but as dangerous tools for subterfuge and rebellion. The ban on masks marked the beginning of a carnival twilight that would last nearly two centuries. During this dormant period, Carnevale lived on only in wistful paintings and the fading memories of Venetians who recalled the festival's former glory.

Venetian artists, historians, and leaders joined forces in 1979 to bring back the tradition. Their efforts breathed new life into ancient customs, and within a decade, the Venice Carnival reclaimed its place as one of the world's most extraordinary celebrations, drawing photographers, filmmakers, and dreamers captivated by its otherworldly beauty.

Throughout the carnival period, Venice hosts many free events, including historical re-enactments, grand parades, water regattas, street performances, live music, and competitions for the best masks and costumes.

For those seeking more exclusive experiences, official dinners, private parties, and masked balls are organized in beautiful Venetian palaces where guests can relive the ancient splendor of Venetian Carnivals past.

Costumes of Carnival

*See the end of this chapter for a Venice Carnival 14 Day Summarized Timeline

Events of Carnival

Opening Week

La Festa delle Marie (Feast of the Mary's)

When: First Saturday of Carnival (procession), with the crowning on Martedì Grasso (Fat Tuesday)

Where: From San Pietro di Castello to Piazza San Marco

The Feast of the Maries, is one of the oldest and most evocative traditions of the Venice Carnival. With roots in a 10th-century legend, this grand parade celebrates beauty, virtue, and the history of the Venetian Republic.

A Legend from the Republic's Early Days

The tradition dates back to 948 AD, during the annual blessing of marriages on February 2nd, the Feast of the Purification of the Virgin (later known as the Presentation of the Lord). According to historical chronicles, the Doge of Venice would bless twelve poor but virtuous brides, selected from the city's humble families, providing them with fine gowns, jewels, and dowries paid for by the Republic. The city would erupt in joyful celebration as the brides walked in procession through the streets, symbolizing Venetian generosity and civic unity.

However, on one such day, tragedy struck: a band of pirates from Dalmatia invaded the city and kidnapped the twelve brides, their dowries, and the ceremonial treasure. The alarm was raised, and Venetian citizens pursued and defeated the pirates, rescuing the women and returning them to safety. This act of heroism further elevated the story into legend.

For centuries, the event was reenacted annually. By the 14th century, it had become a central part of Carnival, drawing crowds from across the Republic. Over time, the celebration faded, but it was revived in the late 20th century and remains a treasured part of today's Venetian Carnival.

The Modern-Day Parade

Each year, twelve local young women, chosen through a selective competition, are named the "Marie" and represent the historical brides. Over several days of Carnival, they attend events, receptions, and photo sessions, always dressed in elaborate Renaissance gowns, often hand-stitched by Venetian artisans and costume houses.

The highlight is the grand public parade, which takes place on the first Saturday of Carnival:

- Starting Point: Church of San Pietro di Castello (a nod to Venice's ancient history)

- Route: Along Via Garibaldi, through Riva degli Schiavoni

- Ending Point: Piazza San Marco, where each Marie is introduced onstage

The parade features flag-throwers, musicians, nobility in period dress, and Doge re-enactors, all accompanied by cheers, music, and camera flashes from the crowd. It's one of the most photogenic and lively daytime events of Carnival.

Crowning of the "Maria dell'Anno"

On Fat Tuesday, during the last day of Carnival, one of the twelve young women is crowned Maria of the Year in Piazza San Marco. She receives gifts, honors, and the opportunity to perform the Flight of the Angel from the Campanile (bell tower) the following year, an enormous and emotional role watched by thousands.

Festival Tips

Best Viewing Spots: Along Riva degli Schiavoni or near the Doge's Palace in the early afternoon

Arrive by 1:30 p.m. to secure a delightful spot; parades usually reach the piazza around 2:30 p.m.

Photographers: This is one of the best chances to capture the rich costumes of Carnival in full daylight

Free Event: No ticket required

Festa Veneziana sull'Acqua (Venice on the Water)

When: Saturday evening.

Where: Rio di Cannaregio

The Festival of Venice on the Water marks the spectacular and theatrical opening ceremony of Venice's world-famous Carnival. Set along the Rio di Cannaregio, one of the city's most charming canals, this waterborne spectacle transforms the historic district into a dazzling open-air stage where Venetian tradition meets modern magic.

As twilight falls, thousands of spectators line the bridges and embankments of Cannaregio. Anticipation builds as the lights dim and the first floating platform appears. What follows is an unforgettable blend of theater, acrobatics, music, and visual storytelling, all performed on boats and floating stages that glide silently across the water.

Each year's theme changes, but the format includes:

- Giant illuminated floats, and artistic barges designed as mythical creatures, carnival masks, or symbolic Venetian figures.

- Live performers on boats, including acrobats, dancers, and actors, all synchronized with haunting music and narration.

- Video projections, colored smoke, and laser lights projected onto surrounding buildings, creating a dreamlike experience that reflects in the water.

The show is usually divided into two or more "acts," each telling a symbolic story tied to Venetian history, culture, or imagination. The atmosphere is festive yet elegant, with both locals and visitors dressed in cloaks, capes, or full Carnival attire. It is free to attend, but arriving at least an hour early is essential to secure a good viewing spot.

Corteo Acqueo del Coordinamento Remiero di Voga alla Veneta (Water Parade and Regatta)

When: Sunday morning of the opening weekend, typically starting around 11:00 a.m.

Where: From the Basin of San Marco, traveling up the Grand Canal to Rio di Cannaregio

The Sunday following the Festa Veneziana sull'Acqua brings a beloved tradition that celebrates Venice's nautical soul: the Corteo Acqueo, or water parade. This event, organized by the Coordinamento Remiero di Voga alla Veneta, pays tribute to the art of Venetian rowing (voga alla veneta) and kicks off the daytime festivities of Carnevale.

Dozens of traditional Venetian boats, including gondolas, caorline, batèle, and sandoli, glide up the Grand Canal, each one lavishly decorated and rowed by costumed oarsmen and women in full 18th-century attire or whimsical Carnival regalia. The parade is a vivid living postcard of Venice's maritime legacy.

Gondolas on the Grand Canal

The route begins at the Basin of San Marco, passes beneath the Rialto Bridge, and continues toward the Cannaregio district, where crowds gather along the Fondamenta della Misericordia and Fondamenta de la Sensa. The spectacle typically arrives in Cannaregio around 11:30 a.m. to noon, where the boats are greeted with cheers, applause, and music.

When the flotilla reaches the Rio di Cannaregio, the waterway becomes a floating stage. Boats dock and participants step ashore to join the festive crowd.

The energy is jovial but respectful, a true celebration of Venetian heritage. There's no entrance fee, and the event draws both Venetians and international visitors.

Insider Tip: Arrive early to claim a viewing spot along the Fondamenta. Some locals set up camp before 10:00 a.m., and many balconies in the area are reserved by residents or hotels. Bring a thermos and enjoy breakfast canal-side as the boats approach.

Il Volo dell'Angelo (Flight of the Angel)

When: First Sunday of Carnival at 12:00 p.m.

Where: Piazza San Marco

Il Volo dell'Angelo is one of the most iconic and emotional moments of the Venice Carnival. At precisely noon on the first Sunday, a young woman dressed in an elaborate Renaissance gown is suspended by a secure harness and glides gracefully on a zipline from the top of the Campanile di San Marco down across the square to a stage in front of the Doge's Palace. The crowd below, often numbering in the tens of thousands, watches with awe, silence, and cheers as the angel "flies" above them, marking the true ceremonial opening of Carnevale.

Historical Background

The origins of this breathtaking tradition date back to the mid-16th century. The first performance wasn't by an "angel," but a Turkish acrobat who amazed Venetian nobles by walking a tightrope from a boat in the Grand Canal to the Campanile. So impressed was the Republic by the feat that it became a recurring act.

By the 18th century, the rope-walker was replaced by a costumed performer, usually a young man representing an angel, and the event was renamed Il Volo dell'Uomo Turco (The Flight of the Turkish Man), later strengthening into Il Volo dell'Angelo. Eventually, the role was assigned to a woman symbolizing purity, grace, and new beginnings, reflecting the spiritual symbolism of Carnival's pre-Lenten period.

Costumed performers, trumpeters, and flag throwers fill the square below. The angel waves and tosses confetti or flower petals into the crowd.

The flight was suspended for many years due to safety concerns but was dramatically revived in 2001, now using modern safety equipment. Since then, it has been performed annually by a Venetian woman, often the winner of the previous year's Festa delle Marie beauty and costume contest.

Event Atmosphere

The performance concludes with a greeting and quick speech onstage, often welcoming visitors to Carnevale and blessing the festivities.

Locals and tourists alike fill Piazza San Marco early in the morning to secure viewing spots. Many wear cloaks, capes, or full costumes, adding to the spectacle and communal energy.

Throughout the Week

Street Performances & Masquerade Magic

When: Daily from 11:00 a.m. to 9:00 p.m.

Where: Piazza San Marco and various locations

Actors, musicians, and dancers fill the piazzas and bridges of Venice, particularly around Piazza San Marco, the Arsenale, and along the Grand Canal.

Mask-Making Workshops & Costume Rentals

When: Daily

Where: Artisan studios throughout Venice

Venice's Carnival is not just a spectacle to observe; it's an immersive experience to wear. Throughout the city, artisan studios and historical ateliers open their doors to visitors who wish to create their own Venetian mask or rent full period costumes to step fully into the pageantry of Carnevale.

Mask of Carnival

*More detail below on masks and how to make costume reservations.

Best Masked Costume Contest (Concorso della Maschera più Bella)

When: Held daily in Piazza San Marco, with finals on the last Sunday

Participants parade across a catwalk in lavish period costumes. Judges select winners based on creativity, authenticity, and artistry.

Il Volo dell'Aquila (Flight of the Eagle)

When: Second Sunday at 12:00 p.m.

Where: Piazza San Marco.

Following the emotional symbolism of the Angel's flight, Il Volo dell'Aquila, or Flight of the Eagle, offers a bolder and often more theatrical aerial descent. Introduced more recently as a complement to Il Volo dell'Angelo, this performance takes place on the second Sunday of Carnival, also at high noon, and represents strength, courage, and renewal, qualities tied to the powerful imagery of the eagle.

While the Angel is traditionally a young woman chosen from the Festa delle Marie, the Eagle is usually a celebrity or prominent public figure, such as a sports champion, actor, or artist. They are dressed in a more modern or dramatic costume and descend by zipline from the Campanile di San Marco to the stage below in Piazza San Marco, thrilling crowds with unexpected flair or personal messages.

The Eagle's flight adds a layer of boldness to the Carnival celebrations and draws a massive crowd just like the Angel, continuing the Carnival's high-flying traditions with energy and spectacle.

Martedì Grasso (Fat Tuesday)

When: Final Tuesday of Carnival

Where: Throughout Venice, especially Piazza San Marco.

Martedì Grasso is the grand finale of Venice's Carnival, an exuberant celebration of indulgence, artistry, and joy before the austerity of Lent begins on Ash Wednesday.

Martedì Grasso, known in English as Shrove Tuesday or Fat Tuesday and in French as Mardi Gras, will be referred to by its authentic Italian name, Martedì Grasso, to honor its rich cultural traditions.

Throughout the day, Venice bursts into life with costume parades, street performers, and open-air concerts. The heart of the action is in Piazza San Marco, which transforms into a theatrical stage filled with dancers, musicians, jesters, and masked revelers in 18th-century splendor. Expect live music from morning through evening, and spontaneous performances erupting in small squares across the city.

The evening typically culminates in a fireworks display, often visible from St. Mark's Basin or along the Riva degli Schiavoni, casting shimmering reflections across the water. The mood is festive but tinged with nostalgia, as Venice bids farewell to its days of masked enchantment.

9:00 a.m. – 5:00 p.m.
Costume Parade & Mask Contest
Location: Piazza San Marco
Throughout the day, costumed participants showcase their elaborate outfits, with judges selecting winners for the "Best Mask" contest.

11:00 a.m. & 3:00 p.m.
Best Mask Contest Finals
Location: Piazza San Marco Stage

Final round of the mask competition, featuring the most creative and intricate designs.

12:00 p.m.
Award Ceremony for "La Maria dell'Anno"
Location: Piazza San Marco
The winner of the Festa delle Marie is crowned, celebrating the most graceful and elegant participant.

2:00 p.m. – 6:00 p.m.
Street Performances & Live Music
Locations: Various squares, including Campo Santo Stefano and Campo San Polo
A variety of performances, from acrobats and musicians to theatrical acts, bring the city's streets to life.

9:00 p.m.
Grand Fireworks Display
Location: St. Mark's Basin
A spectacular fireworks show over the water marks the culmination of carnival festivities.

10:30 p.m. – Midnight
Rowing of Silence (Regata Silenziosa)
Route: From Rialto Bridge to St. Mark's Basin
A serene procession of gondolas glides through the canals, accompanied by soft music and candlelight, offering a reflective end to the celebrations.

Carnival Dates

2026: January 31–February 17

2027: January 27–February 9

2028: February 27–March 7

2029: February 2-February 13

2030: February 23–March 5

Special Carnival Treats
Frittelle, Chiacchiere, Sarde in Soar

Frittelle Veneziane–Fried dough balls with raisins or filled with custard, chocolate, or zabaglione

Galani (or Chiacchiere)–Crispy sweet fried ribbons dusted with powdered sugar

Sarde in Saor–Marinated sardines served with onions, pine nuts, and raisins, a typical Venetian antipasto

---

Additional Detail on Getting Dressed for Carnival

Mask-Making Workshops

Venetian mask-makers invite visitors into their ateliers to experience the centuries-old craft of mask-making. These hands-on workshops typically last 1 to 2 hours, cost between €30 and €60, and include all materials. Under the guidance of expert artisans, participants paint and decorate traditional masks that they take home, a unique souvenir and an expression of personal creativity rooted in Venetian heritage.

Common mask types include:

- Bauta: A white mask with a prominent jawline and no mouth, often paired with a tricorn hat and black cloak, once used to preserve anonymity in both public and private spaces.

- Moretta: An oval-shaped velvet mask worn by noblewomen, held in place by a button between the teeth, evoking silence and mystique.

- Plague Doctor (Medico della peste): A long-beaked mask once worn by physicians during outbreaks, now one of the most iconic symbols of Carnival.

Top Artisan Workshops in Venice:

Kartaruga / Il Canovaccio. Address: Calle delle Bande, 5369, Castello

A respected family-run shop known for its high-quality papier mâché masks and deeply traditional techniques. Their workshops are immersive and friendly, ideal for all ages.

Ca' Macana. Address: Calle Cappeller 3215, Dorsoduro

One of the most famous mask-making studios in Venice, Ca' Macana has created masks for films like Eyes Wide Shut and offers workshops with historical context, step-by-step instruction, and a wide range of designs.

Dressing the Part: Become the Magic of Carnevale

If you're going to visit Venice during Carnival, you might as well dress the part. There are many shops throughout Venice, and even in the surrounding areas, that rent exquisite costumes, from simple period garb to elaborate noble attire worthy of the Doge himself.

Costumes come clean, pressed, and ready to wear, and yes, you can even rent the shoes! Most ateliers also offer wigs, masks, hats, and cloaks to complete your look. Whether you plan to attend a masked ball, join the costume parades, or simply stroll the streets in 18th-century splendor, renting a costume makes you part of the show.

Venice is home to high-end ateliers (design studios) such as:

Atelier Tiepolo (Hotel Danieli).

https://www.meetingeurope.com/costumes/costumes_index.htm

Antonia Sautter Atelier (creator of Il Ballo del Doge).

https://antoniasautter.it/

Vivovenetia (handmade rentals with hotel delivery).

https://www.vivovenetia.com/venice-carnival-costume-rental/

What's Included in a Full Costume Rental: A full costume rental includes a historically styled gown or suit, complete with corsets, vests, petticoats, sashes or waistcoats, and is complemented by hats, gloves, and handbags; optional add-ons such as wigs, cloaks, shoes, and jewelry are also available.

Estimated Rental Cost (3-Day Package):

- Standard Costume: €800 total (€400 first day, €200/day after)

- Luxury Costume: €1,200 total (€600 first day, €300/day after)

- Wigs: €80–€150/day

- Shoes: €50–€85/day

- Capes: €80/day

- Masks: Typically purchased separately for hygiene (€25–€150)

Booking Tips: When booking your costume, be sure to reserve at least three to six months in advance, especially if you plan to attend ticketed events like masquerade balls, and schedule a fitting session the day before your rental begins; many ateliers even offer hotel delivery and pickup, or room fittings with a dresser to assist you.

During the day, you'll see plenty of costumed participants parading through Piazza San Marco, the Palazzo Ducale, or along Campo Santa Maria Formosa, and you can be one of them. Even those not attending a formal event often rent a costume just to stroll and take part in the visual magic of Carnevale.

Venice Carnival Timeline Overview

A 12 Day Guide to the Rhythm of the Celebration

While exact dates vary slightly year to year, Venice's Carnival typically spans two weekends and the weekdays in between, building from intimate early events to a dramatic finale on *Martedì Grasso* (Fat Tuesday). Here's how the days unfold:

Day 1 – Opening Saturday

Festa Veneziana sull'Acqua (evening spectacle on Rio di Cannaregio)

La Festa delle Marie (afternoon historical parade from San Pietro di Castello to Piazza San Marco)

Day 2 – Opening Sunday

Water Parade and Regatta (morning on Grand Canal and Cannaregio)

Day 3–5 – Monday to Wednesday (Week 1)

Mask-making workshops, early costume rentals

Smaller-scale performances in squares like Campo San Polo

Day 6 – Thursday (Giovedì Grasso / Fat Thursday)

Pop-up performances and early balls. Traditional sweets and food tastings begin in earnest.

Day 7 – Friday (Week 2)

Street shows expand across all six neighborhoods

Early masquerade balls and private parties

Day 8 – Main Saturday

Ongoing street performances and live music

Best Mask contest heats up.

Day 9 – Main Sunday

Il Volo dell'Angelo (Flight of the Angel) at 12:00 p.m.

Best Mask contest continues

Day 10–11 – Monday & Tuesday (Week 2)

Final rounds of the Mask Contest

"Maria dell'Anno" crowned

Day 12 – Martedì Grasso

Full-day parades, concerts, and fireworks

Rowing of Silence ends the celebration with elegance.

Best Days to Visit

- For Action & Energy: First Saturday and second weekend (Saturday through Martedi Grasso)

- For Fewer Crowds & Workshops: First Monday–Wednesday

- For Photography & Costumes: Both Sundays and Festa delle Marie day

If you are able, staying for the 12 days of Carnival is an incredible experience. The festivities build in intensity as the event progresses, with each day offering different traditional celebrations and unique performances.

From the opening ceremonies with the Flight of the Angel in St. Mark's Square to the grand finale balls, immersing yourself in the complete Carnival allows you to witness Venice transform completely.

You can do day trips to other Carnival events around the Veneto as outlined in the following chapter, where smaller towns offer their own charming interpretations of this historic celebration without the dense crowds of Venice itself.

CHAPTER THIRTY

Seven Spectacular Veneto Carnivals

Festival Floats & the Gnocchi King

While Venice is the crown jewel of Carnival in Italy, the celebration spills into towns and villages across the Veneto, each adding its own twist of tradition, humor, and community spirit.

These events can be perfect day trips from Venice, offering the chance to explore additional cities while catching parades, costume contests, and local flavor. Or they can serve as standalone Carnival destinations, complete with floats, folkloric characters, and fireworks.

Adding another city to your Carnival week expands your immersion in Veneto's rich heritage, whether you're watching the comical Papà del Gnoco parade through Verona, marveling at floats in Malo's Carnevale del Veneto, or stepping into the medieval charm of Montagnana. Each celebration offers a different lens on what carnival means to the people of this vibrant region.

Seven Not to Miss Carnival Events Across the Veneto: Traditions Worth the Trip

Martedì Grasso, known in English as Shrove Tuesday or Fat Tuesday and in French as Mardi Gras, will be referred to by its authentic Italian name, Martedì Grasso, to honor its rich cultural traditions.

1. Verona: Bacanal del Gnoco

Distance from Venice: 1.5 hours by train (approximately 120 kilometers or 75 miles west).

Carnival Highlight: Venerdì Gnocolar (the Friday before Martedì Grasso)

Verona's Carnival is Italy's oldest documented parade, dating back to 1531, and centers on one of its most beloved figures: Papà del Gnoco. Dressed like a Renaissance king, this jovial character carries a giant fork topped with a gnocco (potato dumpling) and presides over the festivities in the San Zeno district, where the tradition began as a way to distribute food to the poor during a time of famine.

The Bacanal del Gnoco is a humorous, food-themed parade featuring costumed floats, satirical masks, marching bands, and gnocchi for all. It's chaotic, colorful, and absolutely authentic.

Why Go? Verona's Carnival is an energetic, food-loving celebration with deep roots and a lighthearted tone. It's perfect for travelers looking for something quirky, comedic, and truly local. Plus, you'll be in the land of Romeo and Juliet with a plate of gnocchi in hand.

2. Treviso: Carnevale di Treviso

Distance from Venice: 40 minutes by train (approximately 40 kilometers or 25 miles north)

Carnival Highlight: Parade on the Sunday before Shrove Tuesday

Just north of Venice, Treviso offers a more family-oriented, small-town version of Carnival, filled with floats, masks, and local color. The town's Renaissance architecture and winding canals provide a charming backdrop to a large parade organized by local schools, civic groups, and communities, culminating in Piazza dei Signori.

The tradition has flourished since the early 1900s, emphasizing creativity, community participation, and child-friendly festivities like chocolate stands and puppet shows.

Why Go? Treviso is perfect for families, photographers, or travelers looking for a quieter Carnival experience still full of vibrant energy. Its proximity makes it ideal for a half-day trip from Venice.

3. Schio: Carnevale di Schio

Distance from Venice: 2 hours by train (approximately 100 kilometers or 62 miles northwest).

Carnival Highlight: Fat Tuesday (Shrove Tuesday) Parade

Schio, at the base of the Vicentine Alps, is known for its inclusive and joyful Carnival parade, which brings together costumed school groups, artists, and performers. The tradition has grown from a simple community celebration into a major annual event featuring theater performances, mask-making workshops, and children's entertainment leading up to the final procession.

Why Go? If you're traveling with kids or want a Carnival that's full of heart but low on crowds, Schio offers a warm, welcoming atmosphere. It's a creative and inclusive option away from the intensity of Venice.

4. Malo: Carnevale di Malo (Carnevale del Veneto)

Distance from Venice: 1.5 to 2 hours by car (approximately 90 kilometers or 56 miles west; not easily reached by train).

Carnival Highlight: Parades over multiple weekends in February

Known as the "Carnevale del Veneto", Malo's festival is the largest and most famous in the region after Venice. With records dating back to the 17th century, Malo's Carnival is a proud, ongoing expression of local identity. Expect massive allegorical floats, rural-themed characters, humorous satire, music, and fireworks. It's celebrated across multiple weekends, giving travelers flexibility to attend.

Why Go? For a full-on Carnival experience with rural charm, spectacle, and deep tradition, Malo is a must. It's ideal for travelers looking for a lively, crowd-pleasing event with a strong community spirit.

5. Montagnana: Carnevale in Costume

Distance from Venice: 1.5 hours by train or car (approximately 85 kilometers or 53 miles southwest).

Carnival Highlight: Costume parade on the Sunday before Martedi Grasso.

Set within one of the best-preserved medieval walls in Italy, Montagnana's Carnival is an elegant, history-rich celebration. Participants wear Renaissance and Baroque costumes, parading through the cobbled streets to the sounds of classical music, with additional events like fire shows, costume contests, and artisan markets.

The event is a revival of historical processions once held during the town's noble past, and it invites visitors to immerse themselves in the aesthetic splendor of a bygone era.

Why Go? For those drawn to history, architecture, and pageantry, Montagnana offers a quieter yet visually stunning Carnival atmosphere, an ideal escape from the crowds.

6. Feltre: Carnevale Feltrese

Distance from Venice: 2 hours by train and bus (approximately 115 kilometers or 71 miles north, in the foothills of the Dolomites).

Carnival Highlight: Last weekend before Lent

Feltre, in the Belluno province, hosts a Carnival rooted in Alpine folklore and Renaissance tradition. The event features allegorical floats, masked processions, and performers wearing traditional Feltre masks, many representing local characters or legends. The mountain setting adds a dramatic touch to this spirited, community-centered celebration.

Why Go? Feltre is perfect for travelers who want to combine mountain scenery with rich local tradition. It's a great option for a weekend escape from the Lagoon into a Carnival flavored with folklore and festivity.

7. Lendinara: Carnevale di Lendinara

Distance from Venice: 1 hour 30 minutes by train and bus (approximately 95 kilometers or 59 miles southwest, in the province of Rovigo).

Carnival Highlight: Parade and festivities on the Sunday before Lent

Lendinara, known for its neoclassical architecture and strong religious traditions, hosts a vibrant yet intimate Carnival celebration. The Carnevale di Lendinara features a lively parade of floats, masked groups, and community performers winding through the historic town center. Local schools, parishes, and cultural associations organize costume contests, children's activities, and musical entertainment, all infused with small-town charm.

Why Go? Lendinara offers a warm, welcoming Carnival atmosphere perfect for those seeking an authentic local experience away from the tourist path. Its strong community participation and joyful spirit make it an ideal stop for travelers exploring the cultural heart of the Polesine.

Spring Celebrations

March and April

CHAPTER THIRTY-ONE

FestaFusion Venice

Venice in Bloom: The Legacy, Love, & the Festa di San Marco

FestaFusion Venice

#1. Festa di San Marco. The Festa di San Marco, or Saint Mark's Day, is a religious and cultural celebration.

#2. Festa del Bòcolo. The Festa del Bòcolo is an ancient tradition that blends romance, history, and legend.

#3. Festa della Liberazione. Liberation Day is a national holiday that celebrates the country's liberation from Nazi-Fascist rule in 1945.

Where: Venice

When: April 25th

Average Festival Temperatures: High: 16°C (61°F). Low: 8°C (46°F).

#FestaFusion: When two festivals collide in the same town around the same time, your journey becomes twice as magical.

#1. Feast of St. Mark in Venice: A Divine Partnership

Imagine a daring heist in the 9th century Alexandria, two Venetian merchants smuggling sacred relics beneath layers of pork to evade Muslim authorities. This audacious act would forever transform a modest Italian trading post into one of history's most magnificent maritime republics. Welcome to the extraordinary story of Saint Mark and Venice.

Who Was Saint Mark?

Saint Mark, author of the Second Gospel in the New Testament, is celebrated on April 25th by both the Catholic and Eastern Orthodox churches. Believed to be the 'John Mark' mentioned in the Acts of the Apostles, he was the son of Mary of Jerusalem, whose home became a gathering place for the apostles. The Egyptian church claims Mark as its founder, and since the 4th century AD, Alexandria has been known as "the chair of Mark." Several Italian cities, including Aquileia and Venice, also attribute their Christian origins to him.

How Saint Mark Became Venice's Patron

In 828 AD, Saint Mark replaced the earlier patron saint San Todaro (Saint Theodore) as Venice's divine protector. Born in the Levant around 20 AD, Mark became an early Christian convert and founded what is now the Coptic Orthodox Church in Alexandria, Egypt, in 42 AD.

According to historical accounts, two Venetian merchants, Rustico da Torcello and Bono da Malamocco, obtained Mark's relics during a journey to Alexandria in 828. Whether they purchased them from concerned monks, received them for safekeeping from those fearing destruction by Muslim rulers, or cleverly stole them under cover of darkness remains debated. To smuggle the precious remains past authorities, they concealed the saint's bones beneath salted pork, a substance their inspectors wouldn't touch. This ingenious acquisition completely transformed Venice's character and international standing.

The Significance of Saint Mark to Venice

Adopting Mark as patron brought tremendous diplomatic and political advantages to the emerging Republic of Venice. Possessing the body of both an apostle and evangelist was considered exceptional on the international scene. The winged lion, Mark's symbol, became Venice's emblem and remains ubiquitous throughout the city today, adorning buildings, tiles, and proudly flying on flags.

Since the year 828, Venice has celebrated the Feast of St. Mark on April 25th, commemorating the day of his death. Originally, Venice observed three different dates dedicated to the saint, but today only the April celebration endures.

Festival Events

9:00 a.m.

Procession

Before the main Mass, there is a procession that serves as a tribute to the patron saint. Venetians flock to St. Mark's Basilica to participate in these religious ceremonies. The procession can either precede or follow the Solemn Mass, depending on the year's organization.

The festivities actually begin early in the morning, with members of the "Guild of Saint Mark" leading a colorful procession throughout the streets of Venice. Locals and tourists line the historic canals, many waving the iconic "winged lion" flag.

10:30 a.m.

Mass

The principal celebration on April 25th begins with a solemn Mass held at the Basilica di San Marco. This is followed by Vespers, celebrated in the late afternoon, both led by the Patriarch of Venice.

Afternoon

The Regata di Traghetti is a traditional Venetian boat race that showcases the skill and endurance of gondoliers as they compete while transporting passengers in their gondolas. It is part of the larger Venetian regatta tradition, which dates back centuries.

The origins of Venetian regattas can be traced to at least the 13th century, when boat races were held as part of the Festa delle Marie celebrations. However, it is believed that regattas existed even earlier, as Venice has always been a seafaring city, and training oarsmen was a necessity. The first visual depiction of a regatta appeared around 1500, in a map by Jacopo dé Barbari, which included a group of boats labeled "regata".

Over time, regattas evolved from practical training exercises into competitive and celebratory events, often funded by private individuals or foreign princes. Even after the fall of the Republic of Venice in 1797, the tradition endured, with races continuing under different governments. In 1841, the event became publicly funded again, and in 1899, during the Third International Art Biennale, it was officially named the Regata Storica.

Today, the Regata di Traghetti is one of the highlights of the Festa di San Marco, bringing excitement and spectacle to Venice's Grand Canal.

Special Traditions and Costumes

During the procession, people wear special red and gold clothes as they take part in the celebrations. After the religious service at the Basilica, the grand procession includes people wearing traditional costumes and carrying flags, banners, and symbols.

In ancient times, the procession in the Piazza included religious and civil authorities and representatives from artists' guilds. While the celebration is less spectacular than in past centuries, when the entire city would parade through the streets led by the Doge (Venice's highest political authority), it remains an impressive event.

Other Festival Elements

Piazza San Marco comes alive during the festival, filled with street performers, food stalls, and people enjoying the celebratory atmosphere.

On the same day, in the Great Council Chamber of the Doge's Palace, the San Marco Festival Award is presented to Venetian people who have distinguished themselves during the year.

The festivities culminate with fireworks displays, theatrical performances, and other cultural celebrations.

Traditional Festival Foods

The St. Mark's Day celebration offers an excellent opportunity to enjoy traditional Venetian cuisine. The most iconic dish of the celebration is **"Risi e Bisi" (rice and peas),** a creamy dish that falls somewhere between a risotto and a soup. Historically, this dish was presented to the Doge on April 25th as part of the celebrations, making it the official dish of the feast day.

Risi e Bisi's prominence reflects both the importance of rice production in the Veneto region and the seasonal abundance of fresh spring peas. Traditionally prepared with Vialone Nano rice from the Veneto region, the dish is often cooked with pancetta for added flavor and should have a consistency that is neither too liquid nor too dense.

Other traditional Venetian dishes featured during the festival include:

Sarde in Saor: A sweet and sour dish of sardines prepared with onions, vinegar, pine nuts, and raisins. This recipe has Byzantine influences and was popular because it could be preserved for long sea voyages.

Baccalà Mantecato: Creamed salt cod, which became popular in Venetian cuisine from the mid-15th century.

Lasagnette al Nero di Seppia: Pasta colored and flavored with squid ink, reflecting Venice's seafaring heritage.

Polenta e Schie: A dish combining polenta with small lagoon shrimp, seasoned with lemon, garlic, and spices.

Fritto Misto: A popular seafood platter with fried calamari, shrimp, and other seafood from the lagoon.

For dessert, festival-goers enjoy **Fritoe** (delicious pancakes with raisins covered in sugar) and **Buranelli cookies.** Named after the Venetian island of Burano, these biscuits were traditionally packed by sailors for long voyages. Originally round in shape, they now also come in an "S" shape, perfect for dipping in coffee or wine.

The celebration is accompanied by **Prosecco** from the nearby Valdobbiadene area, particularly suited to pairing with the traditional festival dishes.

#2. The Bocolo Tradition: A Story of Eternal Love

The Feast of the Rosebud is one of Venice's most romantic traditions, celebrated alongside the Feast of St. Mark on April 25th. "Bocolo" in the Venetian dialect means "rosebud," and the tradition involves Venetian men giving a single red rosebud to women they love as a symbol of devotion.

The Legend of Tancredi and Maria

The most famous origin story dates back to the early 9th century and centers around a star-crossed love affair. Maria (sometimes called Vulcana for her fiery black eyes) was the daughter of Doge Orso I Partecipazio, who ruled Venice between 864 and 881 AD. She fell deeply in love with Tancredi, a humble troubadour of lower social status.

The Doge strongly disapproved of their relationship due to the social gap between them. Determined to win the Doge's approval, Maria suggested that Tancredi join Charlemagne's army in the war against the Moors in Spain, hoping his valor in battle would elevate his standing.

Tancredi fought bravely and distinguished himself in battle, but his triumph was short-lived. During the Battle of Roncevaux (made famous in the epic poem "Song of Roland"), he was mortally wounded near a rose garden. As he lay dying, Tancredi plucked a white rose that became stained with his blood. He entrusted his friend Orlando to deliver this blood-red rose to his beloved Maria as his final token of love.

Orlando returned to Venice on the eve of St. Mark's Day and delivered the blood-stained rose to Maria. Understanding the tragic message it carried, she was overcome with grief. The next morning, April 25th, St. Mark's Day, Maria was found dead in her bed, the red rosebud resting on her heart. The legend spread quickly throughout Venice, and since then, the tradition of giving a red rosebud on April 25th has symbolized eternal, sacrificial love.

Alternative Legend

Another lesser-known but meaningful legend connects the tradition directly to St. Mark. This story centers around Basilio, a sailor from the Venetian island of Giudecca, who had helped steal St. Mark's relics from Alexandria in Egypt and bring them to Venice. As a reward, he was given a rose plant that grew near St. Mark's tomb.

Basilio planted the roses in his garden on Giudecca, and when he died, the rose plant marked the boundary between the properties inherited by his two sons. When disputes arose between the two branches of the family, the roses stopped blooming. Peace was restored only when two young people from the feuding sides fell in love, at which point the roses flourished again. This version of the legend emphasizes reconciliation and family harmony.

Modern Celebrations

Today, the tradition has expanded beyond romantic partners. Venetian men give rosebuds not only to their wives or girlfriends but to all important women in their lives, mothers, daughters, and sisters, making it a broader celebration of feminine importance.

The Festa del Bocolo has inspired artistic interpretations as well. In 2014, artist Elena Tagliapietra created a stunning public installation called "A Rose for Venice" where over a thousand Venetians dressed in red gathered in St. Mark's Square to form a giant human rosebud when viewed from above. This spectacular display has become a recurring feature of the celebrations, symbolizing Venetians' love for their city and its traditions.

The rosebud tradition has thus strengthened from a romantic legend to become a multifaceted symbol representing love, sacrifice, reconciliation, and civic pride, all elements that are deeply woven into the fabric of Venetian identity.

#3. Liberation Day throughout Italy

I wanted to acknowledge that April 25th is the Festa della Liberazione, or Liberation Day. This national holiday marks the country's freedom from Nazi-Fascist rule in 1945, an event that shaped modern Italy and is commemorated with parades, speeches, and ceremonies throughout the country. In Venice, while San Marco remains the focal point, Liberation Day is observed through reflective gatherings and symbolic gestures, tying together history, resilience, and identity.

CHAPTER THIRTY-TWO

Holy Week and Easter in Vicenza

A Festival of Light and Faith

H oly Week & Easter

Where: Vicenza

When: Week leading up to Easter; dates vary by year but March or April.

Average Festival Temperatures: High: 17°C (63°F). Low 8°C (46°F).

Discover Vicenza: The Renaissance Jewel of the Veneto

Nestled between verdant hills and fertile plains in the northeastern Veneto region of Italy, Vicenza stands as a magnificent testament to the genius of Andrea Palladio, the architect whose vision transformed this ancient Roman settlement into a Renaissance masterpiece. Often overshadowed by its more famous neighbors, Venice and Verona, Vicenza offers visitors an authentic Italian experience rich in architectural splendor, artistic heritage, and profound religious traditions.

The history of Vicenza stretches back to pre-Roman times, with evidence of settlement dating to the 6th century BC by the Veneti people. The Romans established "Vicetia" in the 2nd century BC, and the orthogonal street plan of the ancient city still forms the backbone of Vicenza's historic center. After the fall of the Roman Empire, the city faced successive waves of invasions before coming under Venetian rule in 1404, a relationship that would last nearly four centuries and profoundly shape the city's development.

It was during the Venetian period that Vicenza flourished, as wealthy noble families competed to build ever more impressive palaces. The most significant development came in the 16th century when Andrea Palladio, born Andrea di Pietro della Gondola, emerged as the preeminent architect of the age. His classical-inspired designs transformed Vicenza into what is often called "the city of Palladio," earning it UNESCO World Heritage status in 1994.

Vicenza is located approximately 60 kilometers (37 miles) west of Venice and 35 kilometers (21 miles) east of Verona in the heart of the Veneto region. Monte Berico, rising to the south, forms a dramatic backdrop to the city, its summit offering panoramic views. The Bacchiglione River winds through the city, its banks lined with historic buildings that reflect centuries of prosperity. Artists and architects have been inspired for centuries by the diverse landscape, encompassing the rolling Berici Hills to the south and the pre-Alpine foothills to the north.

With a population of approximately 112,000 residents, Vicenza is a medium-sized Italian city that maintains a perfect balance between urban amenities and small-town charm. While the gold and jewelry industry forms a significant part of the modern economy, Vicenza's rich architectural heritage makes tourism increasingly important. The "Palladian trail" attracts architecture enthusiasts from around the world, while the city's location in one of Italy's most productive regions ensures a thriving manufacturing sector.

Holy Week and Easter

Holy Week and Easter in Vicenza present a remarkable blend of solemn religious devotion and joyful celebration, offering visitors an intimate glimpse into the spiritual heart of northern Italian culture. While perhaps less famous than the elaborate processions of Sicily or the pageantry of Rome, Vicenza's Holy Week traditions possess a quiet dignity and authenticity that speak to the deep-rooted faith of the Veneto region.

The Easter season in Vicenza unfolds against the backdrop of early spring, as the mountains to the north shed their winter snow and the surrounding countryside bursts into bloom. The mild climate of April typically brings pleasant days for exploring both the city's religious traditions and its architectural wonders. While Vicenza serves as our focal point, the surrounding region offers additional Holy Week experiences within easy reach, from the solemnity of Verona's Good Friday procession to the grand Easter celebrations in Venice's St. Mark's Basilica.

For Catholics, Easter represents the culmination of the liturgical year, marking Christ's triumph over death through resurrection. Easter Sunday's date varies annually, falling on the first Sunday after the first full moon of spring, between March 22nd and April 25th. In Vicenza, as throughout Italy, Easter is preceded by Lent (Quaresima), a 40-day period of prayer, penance, and fasting. The solemn observances of Holy Week contrast with the joyful celebrations of Easter Sunday, creating a profound emotional journey for participants.

Holy Week, known as "Settimana Santa" in Italian, represents the most sacred period of the liturgical year in Vicenza's Catholic tradition. These ceremonies attract both the devout and those interested in cultural heritage, creating a unique atmosphere that blends spiritual significance with historical continuity. Even for non-religious visitors, the artistic and cultural dimensions of these events offer a fascinating window into Vicenza's soul and centuries-old traditions.

Palm Sunday Procession

Palm Sunday in Vicenza inaugurates Holy Week with ceremonies that combine solemn remembrance with communal celebration. The day begins with special Masses at all parishes throughout the city, with the most significant celebration taking place at the Cathedral of Santa Maria Annunciata. The Bishop of Vicenza leads this service, where olive branches and palm fronds are blessed, symbolizing the crowds that welcomed Jesus into Jerusalem.

The Procession

Following the morning Mass at the Cathedral, a solemn procession makes its way through the historic center of Vicenza. Beginning in the Piazza Duomo, the procession is led by the Bishop, followed by clergy, religious orders, confraternities, and parishioners. Many carry olive branches or intricately woven palm fronds, creating a sea of greenery that winds through the Renaissance streets.

The procession route typically passes several of Vicenza's most significant landmarks, including Palladio's Basilica Palladiana and the Church of Santa Corona, before returning to the Cathedral. This journey through the city's historic center creates a powerful juxtaposition between Vicenza's Renaissance splendor and the ancient Christian tradition being commemorated.

Throughout the procession, participants sing traditional hymns and recite prayers, creating an atmosphere that is both reverent and communal. At designated stations along the route, readings from the Gospel accounts of Jesus' entry into Jerusalem are shared, allowing participants to reflect on the significance of the day. The palm branches carried during the procession will later be taken home by the faithful and kept until the following year, when they will be burned to create the ashes used on Ash Wednesday.

The Palm Sunday celebrations in Vicenza thus serve as a meaningful beginning to Holy Week, bringing together the community in a shared act of remembrance and devotion. The combination of ancient ritual, communal participation, and the magnificent architectural backdrop of Palladio's city creates an experience that resonates with both religious significance and cultural heritage.

Holy Monday and Tuesday

The early days of Holy Week in Vicenza are characterized by quiet preparation and contemplation rather than public processions. Local parishes hold evening Masses with special readings and prayers focused on Christ's final days. These first days of the week provide an opportunity for the faithful to deepen their spiritual preparation for the more intense ceremonies to come.

Visitors to Vicenza during this time might notice increased activity in the churches as volunteers prepare decorations, clean altars, and arrange flowers for the upcoming celebrations. These days also offer an excellent opportunity to explore Vicenza's numerous churches and chapels, many of which contain remarkable artwork depicting the Passion of Christ.

Holy Wednesday: The Way of the Cross at Monte Berico

As Holy Week progresses, the observances in Vicenza grow more visible and public. On Holy Wednesday evening, one of the most evocative events takes place on Monte Berico, the hill that rises above the southern edge of the city. Here, a torch-lit Way of the Cross (Via Crucis) procession ascends the ancient portico that leads to the Sanctuary of Monte Berico, a pilgrimage church dedicated to the Virgin Mary.

The Monte Berico Sanctuary holds particular significance for the people of Vicenza, as it commemorates two apparitions of the Virgin Mary during plague outbreaks in 1426 and 1428. The Virgin is said to have promised an end to the plague if a church was built in her honor, and the citizens' compliance was followed by deliverance from the disease. This historical connection between faith and communal salvation adds deeper meaning to the Holy Week procession.

The Way of the Cross begins at dusk at the foot of the hill and follows the 700-meter covered arcade with its 150 arches, built in 1746 to shelter pilgrims. At each of the fourteen stations, the procession pauses for readings, prayers, and reflections on Christ's journey to Calvary. The growing darkness, illuminated only by the participants' torches and candles, creates a solemn and meditative atmosphere.

Participants in this procession include representatives from parishes throughout Vicenza, religious orders, and confraternities, many wearing traditional robes or carrying symbols of their organizations. The Bishop of Vicenza often leads this procession, emphasizing its importance in the city's Holy Week observances.

As the procession reaches the summit of Monte Berico, participants enter the sanctuary for a special liturgy. The baroque interior of the church, with its gilded details catching the flickering light of hundreds of candles, provides a dramatic setting for the culmination of this evening ritual. From the terrace outside the sanctuary, participants can look down upon the illuminated city below, creating a powerful visual metaphor for spiritual ascent and heavenly perspective.

This Holy Wednesday tradition on Monte Berico exemplifies how Vicenza's religious observances are uniquely integrated with its topography and architectural heritage, creating experiences that are both spiritually meaningful and aesthetically striking.

Holy Thursday: The Last Supper and Altar of Repose

Holy Thursday in Vicenza marks a significant transition in the Holy Week observances, as the focus shifts to commemorating the Last Supper and Christ's agony in the Garden of Gethsemane. The day's ceremonies are characterized by profound symbolism and a shift from public processions to more intimate liturgical observances.

The Mass of the Lord's Supper

In the evening, churches throughout Vicenza celebrate the Mass of the Lord's Supper (Missa in Coena Domini), with the most solemn celebration taking place at the Cathedral. This liturgy commemorates Christ's institution of the Eucharist and includes the washing of feet (Lavanda dei Piedi), where the Bishop or parish priest washes the feet of twelve people, reenacting Christ's humble service to his disciples.

The ceremony is marked by rich musical accompaniment, with church choirs performing Renaissance and Baroque compositions that have been part of Vicenza's cultural heritage for centuries. The Cathedral choir, in particular, draws on a repertoire of sacred music by composers like Andrea Gabrieli and Claudio Monteverdi, whose works have echoed through Vicenza's churches for generations.

The Altars of Repose

Following the evening Mass, the consecrated hosts are carried in procession to a specially decorated Altar of Repose (Sepolcro), which will remain in place until the Good Friday service. These altars, found in churches throughout Vicenza, are elaborately decorated with flowers, candles, olive branches, and wheat sprouts (symbolizing the bread of the Eucharist).

A tradition unique to Holy Thursday is the "Visita ai Sepolcri" (Visit to the Sepulchers), where the faithful visit seven different churches to pray before their Altars of Repose. This practice transforms the city into a nocturnal pilgrimage route, with families and groups of friends moving between churches illuminated only by candlelight. The tradition of visiting seven churches derives from the commemoration of the seven "stations" or stops that Christ made on the night of his arrest, from the Last Supper to his imprisonment.

In Vicenza, this pilgrimage typically includes the Cathedral, the Basilica of SS. Felice and Fortunato, the Church of Santa Corona (which houses a thorn said to be from Christ's crown), the Church of San Lorenzo, the Church of the Carmini, the Church of San Stefano, and the Sanctuary of Monte Berico. Each church offers a unique artistic interpretation of the Altar of Repose, with some maintaining designs that have been passed down for generations.

The night of Holy Thursday provides one of the most atmospheric experiences of Holy Week in Vicenza, as the darkened streets fill with quiet groups of pilgrims moving between the glowing interiors of ancient churches. The combination of sacred architecture, candlelight, floral decorations, and the hushed voices of prayer creates a timeless atmosphere that connects contemporary participants with centuries of tradition.

Good Friday: Procession of the Dead Christ

Good Friday represents the most solemn day of Holy Week in Vicenza, as the city commemorates the crucifixion and death of Christ. Unlike southern Italian cities that hold elaborate daytime processions, Vicenza's Good Friday observances are characterized by a stark simplicity during the day, followed by an evocative nighttime procession that winds through the historic center.

Daytime Observances

During the day, churches remain undecorated, with crosses veiled and altars stripped bare. The faithful observe a day of fasting and abstinence, and a hushed atmosphere prevails throughout the city. At 3:00 p.m., the traditional hour of Christ's death, parishes throughout Vicenza hold the Celebration of the Passion, which includes the reading of the Passion narrative, veneration of the cross, and communion with hosts consecrated on Holy Thursday.

The Procession of the Dead Christ

As darkness falls over Vicenza, the city's most profound Holy Week tradition begins: the Procession of the Dead Christ. This solemn nighttime procession dates back to the 16th century and is organized by the Archconfraternity of the Good Death, one of Vicenza's oldest religious brotherhoods, founded in 1539.

The procession forms at the Church of San Lorenzo, where a life-sized wooden statue of the dead Christ, crafted by a local artisan in the 18th century, is placed on an ornate platform. The statue is remarkably realistic, with articulated limbs and details that evoke profound emotional responses from viewers. Alongside this figure, a statue of the Mater Dolorosa (Sorrowful Mother) is also carried, dressed in black and with tears carved on her face.

Members of the Archconfraternity, wearing traditional black hooded robes and carrying staffs topped with silver skulls (symbols of mortality), lead the procession. They are followed by representatives from other confraternities and parishes, clergy, and the faithful. Many participants carry candles or torches, creating a river of light that moves slowly through Vicenza's Renaissance streets.

The route of the procession passes through the heart of the historic center, including the Corso Andrea Palladio, Piazza dei Signori, and Piazza Duomo. The narrow medieval streets and majestic Renaissance architecture provide a dramatic backdrop for this solemn journey. Along the way, the procession stops at several churches for brief prayers and reflections on Christ's suffering.

What makes Vicenza's Good Friday procession particularly moving is the musical accompaniment. A brass band plays funeral marches composed specifically for this occasion, their somber melodies echoing off the ancient stones of the city. In addition, members of the Cathedral choir sing traditional lamentations and motets, including settings of the "Stabat Mater" that date back centuries.

The procession concludes at the Cathedral, where the statues of Christ and the Virgin Mary are placed before the main altar for veneration until Easter Sunday morning. The Bishop offers a final blessing, and participants disperse in silence, carrying the solemnity of the evening with them.

For visitors to Vicenza, the Good Friday procession offers a profound cultural and spiritual experience. The combination of Renaissance architecture, traditional sacred music, ancient religious symbolism, and genuine communal devotion creates a timeless atmosphere that transcends the boundaries between art, history, and lived faith.

Holy Saturday: The Day of Silence

In Vicenza, Holy Saturday is traditionally a day of quiet anticipation. The day is characterized by quiet preparation rather than public ceremonies, as the Church waits in vigil at the symbolic tomb of Christ.

Daytime Stillness

During the day, Vicenza's churches remain in a state of symbolic mourning. Altars remain stripped, statues are covered with purple cloths, and there are no Masses celebrated. The tabernacles stand empty, with their doors ajar, signifying Christ's absence from the world. This atmosphere of sacred emptiness creates a powerful sensory experience for visitors, as the normally resplendent interiors of Vicenza's churches are transformed into spaces of stark simplicity.

Despite the absence of liturgical ceremonies, there is considerable activity behind the scenes. Throughout the city, families engage in traditional Easter preparations, cleaning their homes and preparing food that will be blessed and consumed on Easter Sunday.

Bakeries work through the night to produce the traditional Easter bread known as "la colomba" (the dove), a sweet leavened cake formed in the shape of a dove to symbolize peace and the Holy Spirit.

In the churches, volunteers and clergy prepare for the Easter Vigil, arranging flowers that have been kept hidden during the austere days of Holy Week. White lilies, symbolic of resurrection and purity, are positioned near altars but kept covered until the joyful moment when they will be revealed during the Easter Vigil.

The Easter Vigil: Bells at Midnight

As darkness falls on Holy Saturday, the most important liturgical celebration of the Christian year begins: the Easter Vigil. In Vicenza, the most solemn celebration takes place at the Cathedral, though every parish church holds its own vigil. Beginning no earlier than sunset (typically around 8:00 p.m.), these ceremonies traditionally continue past midnight, welcoming Easter Sunday in the first moments of the new day.

The Easter Vigil begins outside the Cathedral, where a new fire is kindled and blessed by the bishop. From this fire, the Paschal Candle, a large decorated candle that represents the light of Christ, is lit. The Bishop carves symbols into the candle: a cross, the Greek letters Alpha and Omega (symbolizing Christ as the beginning and end), and the numerals of the current year.

Then the congregation walks into the dark cathedral, led by the Paschal Candle. The deacon carries the candle through the church, stopping three times to chant "Lumen Christi" (Light of Christ), to which the people respond "Deo gratias" (Thanks be to God). The light from the Paschal Candle is gradually shared with the congregation, each person holding a small candle, until the entire cathedral is illuminated by hundreds of flickering flames, a powerful visual metaphor for how Christ's light spreads throughout the world.

The Exsultet, an ancient hymn of praise, is then chanted, followed by a series of readings that trace salvation history from Creation through the Exodus and the prophets. These readings are significant in Vicenza, where they are often accompanied by Renaissance polyphonic music performed by the Cathedral choir, creating a seamless blend of sacred text and artistic expression.

The Gloria is sung for the first time since the beginning of Lent, accompanied by the ringing of bells that have been silent since Holy Thursday. This moment of transition from darkness to light, from silence to jubilant sound, creates a profound sensory experience for all present.

A highlight of the Easter Vigil in Vicenza is the Baptismal Liturgy, during which adults who have been preparing for initiation into the Church receive the sacraments of Baptism, Confirmation, and Eucharist. The Cathedral's ancient baptismal font, which dates to the 15th century, becomes the focal point for this ritual of spiritual rebirth.

As midnight approaches, the Easter Vigil concludes with the Liturgy of the Eucharist, celebrated with special solemnity. At the end of the Mass, the Bishop processes throughout the Cathedral bearing a statue of the Risen Christ, which replaces the dead Christ that had been venerated on Good Friday. This symbolic action marks the transition to Easter and the beginning of the celebration of Christ's Resurrection.

The Easter Vigil in Vicenza, with its rich symbolism and ancient rituals set against the backdrop of Renaissance architecture, offers visitors one of the most profound experiences of Holy Week. The ceremony's progression from darkness to light, from mourning to celebration, creates a powerful narrative that resonates beyond religious boundaries, touching on universal themes of renewal and hope.

Easter Sunday: Celebration of the Resurrection

Easter Sunday in Vicenza dawns with an atmosphere of celebration that contrasts dramatically with the solemnity of the preceding days. Church bells, silent since Holy Thursday, ring out joyfully across the city, announcing the Resurrection. The strict observance of Lent and Holy Week give way to festive meals, family gatherings, and public celebrations that blend religious significance with cultural traditions.

Morning Mass and Procession

The day begins with solemn Easter Masses in every parish, with the most significant celebration taking place at the Cathedral. Unlike the stark decorations of Holy Week, churches are now adorned with white lilies, spring flowers, and gold vestments, creating a visual expression of joy and new life. The Cathedral choir performs special Easter compositions, often including works by composers with connections to Vicenza's musical heritage, such as Antonio Vivaldi, who was active in the nearby Venetian Republic.

Following the High Mass at the Cathedral, a joyful Easter procession winds through the historic center of Vicenza. Unlike the solemn processions of Holy Week, this celebration is marked by festive music, children dressed in their finest clothes, and the carrying of a statue of the Risen Christ adorned with flowers. The procession typically passes through Piazza dei Signori, allowing participants to admire Palladio's Basilica Palladiana in its Easter splendor, with the building's harmonious proportions serving as a Renaissance expression of divine order, a fitting backdrop for celebrating resurrection.

One unique tradition in Vicenza is the "Incontro" (The Meeting), where statues of the Risen Christ and the Virgin Mary are carried in separate processions that converge in Piazza Duomo. When the two statues "meet," the Madonna's black mourning veil is removed to reveal her blue mantle beneath, symbolizing her joy at being reunited with her resurrected son. This moment is greeted with applause, the release of white doves, and sometimes even fireworks, creating a dramatic climax to the morning's celebrations.

Easter in the Piazza / Sbatarò Festival

By midday, the celebrations move from the religious to the communal, as Vicenza's piazzas become centers of festivity. In Piazza dei Signori, local bands perform traditional Easter music, while food vendors offer seasonal specialties. Families and friends gather to promenade in their Easter finery, taking part in the traditional "pasquetta" (little Easter stroll) that has been a part of Italian culture for centuries.

One beloved Easter tradition unique to Vicenza is the "Sbatarò Festival" held in Piazza delle Erbe. This playful competition involves hard-boiled eggs that have been dyed in bright colors. Participants take turns tapping their eggs against those of their opponents; the last person with an uncracked egg is declared the winner and is said to have good fortune for the coming year. The festival's name comes from the local dialect word "sbatare," meaning to knock or tap, and reflects the distinctly Vicentine character of this Easter celebration.

Family Celebrations

While the public festivities are vibrant and engaging, Easter in Vicenza is a family holiday. After attending morning Mass, extended families gather for elaborate lunches that often last well into the afternoon. Traditional Easter dishes in Vicenza include "torta pasqualina" (a savory pie filled with greens, eggs, and cheese), roast lamb with artichokes, and "risi e bisi" (a risotto with peas that celebrates spring's arrival).

The Easter meal concludes with "colomba pasquale," the dove-shaped sweet bread that symbolizes peace and resurrection. Another Easter sweet particular to Vicenza is "fugassa," a leavened cake enriched with butter and eggs that had been forbidden during Lent. These traditional foods reflect the region's agricultural heritage and the significance of ending the Lenten fast with celebratory abundance.

For visitors to Vicenza, Easter Sunday offers a perfect blend of religious observance, cultural tradition, and communal celebration. The day's progression from solemn liturgical ceremonies to joyful public festivities creates a comprehensive experience of how Easter is celebrated in this Renaissance city. The backdrop of Palladio's architectural masterpieces adds a dimension, as the harmony and proportion of these buildings provide a visual counterpart to the theological themes of divine order and resurrection being celebrated.

Easter Monday: La Pasquetta

The Monday after Easter, known as Pasquetta ("Little Easter"), is a national holiday in Italy and a cherished day for relaxation and socializing. Unlike the solemnity of Holy Week, Pasquetta is all about spending time outdoors with family and friends. Italians traditionally mark the day with picnics in the countryside, barbecues, or day trips to the beach, mountains, or historic towns.

Parks and public spaces fill with people enjoying nature, playing games, and sharing festive foods like hard-boiled eggs, savory pies (such as torta pasqualina), and leftover lamb from Easter Sunday.

Vicenza Walking Tour

#1. Piazza dei Signori

Begin your exploration in Vicenza's main square, the elegant Piazza dei Signori, dominated by Palladio's masterpiece, the Basilica Palladiana. During Holy Week, this square serves as a gathering point for many of the religious processions. Notice the slender Torre di Piazza (clock tower) that dates back to the 12th century and whose bells mark the hours of the Holy Week ceremonies.

#2. Duomo di Vicenza (Cathedral of Santa Maria Annunciata)

Just a short walk from Piazza dei Signori, the Cathedral serves as the heart of Holy Week religious celebrations. This Gothic-Renaissance church, consecrated in 1467, features a single nave with impressive side chapels.

The Cathedral houses Bartolomeo Montagna's masterpiece "Pietà" (1505), which becomes a focal point for meditation during Holy Week. The Cathedral Museum next to the church displays valuable religious artifacts, including processional crosses and reliquaries used in Holy Week processions.

#3. Chiesa di San Lorenzo (St. Lawrence)

This 13th-century Gothic church is notable for its distinctive striped façade of brick and white stone. During Holy Week, San Lorenzo is the starting point for the Good Friday procession of the Dead Christ. Inside, visitors can admire Lorenzo Veneziano's "Madonna and Child" and the "Adoration of the Magi" by Marcello Fogolino, as well as the atmospheric crypt where penitential services are held during Lent.

#4. Corso Andrea Palladio

Stroll along Vicenza's elegant main street, named after its most famous architect. During Holy Week, this corso serves as the principal route for religious processions. Notice the numerous Palladian palaces lining the street, including Palazzo Thiene and Palazzo Chiericati, whose harmonious façades create a magnificent backdrop for the sacred pageantry of Easter.

#5. Chiesa di Santa Corona

Built between 1261 and 1314 by the Franciscan order to house a relic of St Corona, this Gothic church is a cornerstone of Vicenza's spiritual and artistic heritage. Andrea Palladio added a monumental two-story portico of giant Corinthian pilasters in 1549–1551 giving the Gothic structure classical proportions.

Above the main portal is a delicate rose window carved to resemble a blooming crown of stone petals that bathes the nave in soft colored light.

Inside you will find Paolo Veronese's *Adoration of the Shepherds* (circa 1573) celebrated for its luminous palette and graceful figures, along with Jacopo Bassano's *Deposition from the Cross* (circa 1543) noted for rich earthy tones and emotive realism. The church also contains works by Francesco Maffei and a rare wooden crucifix from the 13th century. In the left aisle, a silver-clad chapel built in 1681 enshrines St Corona's relic amid marble columns and baroque ornamentation.

#6. Palazzo Leoni Montanari

This baroque palace, now housing an important art gallery, contains a significant collection of Russian icons, including several depicting the Passion of Christ. During Holy Week, the museum often hosts special exhibitions related to Easter themes in art, with guided tours focusing on representations of the Passion across different artistic traditions.

https://www.gallerieditalia.com/en/vicenza/

#7. Santuario di Monte Berico

Conclude your tour with a climb to this important pilgrimage site overlooking the city. The sanctuary, dedicated to the Virgin Mary who reportedly appeared here during a plague epidemic in 1426, offers panoramic views of Vicenzo and beyond.

Logistics

Train: Vicenza sits on the high-speed Milan–Venice corridor, served by Trenitalia's Frecciarossa, Frecciargento and Frecciabianca trains and Regionale Veloce and Intercity services. From Venice Santa Lucia or Mestre you can reach Vicenza in about 30 to 45 minutes; from Milan Centrale in roughly 90 minutes. The station lies just east of Corso delle Filande, a five-minute walk from Piazza dei Signori.

Bus: Vicenza's local bus network is operated by APS and radiates from Piazza Castello and Piazza Biade into the surrounding neighborhoods and suburbs. Single-ride tickets must be validated on board and can be bought at newsstands or via the MyCicero mobile app. For travel beyond the city, for example, to Batignano or the Colli Berici hills, regional coaches depart from the bus terminal next to the railway station. Schedules are posted at each stop and on the APS website.

Car: Traveling by car, Vicenza is easily reached via the A4 "Serenissima" motorway. Take the exit Vicenza Est for eastern districts or Vicenza Ovest for access to the hospital and western neighborhoods. Be aware that the centro storico is subject to a Zona a Traffico Limitato; traffic is restricted to permit holders Monday through Saturday from 7:30 until 19:30. If you plan to drive into town, arrange any necessary temporary permits in advance through the municipal website or your hotel.

Parking: Ample paid parking lies just outside the ZTL. The Parcheggio Stazione FS (P4) is directly behind the railway station and offers both open-air and covered spaces at about one euro per hour. Closer to the center you'll find the multi-story Garibaldi and Garage Zentrum facilities, which charge around two euros per hour but eliminate the need to navigate narrow streets.

Restaurant Recommendations

CUCU. Address: Piazza delle Erbe 7
Cucù occupies a prime corner beneath the loggias of the Basilica Palladiana, where you can linger over breakfast, lunch or dinner amid three airy floors and a large street-side stall. The menu leans on Italian tradition, fresh pasta, regional salumi and cheeses, but winks at global flavors through creative small plates, gourmet canapés and inventive cocktails. An all-day café vibe is punctuated by natural and organic wines, craft beers and local grappas, making it an ideal spot for people-watching or a relaxed aperitivo in the heart of Vicenza.

Julien. Address: Contrada Jacopo Cabianca 13
Julien is a sleek, metro-inspired bistro just steps from the central piazzas. Its pared-back interior sets the stage for a menu of contemporary Italian classics, think perfectly seared filletto, house-made pastas and seasonal vegetables, served with attentive, informal hospitality. The wine list highlights Veneto labels, while a concise cocktail selection makes it a favorite for both dinner and pre-theater drinks.

Matteo Grandi. Address: Piazza dei Signori 1
Housed within Palladio's Basilica Palladiana, Matteo Grandi brings a farm-to-table ethos to Vicenza's historic center. Chef Grandi sources local produce, meats and seafood to craft refined tasting menus alongside seasonal à la carte dishes.

Accommodation

Hotel Campo Marzio/ Address: Viale Roma 21
Hotel Campo Marzio is a four-star property housed in a 19th-century villa just steps from the pedestrian zone and the train station. Its classic elegance and modern amenities make it ideal for both leisure and business travelers, with Piazza dei Signori and the Basilica Palladiana less than a ten-minute stroll away.

Relais Santa Corona. Address: Contrà Santa Corona 19
Relais Santa Corona is a boutique four-star hotel set in a restored 18th-century palazzo in the heart of the centro storico. Each room blends minimalist contemporary décor with antique accents and many overlook the quiet cobbled street next to the Gothic church. Guests enjoy breakfast, bike rentals, concierge service, laundry, and optional airport transfers. Its central location places you within easy walking distance of Teatro Olimpico, Palazzo Chiericati, and all of Vicenza's Palladian treasures.

The Glam Boutique Hotel & Apt. Address: Viale Antonio Giuriolo 10
The Glam Boutique Hotel & Apt. is a four-star Art Deco–inspired inn blending bold design with personalized service. Stylish rooms and suites feature rainfall showers, minibars, and flat-screen TVs, while the ground-floor café serves specialty coffee by day and handcrafted cocktails by night.

Day Trips: Nearby Sites, Cities and Towns

Soave. 35 kilometers (22 miles) from Vicenza. Times immemorial have made Soave synonymous with both wine and walled hilltop villages. Its medieval fortress perches above vine-covered slopes, offering sweeping views of the Veneto plain. Within the walls you'll wander cobbled lanes lined with pastel houses and pop into family-run cantine for tastings of Soave Classico, a crisp white wine grown on the volcanic soils of Mount Lessini.

The 13th-century castle's enceinte and tall battlements loom above the village, and inside the Rocca Scaligera you'll find a small museum tracing the town's strategic role on the Venetian frontier.

Cittadella. Distance from Vicenza is 25 kilometers (15.5 miles). Cittadella is one of Italy's most perfectly preserved medieval towns, entirely encircled by a 13th-century wall you can walk in its entirety. The elevated walkway spans nearly 1.5 kilometers and offers panoramic views over tiled rooftops and the surrounding countryside. Inside the walls, you'll discover a grid of cobbled streets, elegant palazzi, and a central piazza alive with local markets and cafes.

Originally built as a military outpost by Padua, Cittadella's strategic position made it a battleground between rival city-states. Today, it's a peaceful place to explore Veneto's layered past from the ramparts of a town that still feels fortified by history.

Vicenza Festivals and Sagre Throughout the Year

Festa di San Giuseppe (St. Joseph)

March 19

Saint Joseph, the patron saint of workers and fathers, is honored in Vicenza with local Masses and smaller neighborhood events. Though not a citywide festival, some parishes organize food stands or charity markets. Traditional sweets such as zeppole di San Giuseppe may be available in bakeries. The celebration is quieter compared to southern regions but still holds importance in religious communities.

Abilmente Vicenza (Art)

Held twice annually, in spring and autumn.

"Abilmente Vicenza" is a premier arts and crafts fair that celebrates creativity and manual skills. Hosted at the Fiera di Vicenza, the event showcases a wide array of handmade products, DIY workshops, and exhibitions. It attracts artisans, hobbyists, and craft enthusiasts from across Italy and beyond, offering a platform to explore the latest trends in the arts and crafts sector.

https://www.abilmente.org/en/vicenza

New Conversations – Vicenza Jazz

Annually in May

Since its inception in 1996, the "New Conversations – Vicenza Jazz" festival has transformed Vicenza into a vibrant hub for jazz enthusiasts. Under the artistic direction of Riccardo Brazzale, the festival spans ten days, featuring performances by international jazz legends and emerging talents. Concerts are held in iconic venues such as the Teatro Olimpico, Teatro Comunale, Basilica Palladiana, and various city squares and cafes, creating an immersive musical experience throughout the city. https://www.vicenzajazz.org/

Vicenza in Festival

Late July to early September

Coinciding with the city's patronal feast, the "Festa dei Oto," "Vicenza in Festival" is a cultural event that brings music, theater, and comedy to the heart of Vicenza. The festival features performances by renowned artists and emerging talents in various genres, offering entertainment that appeals to a broad audience. https://vicenzainfestival.it/

La Festa dei Oto (Feast on the Eighth)

September 8

Held in honor of the Madonna di Monte Berico, the patroness of Vicenza, this is the city's most important religious celebration. The origins of the devotion date back to the 15th century, when the Virgin is said to have appeared twice during a plague, promising to end the suffering if a church was built in her name. That church, the Sanctuary of Monte Berico, has become a major pilgrimage site. On September 8, thousands of pilgrims walk or drive up the hill to attend special Masses and pray before the Madonna's statue.

CHAPTER THIRTY-THREE

Seven Sacred Holy Week Events–Veneto

Candelight, Crosses and Choirs

Seven Renowned Holy Week Events Throughout the Veneto

While Vicenza offers a rich tapestry of Holy Week traditions, the surrounding Veneto region is home to numerous other significant and distinctive Easter celebrations. Each city and town brings its own historical and cultural context to these sacred days, creating unique expressions of faith that have strengthened over centuries.

1. Venice: The Silent Processions

Holy Thursday and Good Friday Processions in Silence

Venice, despite its reputation for carnival festivities and ornate celebrations, observes a markedly austere Holy Week. The city's narrow calli (streets) and expansive campi (squares) become venues for solemn processions that wind their way through the labyrinthine urban fabric.

The most distinctive feature of Venice's Holy Week is the "Processioni Silenziose" (Silent Processions) held on Holy Thursday and Good Friday. These processions date back to the 14th century, when Venice was at the height of its power as a maritime republic. Unlike the more elaborate celebrations in southern Italy, Venetian processions are characterized by their solemnity and restraint, reflecting the reserved character of Venetian religious expression.

On Holy Thursday evening, members of the ancient Scuole Grandi (Grand Schools), Venice's historic confraternities, process in silence through San Marco and the surrounding districts. These confraternities, dating back to the 13th century, originally served as mutual aid societies and played crucial roles in the city's social and religious life. Dressed in traditional white robes with distinctive colored sashes that identify their scuola, the participants carry lanterns and ornate crosses but no statues, another aspect that distinguishes Venetian processions from those in other regions.

The Good Friday procession is even more austere, conducted in complete silence and darkness, with only candles illuminating the way. The procession begins at the Basilica di San Marco and visits seven churches throughout the city, symbolizing the seven stations where Christ fell while carrying his cross. An atmosphere of profound contemplation, shaped by the city's unique acoustics of water and stone, is created by the occasional mournful tolling of church bells.

In recent years, the Patriarch of Venice has revived the ancient tradition of the Via Crucis (Way of the Cross) on Good Friday, which processes across the Ponte della Libertà, the bridge connecting Venice to the mainland, symbolizing Christ's journey to Calvary and emphasizing the unity between the island city and its mainland territories.

2. Verona: The Living Stations of the Cross

Good Friday Passion Play on Verona's Ancient Streets

The city of Verona, known worldwide for its Roman arena and the legend of Romeo and Juliet, hosts one of the Veneto's most visually striking Good Friday ceremonies. The tradition of the "Via Crucis Vivente" (Living Stations of the Cross) dates back to the Counter-Reformation period in the 16th century, when the Church sought to make religious narratives more accessible to the common people through dramatic presentations.

This elaborate Passion Play begins at dusk on Good Friday in Piazza Bra, the expansive square dominated by the Roman Arena. Hundreds of participants in period costumes recreate the events of Christ's condemnation, carrying of the cross, and crucifixion. What makes Verona's Via Crucis particularly distinctive is how the dramatic narrative unfolds against the backdrop of the city's remarkably preserved ancient and medieval architecture, creating a powerful juxtaposition of sacred drama and historical setting.

The procession winds through the narrow streets of the centro storico, with key scenes enacted at significant landmarks: Christ's condemnation takes place before the medieval Palazzo della Ragione; Simon of Cyrene helps Jesus carry the cross near the Casa di Romeo; and the crucifixion scene is staged on the steps of the Romanesque San Zeno Basilica. The entire city becomes a stage for this sacred drama, with thousands of spectators lining the route.

3. Chioggia: The Procession of the Dead Christ

An Ancient Maritime Tradition of Faith

Chioggia, often described as "little Venice," is a fishing town at the southern end of the Venetian Lagoon with Holy Week traditions strongly connected to its maritime heritage. The town's Good Friday "Processione del Cristo Morto" (Procession of the Dead Christ) has distinctive elements that reflect its identity as a community of fishermen and seafarers.

Dating back to the 16th century, Chioggia's procession begins at the Cathedral of Santa Maria Assunta after the evening liturgy on Good Friday. The focal point is a 17th-century wooden statue of the dead Christ, remarkably realistic in its depiction of the crucified body, carried on a bed of red carnations. Alongside the statue of Christ, an image of the Madonna Addolorata (Sorrowful Mother) is carried by the women of the town, many dressed in traditional black lace veils that have been passed down through generations.

What makes Chioggia's procession unique is the participation of the local fishing community. The fishermen's confraternity, established in 1508, leads the procession wearing distinctive blue capes that symbolize the sea. Following maritime tradition, they carry large ship lanterns rather than the candles or torches typical of inland processions. The route includes a significant pause at the port, where prayers are offered for those who have lost their lives at sea, connecting Christ's sacrifice with the dangers faced by the local fishing community.

Another distinctive element is the musical accompaniment. Rather than the somber funeral marches common in many Italian Good Friday processions, Chioggia's procession features ancient seafaring laments sung in the local dialect. These songs, known as "bitinici," blend Venetian, Greek, and Dalmatian influences, reflecting the town's history as a crossroads of Mediterranean cultures.

4. Marostica: The Procession of the Mysteries

Medieval Symbolism in the City of the Chess Game

Marostica, famous for its biennial living chess match and impressive medieval walls, preserves a Holy Week tradition with strong medieval symbolism. The Thursday evening "Processione dei Misteri" (Procession of the Mysteries) differs from many others in the Veneto by focusing on symbolic objects of the Passion rather than statues.

Established by the Dominicans in the 14th century as a catechetical tool for teaching the faith to a largely illiterate population, the procession features fifteen symbolic objects carried on velvet cushions by members of the local confraternities. These symbols, known as the "Arma Christi" (Weapons of Christ), include items from the Passion narrative: the chalice representing the Last Supper, the thirty silver coins of Judas's betrayal, the crown of thorns, the nails of the crucifixion, and so on.

Each symbol is presented with an accompanying biblical reading and hymn, creating a mobile meditation on the Passion of Christ. What makes Marostica's procession distinctive is its setting within the town's perfectly preserved medieval walls and streets, with the procession route illuminated only by torches. The dramatic shadows cast against the ancient stone buildings create a powerful visual effect that evokes the medieval era when this tradition began.

The procession concludes in the central square, the famous chessboard square, where the final meditation is accompanied by a medieval rendering of the Miserere, performed from the loggia of the Lower Castle by the town's Renaissance music ensemble, which specializes in historically informed performance practices.

5. Bassano del Grappa: The Burning Boats of Holy Saturday

Bassano del Grappa, situated where the Brenta River emerges from the mountains to meet the Venetian plain, has a distinctive Holy Saturday tradition that incorporates the natural elements of fire and water, symbolizing both destruction and rebirth. The "Rogo delle Barche" (Burning of the Boats) dates back to the 16th century, combining Christian symbolism with pre-Christian spring rituals.

On Holy Saturday evening, as darkness falls, the community gathers at the town's iconic wooden bridge, the Ponte degli Alpini (designed by Andrea Palladio in 1569). Small wooden boats, crafted by local artisans and filled with branches of juniper and laurel, are set aflame and released into the Brenta River. As they float downstream, creating a river of fire, the community sings traditional hymns that blend religious themes with references to spring's renewal.

The burning boats symbolize the destruction of winter and sin, while also representing the light of Christ breaking through the darkness of death on Easter. The ritual also has historical significance: in the 16th century, when the tradition began, Bassano suffered from recurrent plague epidemics, and the burning boats were seen as a way to purify the town and ward off disease.

The ceremony concludes with the lighting of the Easter fire on the riverbank, from which the Paschal Candle will be lit during the Easter Vigil that follows. This blending of natural elements, historical memory, and religious symbolism makes Bassano's Holy Saturday celebration an evocative example of how local communities in the Veneto have created distinctive expressions of universal Christian themes.

6. Padua: The University Holy Week and Botanical Symbolism

Padua, home to one of the world's oldest universities (founded in 1222) and the magnificent Basilica of St. Anthony, combines intellectual and botanical traditions in its Holy Week observances. Easter in Padua is unique because of the city's connection to botanical studies, stemming from the University of Padua's oldest academic botanical garden, founded in 1545.

The Palm Sunday procession in Padua begins at the Botanical Garden, where special palm fronds and olive branches are cultivated specifically for this purpose. Rooted in Padua's Renaissance history as a center for studying medicinal and symbolic plants, the university's botanical experts cultivate these plants using time-honored techniques. Next, the procession goes to the cathedral; university professors in academic robes join in, visually representing the unity of faith and learning.

On Good Friday, Padua's tradition centers on the Basilica of St. Anthony, where a solemn procession carries a relic of the True Cross through the city streets. What distinguishes this procession is the participation of students and faculty from the university, who read meditations on the Passion composed by historical figures associated with the university, including Galileo Galilei, who taught at Padua from 1592 to 1610.

Another distinctive feature of Padua's Holy Week is the "Via Crucis degli Intellettuali" (Way of the Cross of the Intellectuals) held within the university's historic Palazzo Bo on Wednesday of Holy Week. Originating in the 1950s, this modern practice involves selections from sacred and non-sacred texts that examine suffering, sacrifice, and renewal, demonstrating the ongoing interaction between religious belief and logic in this place of study.

7. Este: The Procession of Holy Week

Faith and Ancient Roots in a Walled Town of Devotion

Nestled at the edge of the Euganean Hills and steeped in pre-Roman and medieval history, Este offers one of the most evocative Holy Week experiences in the southern Veneto. This ancient town, once home to the powerful Este family, blends spiritual solemnity with deep-rooted local traditions that reflect its long-standing Catholic devotion and close-knit community.

The highlight of Holy Week in Este is the Good Friday Procession of the Dead Christ, a moving and centuries-old event that winds through the cobbled streets of the historic center. Beginning at the Duomo of Santa Tecla, the procession features life-sized statues of the Dead Christ and the Sorrowful Madonna, carried on the shoulders of members of religious confraternities dressed in traditional robes. The atmosphere glows with reverence as hymns and candlelight accompany hundreds of townspeople following the sacred path through medieval gates and piazzas.

What makes Este's Holy Week truly special is the communal participation that connects generations. Local families adorn their balconies with lanterns and mourning black cloths, while children walk alongside their grandparents in the candlelit procession. The town's religious and civic leaders march together, symbolizing the beautiful unity between sacred traditions and community life.

The procession's route passes by Castello Carrarese, the remnants of Este's medieval castle, creating a powerful visual contrast between ancient ruins and living tradition unfolding below, a testament to the town's journey from pagan and feudal origins to its vibrant Catholic present.

Throughout the days leading to Easter, churches across Este host Lenten reflections and musical meditations, often featuring enchanting Gregorian chant or classical sacred music, inviting visitors into profound experiences of contemplation and beauty.

Este's Holy Week traditions aren't merely performances for tourists; they are intensely heartfelt and participatory, offering visitors an immersive opportunity to witness a community where history, faith, and fellowship converge in a meaningful celebration of Christ's Passion.

Navigating Venice and the Veneto

From Its Vibrant Past to Practical Travel Tips

CHAPTER THIRTY-FOUR

Regional Dishes and Venetian Specialities

A Culinary Journey

The Flavors of Venice

Venice's cuisine is a fascinating reflection of its unique geography, maritime heritage, and historical trading connections. As a powerful maritime republic that dominated Mediterranean trade for centuries, Venetian food culture combines local lagoon ingredients with exotic spices and influences from the East.

Whether you're dining in a traditional bacaro, a family-run trattoria, or a sophisticated restaurant overlooking the Grand Canal, you'll experience the essence of Venetian hospitality through its seafood-centric dishes, hearty rice and polenta specialties, and delightful small plates called cicchetti.

Venetian Specialties: What to Eat in Venice and Veneto

Cicchetti & Starters

Cicchetti are small, traditional snacks or side dishes served in the Veneto. They are similar to Spanish tapas and are often enjoyed at local bars called bacari. These bite-sized delights can include a variety of options with fish, meat or vegetarian, such as:

- Small sandwiches or crostini topped with seafood, meats, or vegetables.

- Fried snacks like meatballs (polpetta) or seafood (sarda fritta are fried sardines, calamari fritti).

- Polenta squares with flavorful toppings.

Cicchetti are usually paired with a small glass of wine, known locally as an ombra. They are a cornerstone of Venetian social life, offering a casual and delicious way to enjoy local flavors.

Cicchetti

Bacalà Mantecato: Creamed salt cod whipped with olive oil and served on polenta or bread, a quintessential Venetian appetizer found in virtually every bacaro.

Sarde in Saor: Sweet and sour sardines marinated with onions, pine nuts, and raisins, a centuries-old dish that reflects Venice's trading history with the East.

Polpette: Small meatballs made with various ingredients such as beef, fish, or vegetables, perfect for snacking with a glass of wine.

Nervetti: Tender beef cartilage salad dressed with onions and vinegar, a traditional appetizer especially popular in mainland Veneto.

Pasta & First Courses

Bigoli in Salsa: Thick, whole-wheat spaghetti served with a sauce of onions and salt-cured fish (usually anchovies), a Venetian classic particularly popular during Lent.

Risotto al Nero di Seppia: Risotto made with cuttlefish ink, giving it a dramatic black appearance and rich seafood flavor.

Risi e Bisi: A springtime specialty of rice and fresh peas, somewhere between a soup and a risotto, traditionally served to the Doge on St. Mark's Day.

Pasta e Fagioli: A hearty pasta and bean soup common throughout the Veneto region, especially popular in Verona and the mainland.

Seafood & Second Courses

Fritto Misto: A mixed fry of seasonal lagoon fish and seafood, often including calamari, shrimp, and small local fish.

Fegato alla Veneziana: Thinly sliced calf's liver cooked with onions, a signature Venetian dish that dates back to Roman times.

Baccalà alla Vicentina: Salt cod slowly cooked with milk, onions, and Parmesan, a specialty from Vicenza in the Veneto mainland.

Moleche: Soft-shell crabs from the Venetian lagoon, available only during their molting season in spring and autumn, typically fried.

Rice, Polenta & Side Dishes

Risi e Bisi: A springtime specialty of rice and fresh peas, somewhere between a soup and a risotto, traditionally served to the Doge on St. Mark's Day.

Polenta e Schie: Creamy polenta topped with tiny gray shrimp from the lagoon, dressed with olive oil and parsley.

Radicchio di Treviso: The famous bitter red chicory from Treviso, often grilled and dressed with olive oil and salt.

Piselli alla Veneziana: Fresh peas cooked with pancetta and onions, a simple but delicious side dish.

Desserts & Sweets

Baicoli: Thin, oval-shaped cookies designed to last during long sea voyages, traditionally dipped in coffee or sweet wine.

Bussolai Buranelli: Ring-shaped butter cookies from the island of Burano, often flavored with lemon or vanilla.

Frittelle Veneziane: Venetian fritters with pine nuts and raisins, traditionally eaten during Carnival season.

Tiramisu: While claimed by several regions, this coffee-flavored dessert with mascarpone cream and ladyfingers is said by many to have originated in Treviso, Veneto.

Wines & Drinks

Prosecco: The famous sparkling wine produced in the hills of Conegliano and Valdobbiadene, perfect as an aperitif.

Soave: A crisp white wine from the province of Verona, ideal with seafood and lighter dishes.

Valpolicella: A vibrant red wine from the province of Verona, ranging from light table wines to rich Amarone.

Spritz: Venice's iconic aperitif cocktail made with Prosecco, Aperol or Campari, and a splash of soda water.

Bellini: A cocktail created at Harry's Bar in Venice, made with Prosecco and fresh peach purée.

Insider Tips for Dining in Venice and Veneto

Try the cicchetti tour! Hopping between bacari for small plates and wine is a quintessential Venetian experience.

Embrace the spritz culture. Join locals for the traditional pre-dinner aperitivo hour.

Venture beyond Venice. Some of the best food in the region is found in smaller towns like Treviso, Vicenza, and Verona.

Book ahead in high season. Restaurants in Venice fill up quickly..

From delicate seafood from the lagoon to hearty dishes from the mainland, Venetian and Veneto cuisine offers a diverse taste of Northern Italy's culinary traditions.

Buon appetito!

CHAPTER THIRTY-FIVE

Best Dining, Gelato & Drinks in Venice

Chicchetti, Aperitivi, & Gelati

Where to Eat and Drink in Venice, A Neighborhood Guide

Venice and the Veneto region offer a variety of dining experiences, from humble bacari to refined restaurants. Here's what to look for:

Bacaro: Traditional Venetian wine bars serving cicchetti (small plates) and local wines by the glass, perfect for a light lunch or pre-dinner snack.

Osteria & Trattoria: Casual, family-run restaurants serving traditional Venetian and Veneto cuisine.

Ristorante: More formal establishments, often with canal views in Venice or scenic settings in the countryside.

Pasticceria: Bakeries where you can find traditional sweets, pastries, and often excellent coffee.

Enoteca: Wine shops that often serve small plates alongside local wines.

Finding the Best Cicchetti and Aperitivi in Venice

When searching for the best cicchetti in Venice, let your ears and eyes guide you. Listen for Italian being spoken; this is one of the best indicators that locals frequent the spot. Also, take a moment to observe who's running the bacaro. If it looks like an Italian family is behind the counter and regulars are chatting over glasses of wine, chances are you've found a good one. Venice's aperitivo culture centers on these lively bacari, where locals gather in the late afternoon to enjoy a small glass of wine (ombra) or a classic spritz paired with savory cicchetti.

Whether you're sampling marinated anchovies, creamy baccalà mantecato, vegetarian options, or fried meatballs, the real magic happens when you stand elbow to elbow with Venetians at the counter or along a quiet canal, soaking in the rhythms of daily life.

Cicchetti in Santa Croce

Al Rivetta. Address: Calle Secchera 637a.

Located near Piazzale Roma, this family-run bacaro is a favorite among locals for its budget-friendly prices and authentic atmosphere. Well-managed and unpretentious, it's a great first or last stop if you're arriving or leaving Venice via the bus terminal or train station.

Cantina Arnaldi. Address: Salizada San Pantalon 35

Tucked away off the beaten path near the Frari Church, Cantina Arnaldi is a hidden gem known for its thoughtful wine selection and beautifully crafted cicchetti. With a welcoming ambiance and modern touches, it's the perfect place to relax and savor the best of Venice's food and wine culture.

Cicchetti in San Polo

Do Mori. Address: Calle Do Mori 429

Founded in 1462, Cantina Do Mori is the oldest bacaro in Venice and is steeped in history. With its low wooden ceilings, hanging copper pots, and dim lighting, it offers a quaint, old-world atmosphere. Their selection is outstanding, especially the traditional baccalà mantecato and meatballs.

All'Arco. Address: Campo San Polo 436

Arguably the most famous bacaro in San Polo, All'Arco is celebrated by both locals and travelers for its fresh, seasonal cicchetti. The small crostini are carefully prepared with ingredients like marinated anchovies, artichoke hearts, and cured meats. Expect a crowd; this spot is almost always buzzing.

Al Merca. Address: Campo Bella Vienna 213

Standing-only and located just beside the Rialto Market, Al Merca is known for its mini panini and quality wine by the glass. It's a quintessential bacaro experience, grab your bite, sip your drink, and lean against a barrel or stone wall while watching the bustle of market life.

Cicchetti in Dorsoduro

Osteria Al Squero. Address: Fondamenta Nani 943

One of our favorite lunch spots in all of Venice. This bacaro offers a generous selection of seafood-based cicchetti, with fresh flavors that change seasonally. It's located directly across from the historic Squero di San Trovaso, where gondolas are still built and repaired by hand, a fascinating view while you eat. Be warned: the seagulls here are bold (one may or may not have stolen a sandwich from me), but it's all part of the Venetian experience.

Cantine del Vino Già Schiavi. Address: Fondamenta Nani, 992

A must-stop in Dorsoduro, this historic bacaro has been serving affordable, high-quality wine and cicchetti for generations. There's no seating, you'll stand or perch by the canal like the locals do, but the lively atmosphere, thoughtful wine pairings, and inventive toppings make this one of the best cicchetti bars in the city.

Cicchetti in Castello

Salumeria. Address: Via Garibaldi 1769

This modern-style cicchetteria is praised for offering high-quality bites at great value. Fresh fish, cured meats, and creative veggie options are served with flair, and the welcoming staff make it feel like a local hangout. It's a wonderful stop just a few minutes from the Arsenale and the Biennale Gardens.

Al Portego. Address: Calle de la Malvasia, 6014

Tucked into a quiet side street, Al Portego is often featured in local guides as one of Castello's hidden gems. Expect tiny plates of stuffed squid, fried meatballs, marinated peppers, and other Venetian specialties. There's no seating, but the crowd spills out onto the street, chatting over wine and cicchetti while leaning on barrels or stone walls—an experience as authentically Venetian as it gets.

Cicchetti in San Marco

Bacarando in Corte dell'Orso. Address: Corte dell'Orso, San Marco (near Campo San Bortolomio)

Cozy and lively, with a curated wine list and a strong local following. Called out by locals as a hidden gem in the San Marco neighborhood, delivering a warm ambiance and quality cicchetti.

I Rusteghi. Address: Corte del Tentor, 5513 (just south of Rialto)

Known for premium cicchetti and an impressive wine list. Try their signature meraveje, tiny truffle and ham panini, and browse from over 875 wine labels. A chic atmosphere with seated options makes it a great stop for a refined aperitivo.

Cicchetti in Cannaregio

Al Timon. Address: Fondamenta dei Ormesini, 2754

A beloved local favorite with good cicchetti, think crostini with prosciutto, tuna, polenta bites, and fried fish, served alongside wine (and even steak if you fancy!), all enjoyed canal-side on a traditional wooden boat or at a few outdoor tables.

Vino Vero. Address: Fondamenta Misericordia, 2497

A chic yet casual gem with stunning canal views, minimalist design, and artisanal cicchetti like fried calamari, anchovies with butter, stuffed zucchini flowers, and liver pâté. Excellent wine pairings from a carefully curated list.

Antica Osteria Vedova (Trattoria Ca' d'Oro). Address: Strada Nuova near Palace Ca' d'Oro

Famous for its "Vedova Meatballs", a comforting Venetian classic, served in a warm, local osteria setting.

Where to Enjoy a Memorable Aperitivo in Venice

Harry's Bar. Address: Calle Vallaresso, 1323, near Piazza San Marco

Perhaps the most famous aperitivo spot in Venice, Harry's Bar has been a symbol of old-world glamour since it opened in 1931. Inventor of the Bellini and favorite haunt of Hemingway, this legendary bar exudes charm and exclusivity. The setting is simple and understated, but the history is rich. Drinks are pricey, but you're paying for the legacy, the ambience, and the chance to sip a Bellini where it was born.

Gritti Palace Bar Longhi. Address: Campo Santa Maria del Giglio, 2467

Set inside one of Venice's most opulent hotels, Bar Longhi at the Gritti Palace offers an unforgettable aperitivo experience on a terrace overlooking the Grand Canal. The décor is lavish; the cocktails are artfully crafted, and the views of Santa Maria della Salute are breathtaking. A favorite for special occasions or for those seeking a glamorous Venetian evening.

Hotel Danieli, Bar Terrazza Danieli. Address: Riva degli Schiavoni, 4196

The rooftop bar at the Danieli boasts one of the most iconic views in Venice, with sweeping panoramas of the lagoon and San Giorgio Maggiore. The setting is cinematic, the service polished, and the wine list impressive. This is the kind of place where you order a spritz or prosecco just to linger and watch the sun set over the water. Dress smartly and expect high-end prices with high-end elegance.

Aman Venice, The Bar at Aman. Address: Palazzo Papadopoli, Calle Tiepolo 1364

We personally enjoyed this refined and tranquil location for an evening aperitivo. The service was impeccable, the cocktails superb, and the setting, a 16th-century palazzo with lush private gardens and historic interiors, felt like a retreat from the bustle of Venice. You must have a reservation, but if you're looking for a quiet, upscale aperitivo away from the crowds, this is one of the best-kept secrets in the city.

Terrazza Panoramica, Hilton Molino Stucky. Address: Giudecca, 810

Located on top of the Hilton hotel across the canal on Giudecca Island, this rooftop bar offers one of the best panoramic views in Venice. You'll see all of the major domes and bell towers across the water as the sun sets. The atmosphere is modern and lively, and the cocktail menu includes both classics and creative seasonal specials. A perfect choice for sunset and photos.

Skyline Rooftop Bar, H10 Palazzo Canova. Address: Riva del Vin, 744, near Rialto

This stylish rooftop spot, located in a boutique hotel near the Rialto Bridge, is perfect if you're looking for magnificent views without leaving the main island. Overlooking the Grand Canal, it offers a more intimate experience than some of the larger hotel bars. The spritz is well made, the wine list is thoughtful, and the setting is ideal for a romantic or relaxed early evening drink.

Artisanal Gelato and Sweet Treats in Venice

No trip to Venice is complete without indulging in a scoop (or two) of gelato. While the city has its share of touristy stands, true artisanal gelato is made fresh daily with natural ingredients and a passion for flavor. From creamy classics like pistachio and hazelnut to bold combinations like chocolate-orange-Grand Marnier, Venice's gelaterie offer a delicious way to cool off as you wander through sunlit squares and canal-lined streets. Whether you're savoring a cup beside the Giudecca Canal, exploring hidden campos, or enjoying dessert under the arcades of Piazza San Marco, these sweet spots deliver a taste of Venetian dolce vita.

Gelateria Nico. Address: Fondamenta Zattere al Ponte Lungo 922

Recommended by our Venetian friend Vanja, Gelateria Nico is a beloved institution along the Zattere promenade. Known for its generous portions and stunning views of the Giudecca Canal, this spot is perfect for those who prefer to sit and savor their gelato rather than stroll. It's also a popular location for an afternoon aperitivo. With plenty of outdoor seating, you can linger with a creamy scoop (don't miss the gianduiotto) and watch the boats drift by. I believe this is the best waterfront gelato experience in Venice.

Gelateria Il Doge. Address: Campo Santa Margherita, 3058/A, Venice (Dorsoduro)

Tucked into lively Campo Santa Margherita, Gelateria Il Doge has earned a reputation among locals and students for offering some of the best artisanal gelato in Venice. Their Crema del Doge flavor, a rich combination of chocolate, orange, and Grand Marnier is a must-try. They also offer dairy-free and fruit-forward options. This is a brilliant spot if you want to explore the Campo, enjoy a relaxed atmosphere, and try flavors that reflect Venice's flair for blending tradition with decadence.

Gelateria di Natura. Address: Multiple locations including Salizada San Lio, 5726 (near Rialto/San Marco)

This modern gelateria chain focuses on natural ingredients and sustainability, earning rave reviews for its creamy texture and bold flavors. Whether you opt for pistachio, Sicilian lemon, or seasonal fruit blends, you'll taste the difference in every bite. With elegant branding and eco-conscious materials, it's a great stop for quality-conscious travelers exploring the San Marco or Rialto areas.

Caffè Florian. Address: Piazza San Marco, 57 (San Marco)

Established in 1720, Caffè Florian is the oldest café in Italy and one of the most elegant in Europe. Located under the porticoes of Piazza San Marco, it offers a timeless experience with frescoed salons, mirrored walls, and gilded decor. Enjoy refined offerings like rich hot chocolate, espresso served on silver trays, gelato, and delicate pastries, all with live orchestral music in the background. Though it's a splurge, the café's historical significance and dramatic setting make it a must-visit for anyone wanting to experience Venice at its most glamorous.

CHAPTER THIRTY-SIX

Best Coffee and Pastries in Venice

A Taste of Tradition

The Coffee Tradition in Venice

Venice was one of the first European cities to embrace coffee, with beans arriving here in the early 1600s through trade with the Ottoman Empire. By the late 1600s, coffee houses began opening and quickly became places of intellectual exchange and social life. The most famous, Caffè Florian, opened in 1720 in Piazza San Marco and continues serving today. It is the oldest operating café in Italy and a symbol of Venetian elegance and tradition.

Coffee in Venice is more than a beverage. It is a daily ritual, a moment of pause, a connection to place and people. Venetians may take their caffè standing at the bar, chatting briefly with the barista, or linger in a historic caffè, savoring both their espresso and the atmosphere.

How to Order Coffee in Venice

To order like a local, simply say:

"Vorrei un caffè, per favore."

(I would like a coffee, please.)

Keep in mind that "un caffè" means espresso in Italy. There is no need to ask for an espresso unless you want to sound like a tourist. If you're looking for something different, try:

- Caffè lungo (a milder espresso with more water)

- Caffè macchiato (espresso with a splash of milk)

- Cappuccino (milk and foam added to espresso, usually for breakfast only)

- Caffè americano (espresso with added hot water)

- Caffè corretto (espresso with a shot of liquor)

Most Italians drink coffee standing at the bar, where it costs less and the service is quick. Sitting down at a table usually involves a service charge, but it allows you to relax and enjoy the setting.

Where to Go for Coffee and Pastries in Venice

San Marco Neighborhood

Caffè Florian. Address: Piazza San Marco, 57

Established in 1720, this is the most famous café in Venice and one of the oldest in Europe. Elegant salons with gilded decor, mirrored walls, and frescoes invite you to linger over espresso, hot chocolate, or delicate pastries. Outdoor seating includes live orchestral music in the piazza. It is expensive but unforgettable.

Marchini Time. Address: Calle Specchieri 4347, San Marco

A sleek, modern pastry shop just steps from Piazza San Marco, known for its beautifully presented desserts and quality espresso. Try a fruit tart or chocolate mousse cake with your cappuccino. Prices are reasonable for the area, and service is quick.

Rosa Salva. Address: Calle Fiubera, 951 and Sestiere di San Marco, 950.

A Venetian classic since 1879, Rosa Salva is known for elegant pastries, fruit tarts, and well-crafted espresso. The café blends historic charm with refined simplicity. It's an ideal spot for a sweet break near San Marco without the heavy tourist traffic of the piazza.

Cannaregio Neighborhood

Pitteri Pasticceria**. Address: Rio Terà S. Leonardo, 1586

Our personal favorite. We visited every morning for a cappuccino or macchiato and a fresh pastry, always greeted with warmth and kindness by the family who runs it. The coffee is excellent; the pastries are delicious, and the sense of community here made us never want to leave the neighborhood.

Torrefazione Cannaregio. Address: Fondamenta dei Ormesini 2804

A favorite among locals, this is one of the few places in Venice that roasts its own coffee beans. The aroma hits you before you walk in. Order at the counter and enjoy a strong espresso or cappuccino with a fresh pastry. The vibe is relaxed and authentically Venetian.

Pasticceria Dal Mas. Address: Rio Terà Lista di Spagna, 149

Near the train station, this pastry shop is known for its croissants, flaky sfogliatelle, and quality espresso. Perfect for a quick breakfast or a sweet bite before boarding a train. Locals and tourists alike pack in during the morning rush.

Caffè del Doge. Address: Calle dei Cinque, 609, near the Rialto Bridge

Though just beyond Cannaregio in San Polo, this café is worth the walk. Known for house-roasted beans and bold espresso, it's a favorite among coffee lovers. Choose from several blends, including organic and single-origin options. Order at the bar or sit inside for a quiet moment away from the bustle.

Dorsoduro Neighborhood

Caffè Rosso. Address: Campo Santa Margherita, 2963

A longtime student favorite, this café has been serving coffee and snacks since the 1800s. Enjoy a cornetto and coffee while watching local life unfold in one of Venice's liveliest squares. There is indoor and outdoor seating.

Bar alla Toletta. Address: Calle Toletta, 1191

Small and unassuming, this café is beloved for its fresh panini and quick coffee service. A good choice for an early stop before visiting the nearby Peggy Guggenheim Collection or walking along the Zattere.

Pasticceria Tonolo. Address: Calle S. Pantalon, 3764, Dorsoduro

A historic pastry shop near the Frari and San Pantalon churches, Tonolo is famous for its cream-filled pastries, seasonal specialties like frittelle, and consistently good espresso. Expect a line in the mornings, it's that good.

Castello Neighborhood

Pasticceria Da Chiusso. Address: Via Giuseppe Garibaldi, 1485

A neighborhood favorite known for excellent coffee, friendly service, and a variety of sweet and savory pastries. It's an ideal stop while exploring the more local side of Venice near Via Garibaldi or the Biennale.

Caffè La Serra. Address: Giardini della Biennale, Viale Giuseppe Garibaldi 1254

Set inside a restored greenhouse in the public gardens, this peaceful café offers espresso, herbal teas, cakes, and a relaxing green escape from the city. A lovely stop before or after visiting the Biennale.

Lido di Venezia

Pasticceria Le Garzette. Address: Via G. Garibaldi, 125, Lido di Venezia

This cozy neighborhood pasticceria offers excellent coffee, beautifully crafted pastries, and a welcoming local vibe. It's a perfect morning stop before heading to the beach or exploring the quieter corners of the Lido. Their cornetti and fruit tarts are fresh and flavorful, and the cappuccino is consistently well made.

Pasticceria Santi. Address: Gran Viale Santa Maria Elisabetta, 23a, Lido di Venezia

A longtime favorite on the Lido, Pasticceria Santi is known for its classic Venetian sweets, including bussolai and zaeti, as well as creamy gelato and quality espresso. Located on the main pedestrian thoroughfare, it's easy to access and perfect for people-watching with a sweet treat in hand.

Giudecca Island

Majer Giudecca. Address: Fondamenta Sant'Eufemia, 677, Giudecca

This elegant branch of the well-known Majer bakery chain offers fresh bread, artisanal pastries, and expertly pulled espresso right along the Giudecca canal. The interior is modern and polished, but the flavors are rooted in tradition. Great for a light breakfast or late-morning break with a view of the water.

Caffè La Palanca. Address: Fondamenta Sant'Eufemia, 448, Giudecca

A true local gem, La Palanca is both a café and a bacaro, popular for its morning espresso and later for cicchetti and spritz. In the morning hours, it's a peaceful spot to enjoy coffee and a pastry while watching boats pass by. Friendly service and authentic atmosphere make it worth seeking out.

CHAPTER THIRTY-SEVEN

Itineraries for Venice and Must-See Sights

Smart, Walkable Itineraries

Explore Venice at Your Own Pace

Venice is a city best discovered on foot and by boat, where every canal crossing and hidden campo holds surprises. These itineraries are designed to maximize your time by grouping nearby sites together, minimizing travel time, and including strategic breaks. Whether you're here for 3, 5, or 8 days, you'll experience Venice's artistic and cultural treasures while navigating efficiently between locations.

Three Perfect Days in Venice: An Insider's Guide

Day 1: St. Mark's Splendor & Grand Canal Journey

Start your Venetian adventure early with a visit to the **Campanile** bell tower, when the morning air is crisp and the city is just waking up. Take the elevator to the top for panoramic 360 degree views across the lagoon, rooftops, and on clear days, the distant Alps. By midmorning, head into the **Doge's Palace** (prebook your tickets to avoid the lines) and explore its gilded halls, grand council rooms, and historic prison cells reached via the haunting Bridge of Sighs.

Pause for lunch at a quiet bacaro away from the tourist crowds. Cantina Do Spade is a local favorite. Then hop on a vaporetto down the Grand Canal from San Marco to San Tomà. This "world's most beautiful main street" offers a front-row seat to the shifting styles of Venetian architecture, from Byzantine and Gothic to Renaissance and Baroque. Disembark and stroll through the peaceful San Polo district, eventually arriving at the **Frari Church** (Santa Maria Gloriosa dei Frari), home to Titian's moving masterpieces and Canova's striking tomb.

As sunset nears, make your way to the **Rialto Bridge** for golden hour photos, then savor dinner at a canal side osteria nearby. But do not end the night just yet. Save the most magical moment for last.

Insider Tip: My family has done the **Basilica di San Marco After Hours Tour** several times, and we absolutely love it. The experience begins in near total darkness, and I remember thinking, "What are we doing here?" And then the magic happened. The lights began to glow, illuminating the golden mosaics one by one. I cried; it was so beautiful. With the crowds gone and silence all around, this after-hours tour reveals the Basilica in a way few ever see. You will stand in awe beneath 8,000 square meters of gold mosaics and get a close look at the breathtaking Pala d'Oro, adorned with 1,300 pearls and 300 emeralds.

A perfect finale to your day. Silent, golden, unforgettable.

The exclusive after-hours tour must be booked in advance and is available through trusted providers such as GetYourGuide, Walks of Italy, Through Eternity Tours, and Viator.

Day 2: Artistic Treasures & Venetian Islands

Greet the day at the **Accademia Gallery** (8:15 a.m. entry recommended) where masterpieces by Bellini, Titian, Veronese and Tintoretto reveal Venice's artistic glory. Or continue to the nearby **Peggy Guggenheim Collection** to contrast Renaissance splendor with cutting-edge 20th-century art in an intimate palazzo setting with Grand Canal views.

By midday, you're ready to escape the crowds. Hop on vaporetto (water bus) #12 from Fondamenta Nove to the island of **Burano**, where a rainbow of brightly painted fishermen's houses creates the perfect lunch backdrop. Continue to neighboring **Torcello** to visit Venice's oldest building, the 7th-century Cathedral of Santa Maria Assunta with its stunning Byzantine mosaics in peaceful, garden-like surroundings.

Return to Venice proper for an aperitivo in the locals' favorite neighborhood of Dorsoduro. Enjoy seafood cicchetti and a spritz along the sun-drenched Zattere waterfront promenade before dinner at one of the authentic restaurants lining the picturesque canals near Campo San Barnaba.

Day 3: Hidden Venice & Panoramic Vistas

Begin at the monumental **Santi Giovanni e Paolo churc**h when its stained glass catches the morning light, illuminating the tombs of 25 Venetian doges. A short walk brings you to the **Scuola Grande di San Marco** with its spectacular marble façade and museum of historic medical instruments.

Meander northward through Cannaregio's authentic neighborhoods, where Venetian daily life unfolds in small squares and family-run shops. Visit the world's first **Jewish Ghetto** and its synagogues before lunch at an osteria filled with locals rather than tourists.

After lunch, follow small canals to one of Venice's most unusual churches, the marble-clad **Santa Maria dei Miracoli,** a Renaissance jewel box. Time your arrival at the rooftop terrace of the Fondaco dei Tedeschi (free entry but reservations required) for sunset views sweeping across the city's terracotta rooftops and bell towers.

End your Venetian holiday with a memorable dinner near the **Rialto Market** before a final passeggiata along the quieter back canals, where the lapping water and distant church bells create the authentic soundtrack of Venice.

Pro Tips:

- Book "skip-the-line" tickets for major sites
- Consider a vaporetto pass for unlimited water bus travel

- Many churches require covered shoulders and knees, be respectful of the faith

- Early morning and evening hours offer the best light for photos and fewer crowds

Five Days in Venice: Cultural & Artistic Immersion

Day 1: St. Mark's & Royal Venice

Begin your journey at **St. Mark's Basilica** when the morning light first touches its Byzantine domes. At 9:45 AM, join the special Secret Itineraries tour of the **Doge's Palace** to access normally restricted areas, including the secret chancellery, torture chambers, and Casanova's prison cell. Afterward, explore the opulent state apartments and Great Council Hall, home to Tintoretto's Paradise, the world's largest oil painting.

After lunch, visit the **Correr Museum** on the opposite side of St. Mark's Square for insights into Venetian history and daily life. As crowds thin in the late afternoon, ascend the **Campanile** for sweeping sunset views across the lagoon.

In the early evening, wander the atmospheric lanes behind St. Mark's. If time allows, visit **Palazzo Grimani**, a hidden Renaissance gem with frescoes and stucco work inspired by ancient Rome. Dine near Campo Santa Maria Formosa, where locals stroll and children play far from tourist crowds.

Option B: Clock Tower Experience. Time, Technology, and Tradition

Instead of (or in addition to) the Secret Itineraries tour at the Doge's Palace, you can book a guided visit to the **Torre dell'Orologio** (St. Mark's Clock Tower), one of Venice's most fascinating Renaissance marvels. Hidden behind the iconic blue-and-gold zodiac clock face, this tower holds centuries-old mechanical ingenuity still in operation today.

Climb the narrow staircase with a small group to see the inner workings of the 15th-century mechanism that powers the astronomical clock and moving figures.

Learn how the winged lion, bronze Moors, and bell system have marked Venetian time for more than 500 years. At the top, enjoy rare views over St. Mark's Square from the very terrace where the clock's automatons strike the hours.

Note: Visits are by reservation only and must be booked through the Musei Civici di Venezia. The tour includes a knowledgeable guide and lasts approximately 45 minutes.

https://torreorologio.visitmuve.it/en/home/

Day 2: Grand Canal & Art Masterpieces

Start at the **Rialto Market** while vendors display their fresh seafood and produce. Cross the Rialto Bridge to visit **San Giacomo di Rialto**, said to be Venice's oldest church. Continue to the **Scuola Grande di San Rocco**, adorned with 60 masterworks by Tintoretto, a visual symphony of spiritual drama.

Next door, enter the **Frari Church (Santa Maria Gloriosa dei Friari)** one of Venice's greatest Gothic churches, home to Titian's Assumption of the Virgin and Madonna di Ca' Pesaro, as well as Canova's monumental tomb.

After a bacaro lunch, board vaporetto #1 to glide down the Grand Canal, admiring centuries of Venetian architecture. Disembark at **Ca' Pesaro**, Venice's museum of modern art set in a grand Baroque palace, housing works by Klimt, Chagall, and Italian futurists. Then visit the **Accademia Gallery**, with its masterpieces by Bellini, Giorgione, Titian, and Veronese.

Conclude the day with dinner in Campo Santa Margherita, where university students and locals gather for vibrant evening life.

Day 3: Artistic Dorsoduro

Begin at the **Peggy Guggenheim Collection**.

Walk to **Santa Maria della Salute,** built in gratitude for Venice's deliverance from the plague, and admire its octagonal design and Titian altarpieces. Continue west to San Sebastiano, where Veronese's frescoes and paintings cover nearly every surface, offering an immersive encounter with Venetian Renaissance art.

After lunch, visit Punta della Dogana, a cutting-edge contemporary art space. Then, take the vaporetto to **San Giorgio Maggiore** and ascend the bell tower (elevator) for sunset views of St. Mark's from across the lagoon.

Stroll the Zattere promenade and enjoy dinner at a canal-side restaurant in Dorsoduro.

Day 4: Island Exploration

Take the vaporetto to **Murano**, visiting the Glass Museum and watching live glassblowing demonstrations. Continue to **Burano** for lunch among its technicolor homes and explore the Lace Museum.

Head to **Torcello**, where you'll find Venice's earliest church, Santa Maria Assunta, famed for its golden Byzantine mosaics.

On the return, stop in Cannaregio for dinner. If time allows, visit **Chiesa dei Gesuiti,** a dramatic Baroque church with green marble inlay and grand illusionistic ceiling frescoes.

Day 5: Hidden Treasures & Jewish Heritage

Begin at **Madonna dell'Orto,** Tintoretto's parish church with some of his most personal works. Explore the Jewish Ghetto, the world's first, with its distinctive tall buildings and rich cultural heritage.

After lunch, walk to the **Ca'd'Oro,** a Gothic jewel on the Grand Canal, now home to the Galleria Giorgio Franchetti, with Renaissance and Baroque art in a breathtaking setting.

End with a sunset aperitivo on the rooftop of **Fondaco dei Tedeschi,** followed by a romantic canal-side dinner and evening gondola ride.

Essential Tips:

- Book "Secret Itineraries" tour and popular museums ahead

- Consider a 3-day vaporetto pass for island exploration

- Dress modestly for churches (covered shoulders/knees)

- Many sites close during lunch (typically 1:00-3:00)

- Early morning and evening offer the best light for photos

- The Museum Pass (Musei Civici) offers good value if visiting multiple civic museums

Eight Days in Venice: A Deep Exploration

Days 1–5 as detailed above.

Day 6: Authentic Eastern Venice

Begin the day at **Santi Giovanni e Paolo**, the majestic Gothic basilica where 25 doges are buried beneath grand tombs. Just next door, admire the **Scuola Grande di San Marco**, its gleaming Renaissance façade now fronting a historical medical museum that surprises many visitors with its quiet beauty and fascinating exhibits.

Wander through the **Castello** district to the serene **Church of San Francesco della Vigna**, where Palladio's classical lines frame a tranquil monastery courtyard often missed by tourists.

From here, head back westward to **Libreria Acqua Alta**, one of Venice's most whimsical and photogenic bookshops. Inside, towering stacks of books rest in bathtubs, gondolas, and even a full-size canoe, all placed to protect the volumes from flooding. A staircase made of old encyclopedias offers a quirky view over the canal, and resident cats keep company with browsers.

Just a short walk away in the **Dorsoduro** district is **San Pantalon**, home to one of Venice's most astonishing artistic surprises: a ceiling painting so large it covers the entire nave, painted on canvas rather than fresco. The Martyrdom and Apotheosis of Saint Pantaleon by Gian Antonio Fumiani took 24 years to complete and is an overwhelming Baroque masterpiece when seen from below.

Finish the day with a walk along the **Riva degli Schiavoni** waterfront and stop in at **San Zaccaria** to admire **Bellini's Madonna and Child with Saints**, glowing in the half-light of this peaceful church. Enjoy dinner at one of **Castello's neighborhood trattorias**, where traditional dishes and local dialect still hold sway.

Day 7: Palladio's Architectural Legacy

Return to **San Giorgio Maggiore** early to visit its serene Benedictine monastery and exhibitions (there is a waterfront cafe next to the church). Then take a vaporetto to Giudecca and admire Palladio's masterpiece, **Il Redentore,** with its light-filled nave and perfect symmetry.

Enjoy lunch at a waterfront spot with views of central Venice, then stroll Giudecca's quiet lanes, discovering artisan shops and a slower rhythm of life.

Return to Dorsoduro for dinner at Osteria ai Cugnai, a local favorite near Campo San Barnaba.

Day 8 (Option 1): Villas of the Brenta Canal

Leave behind the calli and canals of Venice for a day steeped in elegance along the Brenta Canal, once the preferred summer retreat of Venetian nobility. Travel by private car, bus, or board the Il Burchiello, a scenic boat cruise that mimics the 18th-century leisure voyages of the Venetian elite.

Begin at Villa Foscari, known as La Malcontenta, a Palladian masterpiece set beside a tranquil bend in the river. With its classical columns and solemn grandeur, the villa tells a tale of architectural perfection and mysterious legends. Continue to Villa Widmann, a Rococo gem surrounded by romantic gardens, where delicate stucco interiors and crystal chandeliers reflect the playful opulence of the 18th century.

Your final stop is the grand Villa Pisani in Stra, often dubbed the "Versailles of Venice." Once owned by Napoleon, its 114 rooms include a ballroom with Tiepolo frescoes and a mirror-lined hall that dazzles with light. Stroll through the formal gardens and lose yourself in the villa's famous hedge maze, one of the oldest in Europe.

Return to Venice by evening for an aperitivo on the rooftop terrace of Fondaco dei Tedeschi, offering sweeping views over the Grand Canal and Rialto Bridge. Cap off your trip with a candlelit dinner along the canal, savoring classic Venetian dishes as gondolas drift by.

Day 8 (Option 2): Day Trip to Treviso

Trade Venice's crowds for the slower rhythm of Treviso, a charming walled city just 30–40 minutes away by train. Begin your visit at Piazza dei Signori, the historic heart of the city framed by elegant arcades and the stately Palazzo dei Trecento, a former seat of civic power. Just steps away, visit the Duomo di San Pietro, where Titian's Annunciation glows beneath the vaulted dome and a Romanesque crypt whispers of earlier centuries.

Follow the winding Buranelli Canal, where ivy-covered balconies and pastel façades mirror gently in the water. Cross bridges lined with flowers to reach the Isola della Pescheria, Treviso's small fish market island, surrounded by weeping willows and serene reflections.

Spend the afternoon wandering side streets filled with artisan shops and glimpses of medieval frescoes, or simply sip espresso in Piazza San Vito, soaking in the quiet beauty of this well-kept secret.

Return to Venice in the golden light of late afternoon for one final spritz at a quiet bacaro, your heart full of memories and discoveries beyond the guidebooks.

Essential Planning Tips:

- Use a vaporetto for longer distances and save energy for exploring areas on foot

- Schedule indoor activities during the midday summer heat

- Use the Venezia Unica City Pass if visiting multiple museums

CHAPTER THIRTY-EIGHT

Accommodation Detail
Venice

Finding the Perfect Area

Venice's Best Neighborhoods and Accommodations

Venice's magic begins with choosing the right location. The perfect neighborhood can transform your experience from a typical tourist visit into an authentic Venetian adventure. Each area has its own character, and I'll guide you through the best spots to base yourself during your stay.

Understanding Venice's Hotel Options

When searching for the perfect stay in Venice, location and accessibility are key considerations. Venice's unique layout of canals and narrow streets means that luggage transport can be challenging, especially if you're staying far from a vaporetto stop. Platforms like Booking.com for hotels and Airbnb for apartments offer user-friendly tools to narrow your search by area and budget.

Hotel Star Classifications

To help you choose the right accommodation, here's what each hotel rating typically offers in Venice:

Three-Star Hotels strike an excellent balance between comfort and value. Expect comfortable rooms with Venetian decor, often with canal views, breakfast service, and convenient access to major attractions. These properties are ideal for travelers wanting reliable comfort and local character without luxury pricing.

Four-Star Hotels deliver upscale experiences with spacious, well-appointed rooms and premium amenities. These properties typically feature elegant Venetian design, often in historic palazzos, with enhanced services like concierge assistance and water taxi arrangements. They're perfect for travelers seeking luxury touches without five-star prices.

Five-Star Hotels represent the pinnacle of Venetian hospitality, offering impeccable service and world-class amenities. Guests enjoy luxurious rooms with high-end furnishings, often in restored historic palaces, gourmet restaurants, and personalized services. These properties cater to those seeking an exceptional experience where every detail is carefully curated.

Beyond the traditional star system, you'll also find ultra-luxury and boutique properties that offer unique experiences, often in exclusive settings or historic buildings with direct Grand Canal access.

Recommended Hotels by Area

San Marco Area

The heart of Venice and home to its most famous landmark, St. Mark's Square. This area offers easy access to major attractions but can be crowded during peak tourist season.

Hotel Danieli (5 stars). Address: Riva degli Schiavoni, 4196
A legendary luxury hotel housed in a 14th-century palazzo steps from St. Mark's Square. The Danieli features opulent Venetian decor, a rooftop restaurant with

panoramic lagoon views, and impeccable service. Its rich history and prime location make it one of Venice's most prestigious addresses.

Hotel Saturnia & International (4 stars). Address: Via XXII Marzo, 2398
This elegant family-run hotel occupies a historic palazzo near St. Mark's Square and the designer shopping district. With its classic Venetian style, charming internal courtyard, and excellent restaurant specializing in Venetian cuisine, it provides an authentic luxury experience in the heart of the city.

Hotel Anastasia (3 stars). Address: Calle delle Acque, 4557
A charming boutique hotel offering comfortable accommodations just minutes from St. Mark's Square. Despite its central location, it provides a peaceful retreat with traditionally decorated rooms featuring Murano glass fixtures. An excellent value option in Venice's most prestigious area.

Rialto Bridge Area

Centrally located and vibrant, this area offers excellent access to markets, shopping, and dining while being within easy walking distance of major attractions.

Hotel Rialto (4 stars). Address: Riva del Ferro, 5149
Boasting one of the most enviable locations in Venice, directly overlooking the iconic Rialto Bridge and Grand Canal. Rooms feature elegant Venetian decor, and many offer spectacular bridge and canal views. The hotel's terrace provides one of the best vantage points in Venice for watching gondolas and vaporetti pass by.

H10 Palazzo Canova (4 stars). Address: Riva del Ferro, 5625
This beautifully restored historic building offers contemporary luxury with a Venetian twist. Located directly on the Grand Canal with views of the Rialto Bridge, it features a stunning rooftop terrace where guests can enjoy drinks while watching the sunset over the canal. Modern amenities combine with traditional Venetian elements like Murano glass chandeliers.

Hotel Marconi (3 stars). Address: Riva del Vin, 729
A historic hotel with an unbeatable location right on the Grand Canal beside the Rialto Bridge. Many rooms offer direct canal views, and the hotel's traditional

Venetian style with modern comforts creates a warm, authentic atmosphere. Its canal-side breakfast area offers one of the best people-watching spots in Venice.

Dorsoduro Area

Home to important art collections and major universities, this area offers a more local atmosphere with excellent dining options while remaining close to major sites.

Ca' Maria Adele (5 stars). Address: Dorsoduro, 111
A boutique luxury hotel that offers an intimate, romantic retreat in one of Venice's most charming areas. Set in a 16th-century palazzo near the Salute Church, it features exquisitely designed concept rooms with unique themes and decor. Their personalized service and attention to detail create an unforgettable Venetian experience.

Palazzetto Pisani Grand Canal (4 stars). Address: Dorsoduro, 979
This historic noble residence turned boutique hotel offers guests the experience of living in an authentic Venetian palazzo. Located directly on the Grand Canal between the Accademia Bridge and the Peggy Guggenheim Collection, it features original frescoes, antique furniture, and spectacular canal views. Its exclusive position and historic character make it a unique option.

Hotel American Dinesen (3 stars). Address: Dorsoduro, 628
A charming, family-run hotel tucked away on a quiet canal yet just minutes from the Accademia Bridge and Gallery. It offers traditionally decorated rooms, some with canal views, and a lovely terrace where breakfast is served in good weather. Its excellent location provides easy access to both art museums and lively local restaurants.

Cannaregio Area

This is our preferred area for Venice stays. It is a more residential district offering authentic Venetian life, the historic Jewish Ghetto, and excellent local restaurants away from the tourist crowds.

Carnival Palace Hotel (4 stars). Address: Fondamenta di Cannaregio, 929
A modern luxury hotel with a twist of Venetian elegance on the Cannaregio

Canal. The contemporary design incorporates traditional elements like Murano glass and elegant fabrics. Its garden courtyard offers a peaceful retreat, while the canal-front rooms provide beautiful views of Venetian life passing by.

Hotel Ca' Dogaressa (3 stars). Address: Fondamenta di Cannaregio, 1018
A charming mid-range hotel in a quiet part of Cannaregio overlooking the canal. Traditional Venetian style with Murano glass chandeliers and elegant furnishings create a warm atmosphere. Its location offers the perfect balance between accessibility to major sites and authentic local experiences in one of Venice's most vibrant residential areas.

Palazzo Abadessa (4 stars). Address: Calle Priuli, Cannaregio 4011
This magnificently restored 16th-century palazzo offers an authentic aristocratic Venetian experience. Original frescoes, antique furniture, and Murano chandeliers adorn the elegant rooms and common areas. Its hidden garden is a rare gem in Venice, providing a peaceful retreat after a day of exploration.

Santa Lucia Train Station Area

Convenient for arrivals and departures, this area offers easier luggage transport and good connections to the rest of the city.

Hotel Antiche Figure (3 stars). Address: Santa Croce, 686
Directly across from the train station on the Grand Canal, this elegant boutique hotel occupies a beautifully restored 15th-century palazzo. Rooms feature classical Venetian decor, and many offer direct Grand Canal views. The exceptional location combines convenience for travelers with classic Venetian charm and excellent service.

Hotel Carlton on the Grand Canal (4 stars). Address: Santa Croce, 578
This elegant hotel faces the Grand Canal directly across from the train station. Its classically styled rooms evoke 18th-century Venice, and the rooftop terrace offers panoramic views across the city. The convenient location makes it ideal for those who want to minimize luggage transportation while enjoying authentic Venetian luxury.

Santa Chiara Hotel (4 stars). Address: Santa Croce, 548
With the unique distinction of being the only hotel in Venice accessible directly

by car, boat, and train, the Santa Chiara offers modern comfort in a historic setting. Located where the Grand Canal meets Piazzale Roma (the car terminus) and near the train station, it combines ultimate convenience with elegant accommodation and excellent service.

Lido di Venezia

This barrier island offers a beach resort atmosphere just a short vaporetto ride from central Venice, with more spacious accommodations and a relaxed environment.

Hotel Excelsior Venice Lido Resort (5 stars). Address: Lungomare Marconi, 41
A historic luxury beach resort dating from 1908, the Excelsior offers opulent Moorish-inspired architecture, a private beach with cabanas, and spectacular views of the Adriatic Sea and Venice. Its famous terrace restaurant, swimming pool, and elegant rooms make it a sophisticated retreat just a 15-minute boat ride from St. Mark's Square.

Hotel Villa Laguna (4 stars). Address: Via Sandro Gallo, 6
Located directly on the Lagoon side of Lido, this elegant villa hotel offers extraordinary views of Venice across the water. Many rooms feature balconies perfect for watching the sunset over the city's skyline. The hotel combines the relaxed atmosphere of Lido with easy access to central Venice via the nearby vaporetto stop.

Hotel Riviera (3 stars). Address: Piazzale Santa Maria Elisabetta, 1
Perfectly positioned just steps from the vaporetto landing that connects Lido to St. Mark's Square, the Riviera offers comfortable accommodation with panoramic views across the lagoon to Venice. This elegant Art Nouveau building provides a quieter, more spacious alternative to staying in central Venice while maintaining easy access to all attractions.

Accommodation Recommendations in Venice and the Veneto

#1. Hotels

Best for:

- Travelers seeking traditional hospitality services

- Those preferring reliable amenities and 24/7 reception

- Short-term stays and city breaks

- Visitors wanting canal views and historic palazzo settings

Key booking platforms:

- Booking.com: Largest selection of Venetian hotels

- Hotels.com: Offers loyalty rewards and frequent deals

- Expedia.com: Good for package deals with flights

#2. Private Rooms, Apartments, B&Bs

Types available:

- Family-run B&Bs in residential neighborhoods

- Converted historic palazzos and apartments

- Modern guesthouses in quieter districts

- Rooms in traditional Venetian homes

Popular platforms:

- Booking.com: Verified reviews and secure booking

- BedandBreakfast.com: Specialized B&B listings

- Airbnb.com: Largest variety of apartments

- VRBO.com: Focus on entire properties

#3. Rural Accommodations in the Veneto Region

Agriturismo

For Agriturismo experiences in the Veneto countryside, guests can immerse themselves in authentic Italian farming traditions through Prosecco wine production, vegetable gardening, and traditional cooking classes. Many properties offer guided tours of their vineyards and olive groves, particularly in the Prosecco hills and Euganean Hills regions. Traditional food experiences include learning to make regional specialties like risotto, bigoli pasta, and tiramisu from family recipes.

Villas and Country Houses

The Veneto region offers magnificent historic villas, particularly along the Brenta Canal and in the countryside around Verona and Vicenza. Many are former summer residences of Venetian nobility designed by architects like Palladio. These properties combine architectural heritage with modern luxury, often featuring original frescoes, extensive gardens, and swimming pools.

Booking platforms:

- Agriturismo.it: Specialized in farm stays

- ItalyFarmStay: Curated rural experiences

- Direct booking through individual properties

#4. Hostels

Hostels in Venice offer budget-friendly accommodations, often with shared rooms and communal facilities. They're particularly popular with younger travelers looking to meet others while keeping costs down in this expensive city.

- Hostelworld: Largest hostel database

- Hostelling International: Focus on quality standards

#5. Campsites

While not available in Venice itself, the nearby mainland and Lido offer camping options for outdoor enthusiasts, ranging from basic to well-equipped sites with amenities like pools and restaurants.

- Eurocampings: Comprehensive campsite database

- ACSI: Camping card discounts

Booking Accommodations for Festivals

Book Early: Venice hosts world-famous events like Carnival (February), the Biennale (art and architecture), and the Film Festival (September). For these peak periods, aim to book your accommodation at least 8-12 months in advance.

Central Locations: During festivals, staying in San Marco or nearby districts puts you in the heart of the action. These prime locations are in extremely high demand during events like Carnival.

Festival Periods: Plan for higher rates during festival times. The most expensive periods are Carnival, the summer months (June-August), and the Film Festival.

Water Access: Consider proximity to vaporetto stops, as these become extremely busy during festivals. Hotels with private water entrances offer a significant advantage during crowded events.

By planning and securing your accommodation early, you'll be well-positioned to fully enjoy Venice's vibrant festival culture without the stress of last-minute booking scrambles or inflated prices.

CHAPTER THIRTY-NINE

Transportation Detail

Arriving and Getting Around the Veneto

Arriving and Getting Around Venice and Veneto

Airports in Venice and the Veneto

Venice and the Veneto region are served by three main airports, connecting the area to the rest of Italy and major European cities. Each offers different advantages depending on your itinerary and destination within the region.

Venice Marco Polo Airport (VCE)

The main international gateway to Venice, located on the mainland about 13 kilometers (8 miles) from the city. Ideal for reaching Venice, the lagoon islands, and eastern Veneto.

Treviso Airport (TSF)

A smaller airport near Treviso, about 30 kilometers (19 miles) from Venice. Popular with low-cost carriers and best for travelers heading to Treviso, the Prosecco Hills, or northern Veneto.

Verona Villafranca Airport (VRN)

Located southwest of Verona, this airport serves western Veneto and nearby Lake Garda. A convenient option for reaching Verona, Vicenza, and the lake towns.

Choosing Your Landing Spot

When deciding which airport to fly into, consider:

Your itinerary: Are you primarily visiting Venice and the islands (fly into Marco Polo), northern Veneto and the Dolomites (Treviso might work), or Verona and Lake Garda (choose Verona Airport)?

Flight options: Marco Polo has the most international connections, while Treviso serves many low-cost carriers like Ryanair and Wizz Air.

Ground transportation: All airports have connections to their nearby cities, but Marco Polo offers the most seamless links to Venice, including direct water transport.

Budget: Flying into Treviso is often cheaper, though you'll need to factor in additional transportation costs to reach Venice.

Venice and the Veneto region are compact and well-connected, making it relatively easy to reach your destination no matter which airport you choose. Whether you're arriving over the shimmering Venetian Lagoon, the rolling Prosecco hills, or the dramatic foothills of the Dolomites, your Veneto adventure begins the moment you touch down.

Navigating Venice

Venice: Water-Based Transportation

Venice is unique among world cities for its complete absence of cars and roads. Instead, the city relies entirely on boats and pedestrian paths for transportation:

Gondolas

A ride in a gondola is one of Venice's most iconic and memorable experiences. These flat-bottomed, hand rowed boats once served as the primary mode of transportation through the city's canals. Today, they are reserved almost entirely for tourists, but that does not make the experience any less magical.

Gondolas are not a practical way to get around, but they offer a unique and romantic perspective of Venice, especially when drifting through quiet side canals away from the crowds. The official city rate is €90 for a 30 minute daytime ride. After 7:00 p.m., the cost rises to €110. These rates apply per gondola, not per person, and each gondola can carry up to five passengers plus the gondolier. If you request a singing gondolier or a longer custom route, expect to pay more. To save on cost, you can share a ride with other travelers.

Tips for a Better Gondola Experience:

- **Get off the beaten path.** Instead of boarding near major tourist sites like Rialto or Piazza San Marco, head to quieter stations in Castello, Cannaregio, or Dorsoduro. These less crowded areas often offer a more peaceful and authentic ride through smaller canals that reveal a hidden side of the city.

- **Make the most of it**. Gondola rides are expensive, but they are also part of the dream of Venice. Treat it as a special splurge, take photos, ask your gondolier about the history of the canals, and enjoy every moment of the glide.

- **Confirm the price before you board.** Rates are set by the city, but it is still wise to verify the cost and the duration of the ride to avoid misunderstandings.

While gondolas are no longer used by locals as daily transportation, they remain a powerful symbol of Venice and offer a once in a lifetime opportunity to connect with the rhythm and romance of the city.

Vaporetti (Water Buses)

Operated by ACTV, Venice's public water buses serve as the main public transportation system, connecting all areas of the city and nearby islands:

- Grand Canal Line 1–The slow, scenic route along the entire Grand Canal

- Grand Canal Line 2–The express route with fewer stops

- Lagoon routes serving Murano, Burano, Torcello, and other islands

- Lido routes connecting Venice to the Lido beach island

- Seasonal routes to more remote islands and during major festivals

Vaporetti operate 24 hours a day, with night lines (indicated by an 'N' prefix) running at reduced frequency after midnight.

Water Taxis

Private motorboat taxis provide fast, direct service to any location in Venice:

- Available at designated taxi stands throughout the city

- Can be hailed from the canal edge (though this is less common)

- Significantly more expensive than vaporetti but offer door-to-door service

- Essential for reaching locations away from vaporetto stops or when traveling with heavy luggage

Traghetti (Gondola Ferries)

Simple gondola ferries that cross the Grand Canal at seven points between the main bridges:

- Used primarily by locals to save time walking to the nearest bridge

- Inexpensive way to experience a gondola ride (though very brief)

- Passengers typically stand during the crossing

Veneto Mainland: Trains

Trains: Veneto's Rail Network

Operated by Trenitalia and other regional services, Veneto's comprehensive rail network connects all major cities and many smaller towns:

- Venice to Padua, with connections to Bologna and Florence

- Venice to Verona, connecting to Milan and western Italy

- Venice to Treviso and Belluno, reaching into the Dolomites

- Verona to Vicenza and Padua, linking the region's historic cities

- Padua to Rovigo and Ferrara, connecting to southern destinations

High-speed Frecciarossa and Italo trains serve the main Venice, Padua, Vicenza, Verona corridor, while regional trains reach smaller destinations throughout the Veneto plain and foothills.

Trains are ideal for city-to-city travel, with stations typically in or near historic centers.

Trains in Detail: Cities and Towns in Veneto with Trenitalia Stations

Veneto's rail network is primarily operated by Trenitalia, connecting major cities and many smaller towns with efficient service. The region sits on Italy's main east-west corridor, ensuring excellent connections to other parts of the country.

Website: Trenitalia.com

Main Cities with Trenitalia Stations

Venice: Venezia Santa Lucia (in the historic center) and Venezia Mestre (on the mainland)

Padua: Padova Centrale

Verona: Verona Porta Nuova

Vicenza: Vicenza Station

Treviso: Treviso Centrale

Belluno: Belluno Station

Rovigo: Rovigo Station

Smaller Towns with Trenitalia Stations

Bassano del Grappa: Bassano del Grappa Station

Castelfranco Veneto: Castelfranco Veneto Station

Conegliano: Conegliano Station

Portogruaro: Portogruaro-Caorle Station

San Donà di Piave: San Donà-Jesolo Station

Vittorio Veneto: Vittorio Veneto Station

Montebelluna: Montebelluna Station

Chioggia: Chioggia Station

Adria: Adria Station

Legnago: Legnago Station

Dolo: Dolo Station

Pordenone: Pordenone Station (technically in Friuli-Venezia Giulia but serves eastern Veneto)

Peschiera del Garda: Peschiera del Garda Station

Desenzano del Garda: Desenzano del Garda-Sirmione Station

Veneto Mainland: Bus

Bus Services: Reaching Rural Areas

Buses in Veneto connect smaller towns, rural areas, and mountain destinations without direct train service:

- ACTV–Operates urban and suburban services around Venice and

Mestre

- MOM–Provides services in the Treviso province and to the Prosecco hills

- ATV–Serves Verona province and Lake Garda towns

- SVT–Covers Vicenza province and mountain communities

- Dolomiti Bus–Reaches mountain destinations in the northern Veneto

Buses complement the train network and are essential for reaching smaller villages, mountain resorts, and wine regions without rail connections.

Veneto Mainland: Car Rentals

Exploring the Countryside

While cars are prohibited in Venice itself, they're ideal for exploring rural Veneto, the Dolomites, and the region's many wine areas:

- Best for visiting the Prosecco hills, Asolo, Palladian villas, and mountain areas

- Available at all airports and major city train stations on the mainland

- Not needed or allowed in Venice (park at Piazzale Roma or Tronchetto)

- Essential for exploring rural areas where public transportation is limited

Whether you're gliding down the Grand Canal on a vaporetto, taking a high-speed train between historic cities, or driving through the scenic Prosecco hills, Veneto's diverse transportation options help you experience the region at your own pace.

Rental Car Options in Veneto–The Detail

Several well-known car rental agencies operate in Veneto, providing a range of vehicle options across airports, train stations, and city centers.

International Car Rental Agencies

Hertz, Avis, Sixt, Europcar

Locations: Venice Marco Polo Airport, Treviso Airport, Verona Airport, Mestre, Padua, and Verona. Offer a wide selection of vehicles including compact cars and SUVs.

Enterprise, Thrifty, Budget

Locations: Found at Marco Polo Airport and select city locations. Offer a variety of cars, from economy to luxury.

Local Car Rental Agencies

Maggiore

Locations: Found across all major airports and cities in Veneto. One of Italy's oldest car rental companies with excellent customer service.

Locauto, Autovia, Venice Rent a Car

Locations: Available at the major airports and in city centers. Known for a modern fleet and flexible rental options.

Tips for Renting a Car in Veneto

Book in advance: Demand is high during peak travel seasons, especially in summer and during major events in Venice and Verona.

Remember Venice is car-free: If visiting Venice, you'll need to park on the mainland (Mestre) or at terminal points like Piazzale Roma or Tronchetto island.

ZTL zones: Many historic centers (Verona, Padua, Vicenza, Treviso) have restricted traffic areas (Zona a Traffico Limitato). Park outside and walk or use public transportation to enter these zones.

Renting an automatic car: Manual transmissions are standard in Italy, so if you prefer an automatic, reserve early, availability is limited, and prices are higher.

Consider tolls: Many highways (autostrade) in Veneto are toll roads, including the A4 connecting Venice, Padua, Vicenza, and Verona.

Parking challenges: In cities, look for blue-lined spaces (paid parking) or parking garages. White-lined spaces are free but often time-limited.

While Veneto's cities are well-connected by public transportation, a rental car provides the freedom to explore smaller towns, the Prosecco and Valpolicella wine regions, the Dolomite foothills, and the countryside villas at your own pace.

Ferries and Boats in the Veneto

Veneto's position on the Adriatic Sea and around the Venetian Lagoon makes water transport an important part of its transportation network. From Venice's iconic vaporetti to international ferries and recreational boats, the region offers many waterborne options.

Here are some websites for ferry and boat companies that operate in Veneto:

Venice Public Water Transport

ACTV

Operates Venice's public water bus (vaporetto) system within the city and to nearby islands like Murano, Burano, and Lido.

Website: https://actv.avmspa.it/en

Alilaguna

Provides direct water connections between Venice Marco Polo Airport and various stops in Venice, Murano, and Lido.

Website: https://www.alilaguna.it/en

Venetian Lagoon and River Services

Venice Boat Tours

Offers scheduled tours of the Venetian Lagoon islands and specialized excursions.

Burchiello

Historic boat service along the Brenta Canal between Venice and Padua, stopping at Palladian villas.

Website: https://www.ilburchiello.it/en

Delta Tour

Operates boat excursions in the Po Delta region and along the Brenta Canal.

Website: https://www.deltatour.it/en

Lake Garda Ferries

Navigazione Laghi

Operates the extensive ferry network on Lake Garda, connecting towns on all shores.

Website: https://www.navigazionelaghi.it/en

International Ferries

Venezia Lines

Seasonal high-speed ferry service between Venice and coastal destinations in Croatia (Poreč, Rovinj, Pula).

Website: https://www.venezialines.com

SNAV

Operates seasonal ferries between Venice and Croatia.

Website: https://www.snav.it/en

Seasonal & Local Boat Services

In addition to larger operators, smaller boats and specialized services operate in various parts of Veneto:

- Venice-Chioggia–Water buses connect Venice to the "mini-Venice" fishing town of Chioggia in the southern lagoon.

- Lido-Pellestrina–Local ferries connect these barrier islands protecting the southern lagoon.

- Lake Garda water taxis–Private boat services operate in addition to the public ferry network.

Boat schedules vary significantly by season, with much more frequent service during the summer months. It's recommended to book in advance during peak times, especially for international routes.

From navigating Venice's atmospheric canals to cruising across the blue waters of Lake Garda, Veneto's water transport options offer not just practical travel but unique perspectives on this water-rich region.

References and Resources

Calendar, Alphabetical Index, Glossary, and Inspirations

CHAPTER FORTY

Festival Calendar

Dates, Cities, and Celebrations Across Venice and the Veneto

These are the festivals included in this guide, but each chapter offers more information about these events.

Date / City Name / Festival Name

January Events

January 1. Venice. New Year's Concert at Teatro La Fenice

A prestigious classical music concert held at the historic Teatro La Fenice to welcome the new year.

January 1. Venice. New Year's Day Swim (Tuffo del Lido)

Brave swimmers gather at Lido di Venezia for a traditional plunge into the chilly Adriatic Sea.

January 5. Treviso. Brusa la Vecia / Piroea Paroea (Panevin)

Massive bonfire celebrations on Epiphany Eve where an effigy of an old woman is burned to symbolically cast off the past year.

January 5. Conegliano. Panevin

A striking version of the fire tradition, particularly notable near the Piave River with tall flames and wind-blown sparks.

January 5. Jesolo. Panevin with Fireworks and Carnival Rides

A festive version of Panevin featuring bonfires, fireworks, and carnival attractions.

January 5. Burano, Murano, and Sant'Erasmo. Lagoon Bonfires

Smaller Epiphany Eve fires held on these Venetian islands, often paired with weather predictions and traditional foods.

January 5–6. Venice and the Veneto. Epiphany Celebrations (La Befana)

La Befana, the good witch, delivers sweets to children. Towns throughout the region pair this with bonfires and family festivities.

January 6. Venice. Regata delle Befane

A whimsical rowing race on the Grand Canal where participants dressed as La Befana compete, ending under the Rialto Bridge.

January 6. Venice. Festival Epifania

Festivities marking the Epiphany, with events such as fairs, concerts, and fireworks.

January 17. Venice. Feast of St. Anthony the Abbot

Honoring the patron saint of butchers and animals, this day also traditionally marks the start of Carnival season.

January 31. Venice. Pre-Carnival Festivities Begin

Music, street performances, and themed events signal the start of the Carnival period leading into February.

January with Dates that Vary

Treviso. Natale a Treviso

Continues through early January with markets, nativity scenes, concerts, and seasonal displays.

Padua. Natale a Padova

Holiday festivities extend into January with artisan stalls, religious displays, and local culinary traditions.

Verona. Festival Mozart

A month-long music festival celebrating the works of Mozart, with concerts and cultural programming across the city.

February Events

February 8. Belluno. Festa di Santa Apollonia.

Celebrated in the locality of Farra d'Alpago, this festival honors Saint Apollonia, the patroness of dentists.

February 14. Venice. Venice Carnival, Opening Day

The official start of the Venice Carnival, marked by elaborate costumes, performances, and cultural festivities.

February 14. Verona. Verona in Love Festival, Opening Day

A romantic festival celebrating Valentine's Day in the city of Romeo and Juliet.

February 15. Venice. Minuetto of Love

A themed event held in an elegant ballroom featuring dance, music, and costumes.

February 22. Venice. Festa delle Marie

A traditional parade featuring twelve young women, commemorating the historical rescue of kidnapped brides.

February 22–March 4. Venice. Venice Carnival – Main Events

The main period of Carnival, with masked balls, water parades, theatrical performances, and cultural spectacles.

February 23. Venice. Minuetto

A classic dance event set in an elegant ballroom atmosphere as part of the Carnival festivities.

February 27. Venice. Dancing Chocolate

An afternoon event combining dance and chocolate tasting in a refined historical venue.

February 27. Venice. Carnival Official Dinner Show

A dinner with live performances, music, and elegant costumes in one of Venice's grand palaces.

February 28. Venice. Carnival Extravaganza

Another grand masked ball featuring dramatic performances, music, and dance.

February 28. Verona. Bacanal del Gnoco

Verona's traditional Carnival parade led by the character Papà del Gnoco, featuring floats and food celebrations.

February with Dates that Vary

Sarmede. International Children's Illustration Exhibition

An exhibition showcasing original children's book illustrations from around the world, hosted at the Casa della Fantasia.

Veneto Region. Local Carnivals

Numerous towns and villages host their own Carnival celebrations with parades, masked balls, and traditional sweets.

March Events

March 1. Venice. Il Ballo del Doge

A lavish masquerade ball held at Palazzo Pisani Moretta, featuring period costumes, performances, and fine dining.

March 2. Venice. Flight of the Lion (Volo del Leone)

A symbolic event marking the conclusion of the Carnival, where a banner featuring the Lion of Saint Mark is hoisted in St. Mark's Square.

March 4. Venice. Shrove Tuesday (Martedì Grasso)

The final day of Carnival, featuring grand parades, costume contests, and street performances throughout the city.

March 30. Mestre. Via Piave in Festa

A community festival celebrating local culture, food, and music along Via Piave.

March with Dates that Vary

Venice. Classical Concerts and Opera Performances

Various venues host classical music concerts and opera performances throughout the month.

Venice. Vivaldi Concerts

Concerts featuring the works of Antonio Vivaldi are held in historic churches and concert halls.

April Events

April 2. Treviso. Festa di San Liberale

Honoring Treviso's patron saint with Masses at the cathedral, a civic procession, and sometimes classical concerts or historical reenactments.

April 14–17 (2025 dates). Verona. Vinitaly

One of the world's largest wine exhibitions, with tastings, masterclasses, and public events like "Vinitaly in the City" held across Verona's piazzas.

April 20–26 (2025 dates). Vicenza. Holy Week and Easter Events

A week of solemn liturgies, processions, and sacred music centered at Vicenza's churches, especially the cathedral and Basilica di Monte Berico.

April 25. Venice. Festa di San Marco

Venice's most important civic and religious festival, honoring Saint Mark, the city's patron. The day includes Mass at the Basilica, a grand procession, and cultural events.

April 25. Venice. Festa del Bòcolo

An ancient tradition where men give red rosebuds to the women in their lives. Symbolizes eternal love and is deeply rooted in Venetian legend.

April 25. Treviso. Festa della Liberazione

Celebrating Italy's liberation from Fascism with parades, Carabinieri honor guards, and music in Treviso's main squares.

April with Dates that Vary

Treviso. Fiera di Primavera (Spring Fair)

Held in early April, this lively flower and food fair spreads across Treviso and surrounding towns with artisan markets, wine stalls, and performances.

Padua. Holy Week Observances

Processions and liturgies leading up to Easter, with highlights including the Good Friday procession from the Basilica of Saint Anthony.

Riva del Garda. Flicorno d'Oro, European Band Competition

This international wind band competition is held in March or April, with orchestras performing in Riva's concert halls and public spaces.

Abilmente Vicenza (Art)

"Abilmente Vicenza" is a premier arts and crafts fair that celebrates creativity and manual skills.

Two Sundays Before Easter. Belluno. Sagra dei Fisciòt (Festival of the Whistles)

Dating back to 1716, this beloved spring fair takes over Belluno's historic center with lively stalls and handcrafted whistles, a symbol of joy and the arrival of spring.

May Events

May 1. Venice. Labor Day (Festa dei Lavoratori)

A national holiday with parades, concerts, and public celebrations in many towns and cities.

May 4–6. San Zeno di Cassola (Vicenza). Sagra dell'Asparago

A food festival celebrating white asparagus, featuring local dishes and culinary events.

May 4–6 and May 11–13. Torrebelvicino. Sagra della Bondola

A festival dedicated to bondola, a typical pork sausage, with food stands, music, and local traditions.

May 8–11. Jesolo. Venice Festival Days

An international festival showcasing music, dance, and artistic performances.

May 23–Fall. Venice. Venice Biennale

A world-renowned contemporary art exhibition that takes over the city with installations, national pavilions, and curated shows.

May 30-June 1. Rovigo. Rovigoracconta Festival

Art, music and literature festival.

May with Dates that Vary

New Conversations – Vicenza Jazz

Since its inception in 1996, the "New Conversations – Vicenza Jazz" festival has transformed Vicenza into a vibrant hub for jazz enthusiasts.

Venice. Vogalonga

A non-competitive rowing event covering 30 kilometers through the lagoon, promoting traditional rowing culture and environmental awareness.

Veneto Region. Sagra della Fragola (Strawberry Festival)

Strawberry festivals are held in various towns, offering strawberry-based desserts, live entertainment, and local products.

Mid-May. Venice. Festa della Sensa

A traditional festival celebrating Venice's symbolic "marriage to the sea," with a ceremonial boat procession and regattas.

Mid-May. Venice. Mare Maggio

A maritime festival held inside the Arsenale, celebrating Venice's naval history with reenactments and sea-themed events.

Mid-May. Belluno. Belluno Photo Festival

This annual celebration of photography brings together local and international artists for a series of exhibitions held in galleries, palaces, and open-air spaces around Belluno

Late May. Belluno. Lungardo in Fest

Held along Via Lungardo, this community festival features live music, pop-up food stands, and entertainment ranging from children's games to late-night dancing.

June Events

June 1. Venice. Festa della Sensa

A traditional festival celebrating Venice's historic "marriage to the sea," featuring a ceremonial boat procession and regattas.

June 2. Venice. Festa della Repubblica

Italy's Republic Day is celebrated with parades, concerts, and events across the city, including a regatta around Sant'Erasmo.

June 8. Venice. Vogalonga

A non-competitive rowing event covering approximately 30 kilometers through the Venetian Lagoon, promoting traditional rowing and environmental awareness.

June 9. Venice. Laguna Pride

A vibrant LGBT parade through Venice with music, dance, and public celebrations.

June 13. Verona. Opera Season at the Arena di Verona

Opening night of the summer opera season in Verona's ancient amphitheater, offering world-class performances under the stars.

June 13–17. Venice. International Music & Folk Dance Festival "Venice Fest"

An international festival featuring folk groups, choirs, and orchestras performing traditional music and dance.

June 24. Venice. Feast of St. John in Bragora

A neighborhood festival with puppet shows, concerts, and Mass in the Church of Bragora.

June 29. Venice. Feast of San Pietro di Castello

A celebration in the Castello district with traditional food, music, and activities honoring Saints Peter and Paul.

June with Dates that Vary

June, Third Weekend. Cervarese Santa Croce. Palio dello Sparviero.

The Palio dello Sparviero is an annual medieval reenactment festival held in Cervarese Santa Croce.

Venice. Veneto Jazz Festival

A region-wide jazz festival featuring local and international artists in concert halls and open-air venues.

Venice. Vivaldi Four Seasons Concerts

Classical music performances of Vivaldi's works held in historic churches and theaters.

Noale. Palio di Noale

A medieval reenactment with parades in period costume and competitions between town districts.

Albaredo d'Adige. Sagra di Presina

A local food and culture fair with traditional cuisine, music, and carnival rides.

Malcesine. Malcesine Music.

A lively series of free live shows, from pop, blues, funky, soul, hip hop to rock, staged throughout Malcesine's historic center and in the "Padre Mario Casella" gardens.

July Events

July 13-Summer. Verona. Opera Festival at the Arena di Verona

Major opera productions begin nightly in the Roman amphitheater, a world-renowned open-air venue.

July 19. Venice. Festa del Redentore

Venetians prepare with dinners along the Giudecca, lantern-lit boats, and the ceremonial votive bridge to the Church of the Redeemer.

July 20. Venice. Festa del Redentore

Fireworks light up the lagoon at night, and earlier in the day, a regatta and religious services are held. This historic festival dates to 1577 and commemorates the end of the plague.

July with Dates that Vary

July / August. Bassano del Grappa. Operaestate Festival Veneto (Opera Summer Festival)

FestaFusion with nearby River Race (Palio).

Late July to early September. Vicenza in Festival

Coinciding with the city's patronal feast, the "Festa dei Oto," "Vicenza in Festival" is a cultural event that brings music, theater, and comedy to the heart of Vicenza.

Late July. Treviso. Suoni di Marca Festival

Two-week music festival with performances along the city walls, featuring jazz, indie, folk, and more, accompanied by food and craft vendors.

Last weekend of July. Bardolino. Bardolino Air Show (Frecce Tricolori)

Aerial demonstration over Lake Garda featuring Italy's national aerobatic team. Food stands, music, and lakeside festivities round out the day.

Last weekend of July. Riva del Garda and surrounding towns. Garda Jazz Festival

Concerts begin in Riva and nearby towns like Arco and Nago-Torbole, blending jazz music with stunning alpine and lakefront settings.

Malcesine. Malcesine Music.

A lively series of free live shows, from pop, blues, funky, soul, hip hop to rock, staged throughout Malcesine's historic center and in the "Padre Mario Casella" gardens.

August Events

August 1–4. Feltre. Palio di Feltre

Medieval horse race and pageantry in Feltre's historic center, with flag throwers, tournaments, and a costumed parade honoring the town's Renaissance history.

August 9–15. Valli del Pasubio. Sagra della Sopressa

A weeklong food festival celebrating the traditional Veneto salami, with tastings, cooking demos, concerts, children's workshops, and a grand fireworks finale on Ferragosto.

August 10. Treviso. Festa di San Lorenzo

Celebration of Saint Lawrence with outdoor Mass, candlelight processions, and fireworks coinciding with the Perseid meteor shower.

August 15. Venice and throughout Italy. Ferragosto

National summer holiday with beach picnics, processions, concerts, and fireworks. In Venice and surrounding areas, it often overlaps with local sagre and church feasts.

August 23–September 2 (dates vary). Venice. Venice Film Festival (Mostra del Cinema)

Held on the Lido, this is one of the oldest and most prestigious international film festivals, featuring red carpet premieres and screenings by major directors.

August with Dates that Vary

Treviso. Suoni di Marca Festival (Late July to Mid-August)

Two-week music and food festival held along Treviso's historic city walls, featuring diverse live performances, street food, and artisan markets.

Venice. Venice Biennale (May to November)

Major international contemporary art exhibition with national pavilions and curated installations spread throughout Venice.

Various towns. Summer Sagre

August is peak season for sagre in small towns across the Veneto—celebrating everything from polenta and gnocchi to sausages, cherries, and local wines.

September Events

September 1–7 (approximate). Murano. Festa del Vetro (Festival of Glass)

A week-long event centered in Murano featuring open glass furnace demonstrations, nighttime shows, exhibitions, and the famous Night of Glass with fireworks and late-night studio openings.

September 1–11 (approximate). Venice. Venice Film Festival (Mostra del Cinema)

Held on the Lido, this is one of the most prestigious international film festivals, with red carpet premieres, screenings, and award ceremonies.

September 1–7 (overlapping). Venice. Biennale of Dance and Music Events

As part of the broader Venice Biennale, September often includes a rotation of dance and music performances in conjunction with the film and art programming.

September 8. Treviso. Festa della Natività di Maria

A religious feast celebrating the Nativity of Mary with processions, special Masses, and music in the piazzas.

September 10–11 (weekend closest to). Verona. Tocatì – International Festival of Street Games

One of Italy's most unique festivals, where Verona's city center becomes a giant playground. Visitors can try street games from around the world, such as skittles, stilts, and tug-of-war.

September 30–October 1 (weekend). Bardolino. Festa dell'Uva e del Vino (Grape and Wine Festival)

This lakeside celebration marks the grape harvest with wine tastings, concerts, food stalls, and fireworks on the shores of Lake Garda.

September with Dates that Vary

Mid-September for 10 days. Monselice. Giostra della Rocca.

Established in 1986, the event commemorates the 1239 visit of Emperor Frederick II of Swabia, who was warmly received by the local populace. This historical reenactment transforms the town into a medieval spectacle, featuring competitions, parades, and cultural activities that celebrate Monselice's rich heritage.

Mid-September. Verona. Tocati.

The festival promotes the preservation and sharing of traditional games from both Italian regions and international cultures. Over four days, Verona's streets, piazzas, and riverbanks transform into open-air game boards where children and adults alike can play, observe, and learn about dozens of traditional activities.

Fourth Weekend in September. Cittadella. Voci dall Evo di Mezzo.

The Voci dall'Evo di Mezzo (Voices from the Middle Ages) is a captivating medieval reenactment festival held annually in Cittadella, a walled town in the province of Padua.

Various towns. September Sagre

Grape harvest, truffle, fig, and polenta sagre pop up in towns across the Veneto, celebrating the shift from summer to autumn with seasonal dishes, local wines, and artisan markets.

October Events

October 1. Bardolino. Festa dell'Uva e del Vino (Grape and Wine Festival)

Lakeside celebration featuring wine tastings, live music, local cuisine, and fireworks, continuing from the last weekend of September.

October 7. Padua. Festa di Santa Giustina

Religious feast honoring the early Christian martyr Santa Giustina, with Mass and local observances centered at the Basilica of Santa Giustina.

October 12–13 (approximate). Marostica. Festa dell'Uva e dei Vini DOC

Wine and grape festival in the town famous for its human chess match. Includes tastings of DOC wines, concerts, and food stands.

October 15–20 (dates vary). Verona. Verona Jazz Festival

A major music event featuring Italian and international jazz artists, with concerts in theaters and open-air venues across the city.

October 19–20 (weekend closest to). Soave. Festa dell'Uva di Soave

Celebration of Soave wine with medieval-themed events, tastings, music, and parades through the historic wine-producing village.

November Events

November 11. Bardolino. San Martino in Cantina (St. Martin's in the Cellar)

A day for tasting young wines and exploring local wineries. Celebrated around the feast of San Martino, this event invites visitors into Bardolino's cellars for wine, food pairings, and storytelling.

November 11. Belluno. Festa di San Martino and Fiera di San Martino

Belluno's celebration of its patron saint, San Martino, fills the historic center with religious processions, local music, and traditional dishes in honor of the saint known for his charity and kindness.

November 21. Venice. Festa della Madonna della Salute

One of Venice's most important religious festivals. Thousands cross the votive bridge to the Basilica di Santa Maria della Salute to offer candles and prayers. Outside, a festive market lines the streets with candied fruit, fritole, and roasted chestnuts.

November with Dates that Vary

Mid-November. Padua. Padova Jazz Festival.

Founded in 1998, the festival spans several days each November, offering concerts in iconic venues such as Teatro Verdi, Caffè Pedrocchi, and the Sala dei Giganti.

Mid-November (Friday to Sunday). Bassano del Grappa. Festival delle Birre Artigianali & dello Street Food

A lively festival of craft beer and gourmet street food, hosted under the Palladian arcades. Features artisanal brewers, local specialties, and live entertainment.

Mid-November (concurrent). Bassano del Grappa. Expo di Bassano

A large-scale exhibition of food, artisan products, and innovations from across the Veneto. Coincides with the beer and street food festival, creating a festive, multi-event experience.

December Events

First weekend of December. Cortina d'Ampezzo. Cortina Fashion Weekend

An elegant kickoff to the ski season in the Dolomites, featuring runway shows, pop-up boutiques, and holiday events in Cortina's mountain-chic setting.

December 8. Venice, Padua, Verona, and across Italy. Feast of the Immaculate Conception

Start of the Christmas season with Masses, Nativity displays, the lighting of city decorations, and the opening of Christmas markets.

December 13. Verona. Fiera di Santa Lucia

A traditional winter fair honoring Saint Lucy, protector of sight and bringer of children's gifts. The Piazza Bra fills with toy stalls, sweets, roasted chestnuts, and handcrafted gifts.

December 24–25. Throughout the Veneto. Christmas Eve and Christmas Day Celebrations

Churches hold Midnight Mass, especially in Venice's Basilica di San Marco and Padua's Basilica of Saint Anthony. Traditional meals, nativity scenes, and family gatherings fill the region.

December 31. Venice. New Year's Eve in Piazza San Marco

Live music, concerts, and fireworks mark the arrival of the New Year. Couples share a kiss at midnight in St. Mark's Square.

December with Dates that Vary

Cortina d'Ampezzo. Mercatini di Natale (Christmas Markets)

Throughout December, Cortina's center glows with lights, and wooden stalls sell alpine gifts, ornaments, and mountain specialties.

Padua. Natale a Padova

Running from December 8 to January 6, Padua hosts markets in Piazza delle Erbe and Piazza Capitaniato, with concerts and religious events throughout the season.

Verona. Natale a Verona

The city glows with lights and Nativity installations. The Arena hosts a large comet-shaped light sculpture and a display of nativity scenes from around the world. Carolers, roasted chestnuts, and mulled wine fill the streets.

Venice. Christmas Markets and Concerts

Scattered markets across neighborhoods like Campo Santo Stefano and Strada Nuova offer handmade gifts and festive treats. Classical concerts take place in historic churches.

CHAPTER FORTY-ONE

Alphabetical Listing of Cities

Alphabetical Listing of Cities / Chapter Number

CHAPTER FORTY-TWO

Glossary of Key Terms

A Bit of Italian & Key Words to Enhance Your Journey

Agriturismo: An agriturismo, or farm stay, is a type of accommodation in Italy that allows you to enjoy the peace and quiet of the countryside. Often functioning farms, these accommodations often include breakfast, a pool and spa, and luxurious rooms (4 and 5 star) or they an offer affordable accommodation with the family who enjoys having you. This type of stay helps to support farmers. The farm can be olive groves, orange groves, wineries, or farms with animals.

Albergo: The Italian word for "hotel." Traditionally, albergo referred to an inn or lodging house for travelers, but today it is used for hotels of all sizes and categories, from simple family-run establishments to luxury properties. The plural is alberghi.

Aperitivo/Aperitif: Aperitivo is an Italian tradition of enjoying a light drink and small snacks in the early evening to stimulate the appetite before dinner. It is both a social ritual and a relaxing pause in the day, often shared with friends in cafés, bars, or piazzas.

Ascension (Feast of the Ascension): Jesus Christ was taken up to Heaven in body and spirit. Acts of the Apostles (Acts 1:9–11). In Christian belief, the

Ascension refers to the event in which, forty days after His Resurrection. It is described in the, where Jesus blesses His disciples on the Mount of Olives before rising into the sky, received by a cloud and no longer visible to them.

Bàcari (singular: bàcaro): Bàcari are traditional Venetian wine bars known for their casual, friendly atmosphere and small bites called cicchetti. These humble establishments are scattered throughout Venice and are a beloved part of the city's culinary culture.

Basilica: A term derived from the official building of a Greek magistrate, Basileus. In antiquity, it was a roofed building with a double colonnade used for law courts, assemblies, or markets. In the Christian era, it meant a characteristic type of church building with a high nave and two or four aisles. Usually oriented to the west. basilicas usually have windows on the elevated part of the walls (clerestory) where the roof meets the wall. A basilica is the shape of Catholic churches since the 4th century. The Pope has given the basilica special privileges as a major church.

Benedictines: St. Benedict of Nursia (c. 480-547) founded the oldest order of Western monks. 529AD. The Benedictine rule formed the basis of Western monasticism. The primary task was to cultivate liturgy and prayer. Physical labor, scholarly and artistic work supplemented this.

Blue Flag Beaches: The Blue Flag is an international certification awarded to beaches, marinas, and sustainable boating tourism operators that meet high environmental and safety standards. It is granted by the Foundation for Environmental Education (FEE), a non-profit organization, and is recognized worldwide as a symbol of clean and well-managed beaches.

Brotherhoods: The brotherhoods, or "confraternite" in Italian, are religious lay organizations that play a crucial role in preserving and celebrating local traditions of the region. These brotherhoods have deep historical roots, often dating back centuries, and are named after various saints or religious concepts.

Byzantine architecture: This style relates to the architecture developed in the Byzantine or Eastern Roman Empire. Characterized by enormous domes, mosaics, rounded arches, and spires.

Campanile: A bell tower of an Italian church. Sometimes a watchtower for the town. The bell tower grew in importance during the Renaissance.

Campo / Campi: In Italian, campo (plural campi) means "field," but in cities such as Venice the word refers to a public square or open space. Unlike the piazza, which is often large and monumental, a campo is traditionally smaller and more intimate, usually centered around a church, a well, or a marketplace. Campi were historically the heart of neighborhood life, where residents gathered for festivals, trade, and socializing. Today, they remain lively urban spaces filled with cafés, shops, and daily activity.

Centro Storico: The historic center of town.

Cicchetti: Small Venetian tapas-style snacks, typically enjoyed in local wine bars called bàcari. Cicchetti can include crostini topped with seafood or cured meats, fried delicacies, meatballs, or marinated vegetables. They are usually eaten standing at the counter, accompanied by a small glass of wine (ombra). This tradition is central to Venetian social life, offering a casual and flavorful way to experience the city's cuisine.

Chiesa di: Church of followed usually by a saint's name.

Chiesa Madre: Mother church or the most important church in town. This is not a duomo or cathedral.

Cinquecento: A term shortened in Italian from mille-cinquecento. It means the 1500s or the 16th century.

Cistercians: The Cistercians are a monastic Catholic order that has its origins in the reformed Benedictine monastery of Citaeux founded in 1098. The new order set out to achieve fully the ideal from the Rule of St. Benedict.

Confraternite: Religious brotherhoods composed of laypeople dedicated to prayer, charity, and community service, especially within Catholic traditions. Confraternities in Italy, including those in Sicily, are often responsible for organizing and participating in religious processions during major festivals. During events such as the Festa di Santa Rosalia in Palermo, the confraternities don traditional garments—typically long tunics and capes—carrying banners and religious symbols. They play a key role in maintaining the solemnity and spiritual focus of the event, embodying centuries-old traditions of faith and devotion.

Consul: A Roman consul was one of the highest-ranking elected officials in the Roman Republic. After the overthrow of the Roman monarchy, the Romans introduced the office of consul around 509 BC. The Roman Republic elected two consuls each year to serve jointly for a one-year term. They held significant power and responsibilities.

Corpus Domini: Corpus Domini is the Latin term for the Solemnity of the Most Holy Body and Blood of Christ, a major feast in the Catholic Church. Commonly referred to as Corpus Christi in English, this celebration honors the real presence of Jesus Christ in the Eucharist. It is traditionally celebrated on the Thursday after Trinity Sunday or, in many places, moved to the following Sunday to encourage broader participation.

Corso & Via: Street.

DOC: DOC stands for Denominazione di Origine Controllata (Designation of Controlled Origin) in Italian. It is a quality assurance label for Italian wines, cheeses, and other agricultural products. This classification guarantees that the product meets strict production standards and comes from a specific geographic area.

DOCG (Denominazione di Origine Controllata e Garantita): Italy's highest classification for wines, indicating strict government guarantees of quality and origin. The label means "Controlled and Guaranteed Designation of Origin." DOCG wines must meet rigorous standards in terms of grape variety, production methods, aging, and geographic origin.

Duomo or Cattedrale: These are all referred to as the town's Cathedral, but they have different significance. Cathedral means the main church of the diocese where the bishop's seat is located. Duomo is the Italian word for cathedral, but both Duomo and Cattedrale are used when seeking the bishop's seat in Italy.

Loggia: A loggia is an open-sided gallery or corridor, often on the ground floor or upper level of a building, with a series of columns or arches supporting the roof. It is typically open to the air on at least one side and used for shade, shelter, or enjoying views. Loggias are common in Italian Renaissance architecture and can be found in palaces, villas, and public buildings, often facing a courtyard or piazza.

Municipio: Town hall or city hall.

Piazza: Square, as an element of urban layout.

Reformation: A major religious movement from within the Catholic Church that began in Germany in 1517 at the instigation of Martin Luther. His challenge of the practices and doctrines of the Roman Catholic Church ultimately led to the establishment of the Protestant churches.

Rifugio: A rifugio is a mountain refuge or hut, typically found in the Italian Alps and Apennines, that provides shelter, simple lodging, and hearty meals for hikers, climbers, and outdoor enthusiasts. Positioned at strategic high-altitude locations, often near trails, passes, or summits, rifugi are staffed during the trekking season and may offer dormitory-style rooms or bunks, a communal dining area serving regional specialties (polenta, soups, cured meats, cheeses), potable water, and basic facilities (toilets, hot water).

Romanesque: A term used to describe forms of Roman architecture such as rounded arches, columns, capitals, and vaults that were used in buildings in the early Middle Ages. The term Romanesque covers the period from about 1000 to the point when Gothic began.

Scaligeri (della Scala family): The Scaligeri, also known as the della Scala family, were the ruling dynasty of Verona from 1262 to 1387. Rising from wealthy merchants to powerful lords, they transformed Verona into one of northern Italy's most prosperous and artistically vibrant city-states during the Middle Ages. Their reign was marked by ambitious building projects, military expansion, and patronage of the arts. Members of the family included notable figures such as Cangrande I della Scala, remembered as a skillful military leader and a great patron of Dante Alighieri. The Scaliger Tombs in Verona, with their elaborate Gothic design, remain among the city's most iconic monuments, symbolizing the dynasty's wealth, influence, and enduring legacy.

Traghetto: Ferry

Vaporetto / plural Vaporetti: Water bus in Venice

CHAPTER FORTY-THREE

Editing and Photo Credits

A **very special thank you to my editor, Pamela Zale**

Pam, thank you for your sharp eye, steady guidance, and heartfelt enthusiasm throughout this journey. Your insight helped shape every page, and your belief in these Ultimate Festival & Travel Guides project never wavered. I'm deeply grateful for your care, precision, and the joy you brought to the process. This book is all the better because of you. And I save your funny commentary for days when things are not going as well!

Photo Credits

Venice at dusk. Federico Beccari, CC0, via Wikimedia Commons.

https://commons.wikimedia.org/wiki/File:Canals_of_Venice_at_Dusk.jpg

Basilica of St. Anthony in Padua (chapter 2). Gary Bembridge from London, UK, CC BY 2.0 <https://creativecommons.org/licenses/by/2.0>, via Wikimedia Commons

CHAPTER FORTY-FOUR

Select Bibliography

Great Reads for those who Love Italy

Ackroyd, Peter. *Venice: Pure City*. London: Vintage Books, 2010.

Crowley, Roger. *City of Fortune: How Venice Ruled the Seas*. New York: Random House, 2012.

Garland, Alex. *The End of Venice: How the Sinking City is Losing Its Soul*. London: Picador, 2022.

Morris, Jan. *Venice*. London: Faber & Faber, 1993.

Norwich, John Julius. *A History of Venice*. London: Penguin Books, 2003.

Wills, Garry. *Venice: Lion City - The Religion of Empire*. New York: Simon & Schuster, 2001.

Lonely Planet Venice & the Veneto. Lonely Planet Travel Writers. Dublin: Lonely Planet, 2022.

Zucchetta, Emanuela. *Venice: The Golden Centuries*. New York: Ullmann Publishing, 2017.

CHAPTER FORTY-FIVE

Thank You & Please Leave a Review

Reviews Enhance a Book's Discoverability

Thank you for reading this Ultimate Festival & Travel Guide. It is the fifth in the Travel Italy Series.

If the guide enhanced your travel planning, I'd greatly appreciate it if you could leave a review on Amazon. Your feedback not only helps other travelers but also supports this book's success.

I sincerely hope you have enjoyed this tour through Venice and the Veneto via its festivals. I would love to hear about your own travel adventures!

Thank you for being part of this journey, and I look forward to hearing about yours!

Wishing you the safest and happiest travels!

Katerina Ferrara

CHAPTER FORTY-SIX

Connect with Me

Free Festival Resources and More

Newsletter / Travel News

Sign up for my FREE newsletter and stay updated with insider secrets about Venice and the Veneto region, hidden canals, authentic bacari wine bars, lesser-known islands, and seasonal festivals you won't find in standard travel guides. Stay informed about Venetian cultural events, specialized lagoon tours, podcast episodes, and unique insights that go beyond the book!

KaterinaFerrara. com

Immersion Travel by Katerina Ferrara Blog

Looking for even more hidden treasures in Venice and the Veneto? My blog is packed with insider tips, from secluded corners of the lagoon to self-guided walking tours that reveal Venice's authentic neighborhoods far from the tourist crowds. Discover family-run trattorias serving authentic cicchetti, artisan workshops where traditional crafts still thrive, and magical viewpoints for capturing the perfect Venetian sunset. Whether you're planning a romantic escape or a cultural exploration, you'll find everything you need to create unforgettable memories in La Serenissima. Subscribe at KaterinaFerrara.com for exclusive travel insights and start uncovering Venice's best-kept secrets!

Immersion Travel Podcast and YouTube

Looking for the real Italy? Step beyond the tourist trail with the Immersion Travel Podcast and YouTube series, where I take you deep into Italy's most captivating regions. From hidden festivals and authentic food spots to spiritual walks and backstreet wonders, each episode brings you insider stories, expert tips, and cultural treasures you won't find in typical travel guides.

Podcast

https://podcasts.apple.com/us/podcast/immersion-travel-italy/id1795327762

YouTube

https://www.youtube.com/@ImmersionTravelItaly

Katerina on Instagram

@KaterinaFerraraAuthor

Corrections / Updates / Suggestions Oops!

Even with the most careful research, details about Venice's ever-changing events and venues can shift like the tides in the lagoon. I would appreciate your help to keep my content current and accurate. Please visit the book page here: https://katerinaferrara.com/ultimate-festival-and-travel-guide-venice-and-venet o/ and scroll down to the book feedback button.

CHAPTER FORTY-SEVEN

About the Author

Festival Follower and Founder of Immersion Travel Italy

Katerina Ferrara first stepped off a vaporetto into Venice's labyrinthine streets over two decades ago and instantly fell under the spell of La Serenissima. What began as a weekend trip blossomed into a lifelong passion that has seen her return to the floating city dozens of times, in every season and for every festival. From witnessing the ethereal dawn light on the lagoon during winter fog to dancing until sunrise during Redentore celebrations, her connection to Venice transcends typical tourism; it's a love affair written in water and stone.

As the founder of Immersion Travel Italy and author of multiple travel guides, Katerina has spent countless hours uncovering Venice's secrets. She's paddled with local canals in traditional Venetian boats, learned mosaic-making from artisans in hidden Dorsoduro workshops, and formed friendships with Venetians who've shared generations of family stories and hidden canals known only to those born on the water.

The Veneto countryside holds equal allure for her adventurous spirit. Katerina has hiked the rolling Prosecco hills at harvest time, studied with glass masters on Murano, and traced Palladio's architectural legacy from Vicenza to the Brenta Canal villas. Fluent in Italian and Venetian dialect (which she proudly notes is "its own language entirely"), she navigates both grand palazzos and humble bacari with the same genuine enthusiasm, collecting stories and recipes with equal fervor.

An advocate for sustainable tourism, Katerina encourages travelers to venture beyond St. Mark's Square to discover the authentic Venice that still thrives in quieter sestieri and outer islands. Her ultimate mission is to create "Festival Followers", travelers who plan their Venetian adventures around the city's magnificent celebrations and then delve deeper into local traditions that have survived for centuries.

Website: https://katerinaferrara.com/

Follow the Immersion Travel Podcast on Spotify. Also Available on Apple iTunes. Podcast links available at:

https://katerinaferrara.com/video-podcast/

Katerina's YouTube Channel:

https://www.youtube.com/@ImmersionTravelItaly

www.ingramcontent.com/pod-product-compliance
Lightning Source LLC
Chambersburg PA
CBHW051256120626
46547CB00015B/1967